Bill Kaysing's

Freedom Encyclopedia

Bill Kaysing's
FREEDOM
ENCYCLOPEDIA

Bill Kaysing

Instant Improvement, Inc.

Instant Improvement, Inc.
1160 Park Avenue
New York, New York 10128

Manufactured in the United States of America

Library of Congress Cataloging–in–Publication Data

Kaysing, Bill, 1921–
    Bill Kaysing's Freedom encyclopedia.

    Bibliography: p.
    Includes index.
    1. Life style—Handbooks, manuals, etc.
2. Food, Natural—Handbooks, manuals, etc.
3. Self–care, Health—Handbooks, manuals, etc.
4. Dwellings—Handbooks, manuals, etc. 5. Quality
of life—Handbooks, manuals, etc. I. Title.
II. Title: Freedom encyclopedia.
HN18.K34   1988   640   88–864
ISBN 0–941683–02–8

IMPORTANT NOTICE

This book contains material for informational and educational purposes only. In part, it seeks to make people aware of their health needs.

If any person makes a decision to use any of the data found in this book, the decision rests completely with that person.

The health sections of this book are not a substitute for personal medical supervision by a qualified health professional. People with health problems should consult their physician.

Any action taken by any reader concerning therapies or individual substances rests solely with the reader and his or her doctor.

Table of Contents

Shelter Now: A Variety of Ways to Put a Roof Over Your Head without Going Bankrupt 119

Health is Your Responsibility 189

Foreword

Freedom of Choice

We should have this option, but do we? The media are controlled by people whose sole interest is profit. Thus, we are brainwashed daily to believe things that aren't true. Therefore, we don't really have freedom of choice until we learn the truth.

Our real option is to examine all sides of a question or fact. Don't listen to just one person or organization. Research, study, reflect—and then make your own decision. That's the way to have a really effective and relevant freedom of choice.

An example is appropriate. We are told that taking one aspirin per day will prevent strokes and heart failure. But is this true? Frankly, I don't know. I do know that aspirin is a stomach irritant and that overuse has been cited in many cases of illness. I intend to research this new use of aspirin much more thoroughly—and it would be wise if you were to do the same. After all, the makers of Bayer aspirin would profit greatly if all Americans started using one aspirin a day. A good place to start with any research program is to ask yourself,

"If a certain fact is judged to be true, who benefits?"

“Somebody who reads only newspapers and at best books of contemporary authors looks to me like an extremely near–sighted person who scorns eyeglasses. He is completely dependent on the prejudices and fashions of his times, since he never gets to see or hear anything else.”

Albert Einstein
(1879–1955)
Ideas and Opinions

Dedication

No writer works in a vacuum. Thousands of people have contributed to this book directly or indirectly, knowingly or otherwise. Almost every experience I have had in the past sixty-odd years has been valuable to the creation of this work, and most of those experiences involved other people.

Thus, I want to thank everyone that I know for helping me with the preparation of this book.

Special thanks go to Ruth C. Kaysing, my ally, severest critic and most valuable inspiration. She claims that I have a messiah complex, that I want to save the world, and, as usual, she's right. That's really all I intended to do in the first and last place.

Preface

"We are duped by our programmed desires."

In December of 1985, I began work on a forty–foot boat called the *Manna*. This diesel–powered fishing craft was badly rotted and had not been hauled out for repairs in seven years. My approach was to apply what I call "the Kaysite process," a method that incorporated a high–tech metal reinforcement with a flexible, waterproof cement. The technique proved successful, and today the *Manna* is floating high and dry and safe at B–dock, Moss Landing Harbor, California.

While doing this work, I ran short of money. To cut expenses, I arranged to pick up fruits and vegetables that were still edible but were a trifle "over the hill" at a nearby produce stand. Simultaneously, to avoid the drive from Moss Landing to my home in Soquel, I moved onto the *Manna* and lived there for three weeks. My outlay for food and shelter dropped to almost zero, proof that the ideas that are presented in this book are valid.

My major contention is that we can all live so cheaply it's ridiculous. *Most of us spend far more for food, shelter and other basic necessities than we need to.* For example, I often see housewives with their grocery carts loaded to the top with colorful and expensive packages of prepared foods. The actual cost of these foods in basic, natural form is often a *tenth or even a twentieth* of what these hapless shoppers pay.

As another example, I know a number of people who pay $800 a month for an apartment—even more. They are apparently unaware that for far less they could make payments on a luxury yacht at a nearby marina or buy a large, comfortable motorhome and within a reasonable time, *own* it!

Packaged cereals often sell for two dollars or more for a pound box. That's about 12 1/2 cents per ounce. You can buy whole grains that are superior to the packaged variety for as little as 10 cents a pound or 1/20th the cost! Better food value, no chemicals, and no box to toss away. What a bargain!

Alternatives—these are the keys to a better life for less money and effort to earn that money. *Alternatives* can provide anyone with more time, more enjoyment of life, more of everything that makes life worthwhile. I have provided a lot of different alternatives in this book in the hopes that you, the reader, will find those that suit your particular needs.

I wish you good luck in finding ones that will free your mind and your body.

Pokeweed

PHYTOLACCA AMERICANA

Prologue

Many people are struggling to live on limited incomes. For example, millions are receiving only small social security checks; the average in America is three hundred dollars. Unfortunately, that amount does not go very far when *spent in conventional ways*. Rental for a one–bedroom apartment can easily cost that amount. When purchased in supermarkets, food for one person can cost three to five dollars a day. Then there are clothing, transportation, medical and dental and miscellaneous. And we haven't even mentioned entertainment, gifts...all the little things that make life desirable.

Only three hundred dollars? Is that some kind of bad joke that the government is playing on seniors and others with minimal income? How can anyone stretch that small amount to cover living costs?

I can.

I've done it, repeatedly, in many places and circumstances.

Here's proof.

Mendocino County

Redwoods tower into clear blue skies while sparkling clear rivers flow into the nearby Pacific Ocean. That's a one–sentence description of the beauty of this lovely, tranquil county north of San Francisco in the Golden State.

On the invitation of a friend who owned a large parcel of land in the woods between Ukiah and Mendocino, my wife and I towed our travel trailer to a delightful campsite near an old homesteader's cabin. A spring provided water, the river was our bathtub, and we had an abundance of firewood for cooking and heat. We joined with other dwellers on the property to tend a large cooperative garden. It yielded an abundance of fresh vegetables, and the trimmings went to feed a flock of chickens. I had my motorcycle with me and often took exciting rides through the forests to the seashore, where we bought fresh fish and abalone. On the way back, I passed through apple orchards, some long abandoned. They yielded more red and yellow Delicious apples than I could carry in my knapsack.

One day my wife said, "Hey Bill. It's Wednesday, and we've only spent three dollars for the week so far for *everything*"

"Really?" I replied. "How can that be?"

At the time we were amateurs at low–cost living, and this seemed to be a real mystery. After all, we were accustomed to spending bundles of money in conventional living. Upon reflection, we discovered that our economical lifestyle came with the territory. With no rent to pay, little food to buy, and no utility bills, it was actually easy to live so cheaply. It was ridiculous! What we had done was rediscovered what the pioneers had done naturally.

Bradford Island

In the mid–seventies, I piloted my old Coast–Guard cutter/houseboat conversion to the southeast corner of Bradford Island in the California Delta. I had received permission from the owner of the property to park my boat there in exchange for being the watchman of an old floating clubhouse and some water–pump installations on shore. A fifteen–acre parcel of land was also part of the deal. I could use it free.

Several friends joined me to live on the boat, and together we planted a large garden. We grew tomatoes of several varieties, peppers, many salad greens and squash. The harvest was abundant. The rest of the island was planted with corn, and we were welcome to take all we wanted. We ate it fresh and also dried it for future use. All around us were thickets of wild blackberries, and on the north shore of Bradford were many fruit trees, the heritage of an old farm.

Catfish, striped bass, sturgeon and crayfish were plentiful in the nearby canals and rivers. Thus we had protein to balance our mainly vegetarian–fruitarian diet. When other supplies were needed—oil, flour and such—we picked blackberries and traded them for staples at a nearby natural foods store. When the cherry crop was ripe in late June, we added these to our menu and also used them for bartering purposes. To get them, we hired ourselves out as pickers and took our pay in cherries.

Centuries prior to our arrival, the local Indians spent only *an hour or so a day* gathering and processing all the food they needed. We matched or bettered their time schedule. Like the original dwellers in this region, we had no rent or utilities to pay and received our food direct from nature or by barter.

Since we had lots of leisure time, we roamed the island, as well as others nearby. In the process we often gathered wild artichokes or stumbled upon clutches of duck or pheasant eggs. In the evenings we either listened to music or made our own with guitars and harmonicas. Mark Twain would have approved of our life on the river.

In reflecting on this period of my life it occurs to me that with a reduction in financial pressure, I became more creative. I had no trouble in selling books and articles, and I even sold one called "How to live on $1200 a Year!"

The key element in living aboard the old *Flying Goose* was that virtually *everything we needed was ours for the taking*! Could anyone do this? I don't see why not. Large old boats are available in many parts of the world, and the world *is* three fifths water to begin with! (Later I'll explain how one can obtain old boats for free!)

Ash Springs

In the fall of 1980, I received a call from my friend Hank Greenspun who is owner of the Las Vegas *Sun*, the best paper in town. He wanted me to write a series on legal tax avoidance. I hopped into my old '66 GMC pickup camper and drove the five hundred miles to the entertainment capital of the West. The pay for my work was substantial—enough to permit me to enjoy both the city and its fascinating environs.

About one hundred miles northeast of Las Vegas is the vast and nearly uninhabited Pahranagat Valley. At the north end are two fabulous hot springs, Crystal and Ash. The leaves on the cottonwoods surrounding Ash Springs were just turning yellow and gold when I arrived. Beneath them was the great spring itself: thousands of gallons of pure, clear, warm water heated by Mother Nature and poured out at around ninety five degrees Fahrenheit. That's just about perfect for anyone.

Part of Ash Springs is privately owned, and the owner requires a fee for admission (quite modest). But at the north end of the large warm lake created by the springs is a concrete pool with a natural lagoon at one end and a small waterfall at the other. It was night when I arrived, and no one was there. I slipped out of my clothes and into that warm, satin–like water. Aaahhh, paradise! Floating on my back, I could see huge swarms of stars sweeping across the Nevada skies.

In time I felt so relaxed that I almost fell asleep in the water. After a long, luxurious bath, I climbed into my cozy camper and fell into a deep and restful sleep.

I stayed at Ash Springs off and on for several weeks. Nearby, I found a fire pit, and two young willows provided support for my clothes–line. I had brought sufficient supplies with me, so even though there was a small store across the way, I didn't need it. My food was simple fare: oatmeal and bran cereal for breakfast; a salad for lunch; tortillas and beans for dinner. Nothing gourmet, but after a day of hiking in the nearby hills and regular baths in Ash Springs, I had the kind of appetite that makes old boots taste delectable.

Funny thing. As I drove away I realized that this sojourn at one of the finest hot springs in the world, surrounded by spectacular desert scenery had cost me no more than the food I ate (which was simple) and the gas it required to drive there. My supply of one hundred dollar bills stashed in the camper's tool box was still untouched.

Could anyone become a "tire tramp" and enjoy the free life of a gypsy vagabond? Sure—as long as they had their health and could earn the small sums necessary to support such a lifestyle. And keep in mind that Ash Springs is still there, flowing steadily as it has for many centuries. Beyond Ash there are hundreds of other hot springs all over the eleven Western states—about 1,700 in all!

In Summary

We have presented examples of three different situations where an income of three hundred dollars would more than cover the living costs of one or two people. In ensuing chapters, we'll discuss more possibilities as well as provide the details regarding food, shelter and other necessities. I think that Henry David Thoreau was right when he said,

"Simplify, simplify."

Do you have to move to a rural setting to live on three hundred dollars? Not really. In the pages that follow we'll outline how just a small amount of money can provide all you need anywhere!

Waterway Homesites

The California Delta region is located roughly between San Francisco, Stockton and Sacramento. It consists of twenty-five hundred square miles of canals, rivers, bays and sloughs, plus low-lying islands that are mainly used for agriculture. There are few inhabitants. One could travel the Delta for a lifetime and never see it all. It is open to the public all year, and there are virtually no restrictions on anchoring and mooring. Many of the islands are quite small, and people actually plant gardens there for their own use. I knew of one man who lived on a Delta island for the year 1975 and spent about *$10 a month* for everything he needed. While the cost might be higher now, due to inflation, this gives you a picture of what expenditures might be while living like Tom Sawyer and Huck Finn!

Remember that the California Delta is just *one* of many in the world. Our own country has several, including the mighty Mississippi Delta below New Orleans. And recall too that there are thousands of miles of rivers that provide homesites and tie-ups to thousands of free-livers.

As you will learn when you try living afloat, each waterway area is a place where great adventures can happen. Thus, the fact that living on the water is almost free becomes an incidental. You enjoy the best of everything: high adventure and freedom from the rat race.

Eating Better for Less

Introduction

After writing the book, *Eat Well On a Dollar a Day*, I often appeared on TV talk shows and was invariably asked this question: "Tell us, Bill, can you *really* eat well on a dollar a day?"

My answer was always the same: "Of course. It's just a matter of knowing how."

For the past twenty years I've spent almost nothing on doctors—neither time nor money.

Today—just as I have for years—I had a ten cent breakfast, a twenty–five cent lunch, and a sixty–five cent dinner. One dollar for great food for the entire day! And every mouthful was healing food. All natural, healing food, and not a single ounce of additives.

After breakfast, I worked straight through until lunch without the slightest hunger pangs. If I'd squandered five dollars on bacon and eggs, etc., I would have been starved for a Danish—without an ounce of energy in my body—by ten thirty.

How much time did it take me to prepare that breakfast? Far less than you spend on the bacon and eggs. And the same saving of time—as well as health and money—holds for lunch and dinner.

Why? Because I know natural healing food secrets that are sheer impossibilities to you right now. These secrets took me forty years to discover and perfect. And I want to share them with you right now.

And despite inflation, which has caused food prices to escalate, it is *still* possible to not only eat well for a dollar a day, but to eat better.

Here's proof right now!

Breakfast:	A big bowl of freshly ground and simmered whole–grain wheat with skim milk and a bit of honey	.10
Lunch:	A large salad of homegrown sprouts, cabbage and green peppers with oil and vinegar dressing	.25
Dinner:	Two large baked potatoes with herb and yogurt topping, steamed, homegrown zucchini, and fresh apples for dessert	.65
	TOTAL	$1.00

There you have it—whole grains, fresh vegetables and fruits—the best kind of food for people. No processing, no additives—just wholesome, genuine, good food as nature made it for us. The benefits are many:

- You'll have better health and spend little if anything on doctors.

- You'll have to earn less money since good food is almost invariably low–cost.

- You'll have fun growing and making your own food—things like home–grown sprouts and yogurt.

And those are just for starters...

Background

We Americans spend about 250 billion dollars on food every year. But the poor farmers only get about 60 billion of this. So we are paying about 190 billion dollars to have that food processed, packaged, and poisoned. That wouldn't be so bad except that the processors add a lot of unhealthy chemicals to our food to make it have a long shelf life.

Nat Pritikin (rest his energetic soul) once defined supermarket food as being "cosmetized garbage," and that's as good a description as one could ever find. He compared the technique of doctoring up dead food so it would look attractive enough to buy with the process of making a corpse look good in a coffin.

Truly, doesn't it make good sense to *buy your food as fresh and direct* as possible *so that it will have more food value*? While it's important to try to save part of that 190 billion surcharge, it's even more important to put good food in you body. Why spend $2 for a box of colored and candied oat flour when—if you know how—you can buy ten pounds of wholesome, fresh, untouched rolled oats for the same price! Incidentally, if you correct for inflation, oats are now selling for *less* than they sold in 1932, the bottom of the Great Depression.

What we'll talk about in this section is:

- How to eat what your body really needs to be healthy.

- How to obtain food that hasn't been processed to death at your expense.

Eat Well on a Dollar a Day sold well through several printings. I was happy to find it in many libraries across the country. The following is taken directly from the pages of that book. I believe that it is as valid today as when it was written:

To eat well you must learn how to outwit some very clever minds. The food–industry moguls and their hired guns, the dirty rats on Madison Avenue, are very good at what they do. They manage to convince a huge proportion of the American people that we are getting our money's worth when we buy processed foods. They have accomplished this monumental feat (monumental considering the evidence to the contrary) in most cases by suppressing or simply ignoring the truth. To help you deal with these rascals, culprits, and con men, the bulk of this book will elaborate on these basic rules:

1. Plan on changing your entire way of life regarding food. No half–way measures will do if you really want to eat for less than a dollar a day.

2. Develop a sense of humor as well as a sense of strategy. Think of yourself as a guerrilla in a funny/serious war with rats who are trying to profit from your presumed gullibility. But keep in mind that the last laugh will be yours, since you are fully capable of using your head in finding out the truth on your own.

3. Stay out of supermarkets except when shopping for fresh foods and possibly dairy products.

4. Search out and buy from alternative food sources (I cite some good ones in this book).

5. Plan on keeping lots of bulk foods in your home at all times. That way you will reduce your shopping trips and will be protected in case of disaster.

6. Be open–minded. Try new foods, both wild and domestic.

7. Plant a garden; the bigger it is, the better for your pocketbook. There are good books on the subject in your local library and book store, and more are coming out all the time.

8. Learn about harvest times for local crops. Take a weekend drive in the country and make it a food–gathering trip.

9. Think of meat as a condiment, not as a staple.

10. Give up sugar and all sugar–containing products. It's easier to do than you may think, and the reasons for doing it are pressing, as you will learn.

11. Buy international cookbooks. Find out what people in other cultures eat and try their recipes.

12. Eat raw foods or let things cook themselves. Save time and energy (yours and the kind you pay for).

13. Eat less. Determine your own minimum requirements and keep to them.

14. Don't waste anything.

15. Make your own convenience foods. You can even make money doing this.

❝About 95 percent of what you buy in a supermarket is bought because of a lie.**❞**   —*Consumer Advocate*

Supermarket food has been processed to death at your expense. Why not whip together your own "convenience foods"? It's so easy that you can even make money doing it.

The goal should be to obtain food as pure and natural as possible.

Proof Positive

Here's a demonstration of a principle presented on network TV many times. It proves that you can eat well for a dollar a day or less if you know how:

First, acquire a quantity of whole–grain wheat. Put *four ounces* (more won't grind effectively) in your kitchen blender, and turn it to high (be sure the top is on tight as those kernels would love to bounce all over your kitchen). Stick your fingers in your ears as this makes a lot of noise. Wait about thirty seconds, and turn it off. You'll find that the blender has acted just like a small grain mill, turning that hard wheat kernel into a combination of small and medium–sized particles. What you've produced is your own homemade Wheatena!

Boil a pint of water, pour in the fresh–ground grain, and stir vigorously. Turn down the heat to the lowest setting and allow the cereal to simmer slowly with lid on. In about thirty or forty minutes, you'll have the best and freshest hot cereal you've ever tasted.

Add a little cream or milk, a few chopped nuts, a couple of cut up prunes, a tablespoon of raisins and some honey. Mmmmmm, you'll flip over the flavor! We guarantee it.

Your cost was just *four cents* for the cereal! This is on the basis that you bought the whole wheat in bulk form for about twelve to fifteen cents per pound.

Four ounces expands to twelve ounces, so you ended up with a big bowl of healthful food for a mere four pennies. Even if your additions ran fifteen or twenty cents, you would still have enjoyed a big, hearty breakfast *for under a quarter*. And this example is why we are firmly convinced that anyone who wants to can have a better diet than they now have for *lots* less money. And the work involved is minimal and fun to boot!

Had Any BHA Lately

Try this test. Wander through the aisles of any supermarket, and pick up various products from the shelves. Canned, bottled or packaged, you'll find that the majority contain dyes, bleaches, antioxidants, emulsifiers, preservatives, flavors, buffers, acidifiers, drying agents, sweeteners, anti–foaming agents, conditioners, hydrogenators and so forth *ad infinitum*. These take the form of such tasty chemical treats as calcium propionate, sodium benzoate, butylated hydroxianisole, nordihydroguai-aretic acid (NGDA) and Saforale.

Now, it wouldn't be so bad if we just had those to contend with. But what about the *secondary reactions* with the medications that so many people take? What happens when NGDA hits your Valium or BHA starts fighting with a Tums or Rolaid?

To me, the wonder is not that half of America is sick—the wonder is that we're not all dead.

But stay with me dear reader; there's hope. You can avoid most of the dangerous chemicals if you bypass the processors. And that can be done by either growing more of your own food or by getting it direct from a natural foods grower in bulk form.

Try this test. Cut out anything that has a chemical additive for two weeks. Then see if your health doesn't soar.

Health Problems of Processed Foods

❝If we define garbage as food that has been changed to render it harmful, then much of what is being sold as food in a supermarket is not really food at all. It is garbage. It is garbage handsomely packaged and labeled as food, but it is garbage all the same.❞

Live Longer Now
by Leonard, Hofer, Pritikin

❝The food economy used to exist to produce an abundant supply of good food at a reasonable price. Today it exists to produce organizational growth and profits. Product quality is no longer an organizational objective.❞

Eat Your Heart Out
by Jim Hightower

The World's Finest Hand Grain Grinder

Making fresh flour is so easy . . . with the Back To Basics Grain Grinder

The Secret is in the Precision Cone Burrs

The secret of the Back to Basics Grain Grinder is in it's milling mechanism. The cone shaped grinding burrs are self aligning and made of a hardened steel alloy, precision machined to insure long life and smooth even milling. It's adjustable for any desired flour texture from fine to coarse.

It's Versatile

Stone milling has been the standard for years in grain grinders. But times are changing - people are now wanting to grind products not easily milled with stones. Stones can gum up, chip or glaze and because they're porous, are difficult to clean. With that in mind, and through modern technology, a versatile kitchen appliance was designed for today's needs. The Back to Basics Grain Grinder easily grinds and mills wheat, corn, rice, oats, barley, soybeans, seeds, nuts, shells, peppercorns, peanuts, herbs, spices, and the list goes on.

It's Fast and Easy

Simply mount on a table or counter top and secure with the positive clamping screw. A rubber pad protects against marring and scratching. Fill hopper with ingredient to be ground, select the desired texture, then turn the handle. The Back to Basics Grain Grinder makes flour more rapidly and with less power - 1 cup of fine flour per minute and more than twice that quantity on course setting. You'll be delighted with the results.

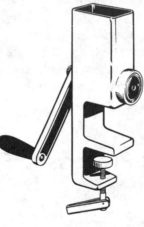

It's Better for you

With the Back to Basics Grain Grinder you have a simple way to substitute the fresh natural goodness of home ground products for the store bought items coated with sugar, salt, preservatives and colorings. Whole grains are intended as the basis of man's diet and contain the natural fiber, vitamins and minerals needed to maintain vibrant good health. You'll experience an infinite variety of new texture and flavor sensations in home baking. Breads, biscuits, pancakes, muffins, cereals, soups, sauces, cakes, cookies, granola, trail mixes, beverages and desserts are more delicious and nutritious when made with freshly ground ingredients.

It's Economical

By making your own delicious whole grain breads and other bakery items, at a fraction of the cost of store bought, your family can save hundreds of dollars year after year. And the difference in taste will astound you. The Back to Basics Grain Grinder will pay for itself many times over while providing great tasting nutritious foods.

It's Practical

The Back to Basics Grain Grinder is easier and more convenient to use than conventional models. Because of its compact, lightweight design it stores easily in a drawer or cupboard and is always handy when you need it. You won't even mind using it for small jobs. Measures 11 1/2'' x 5'' x 2''. Weighs 2 1/2 lbs.

It's Built to Last

A quality designed grinder built to last a lifetime. It's sturdy, reliable and simple to use. Guaranteed a full 2 years against defects in materials and workmanship.

Here's a grinder from Mormon country, the region where they know everything about using whole grains. For more information and prices, write to: Back to Basics Products Inc., Sandy, Utah 84070.

Background

Several years ago I encountered an unusual magazine called *Food Technology*. From an examination of several issues I learned the following facts:

- There is a product called Merlinex that is offered to food processors as a sort of "instant anything," a silly putty of the food world. The manufacturers suggest that it extends cheese, acts as phony fig paste in fig bars or as imitation strawberry filling in pastries. And those uses are just for *starters*.

- One of the larger chemical companies offers a "candy system" replacing natural ingredients with artificial flavors and a bulking agent.

- Synthetic milk used in many ways in food preparation contains sodium caseinate, vegetable fat, emulsifiers, buffers, stabilizers, body agents, sweeteners, flavorings, coloring and preservatives.

- Manufactured from chemicals with not a trace of tomato is a widely used imitation flavor called Fresh Tomato Flavor.

This list could be much longer; in fact it could comprise an entire book. However, I suggest that you obtain a copy of *Food Technology* from a food processor, large library or university and see for yourself how blatantly and crassly the food industry works against our best interests.

During the Korean war, dead soldiers under 21 were autopsied, and it was found that about half had serious arterial damage from plaques. The major cause of these plaques was from the over consumption of fatty foods. Since the men killed in Korea were representative of other young men who didn't go to war, it is safe to assume that damaged arteries are a fact of life for everyone who consumes a typical American diet. And that diet currently consists of about 42 percent fat.

Several years ago, my young nephew's kneecap was removed because it had deteriorated badly. Later I learned that he had been drinking from six to a dozen bottles of a cola beverage daily. Further investigation revealed that a major ingredient of the "coke" was phosphoric acid. It turned out that calcium had been leached from the back of his kneecap to neutralize the acid in the drink.

Dr. Ben Feingold, a distinguished allergist, has linked hyperactivity in children to the heavy doses of synthetic flavorings and colorings that are pervasive in supermarket foods.

"He that will not mind his stomach, will mind little else."
Samuel Johnson

Pie in the Sky

In 1971, National Educational Television ran a funny skit that stripped bare the pretensions of manufactured food. Created by Marshall Efron and Penny Bernstein, the program showed what you would need to make a Morton's frozen lemon cream pie in your own kitchen. Donning a chef's hat, Efron acted the part of a cooking teacher on those how–to–do–it cooking shows, taking the viewer step–by–step through the adding and mixing of such ingredients as sugar, sodium bicarbonate, ammonium bicarbonate, sodium caseinate, more sugar, emulsifiers, polysorbate 60, and artificial coloring and flavoring. "You may wonder what kind of pie we've made here," Efron said at the end of the spoof holding up the Morton's box:

"There it is. A modern lemon cream pie. I'll open it for you. Get it out of the box. Good, factory–fresh, factory–approved. No lemons, no eggs, no cream, just pie."

Morton's, an ITT subsidiary, was not amused.

Let's Get Specific

Your local supermarket stocks about eight thousand different products. You buy 99 percent of them because of a lie. The food processors and their retail outlets would like you to believe that everything in the store is pure and good to eat. That's the way they present their products in all advertising. But let's take a look at some specific items that most people commonly buy.

Sugar and Products Containing Sugar

Sugar is really a drug, not a food. It provides calories *and that's all*...no vitamins, minerals or other food values. It is so alkaline that when it reaches your stomach, a tremendous amount of acid is secreted to neutralize it. Further, when the sugar reaches the bloodstream a great deal of insulin is secreted. If you have a weak pancreas, diabetes results. If your pancreas is strong, it secretes too much insulin, and hypoglycemia (low blood sugar) results. This is a disease that nine out of ten Americans have to some degree.

Sugar leaches the mineral reserves of the body, producing tooth decay, falling hair and weak bone structure.

The Helpers

One of the scams perpetrated on the unsuspecting public is the "helper" concept. There's Hamburger Helper and Tuna Helper and others, but all have one thing in common: cheap, filler–type material and some flavorings, either in an envelope or can or both. You would pay a lot for the "convenience" of this presentation if you were conned into buying it. It's so easy to make your own, especially since you are providing the main and expensive protein ingredients. For help with your hamburger, just add onions, seasonings and cooked pasta to hamburger. To keep tuna in tune, chop up some fresh spuds and add to tuna along with your favorite spices…a little hydrolyzed vegetable protein will help, along with a shake or two of pepper sauce.

And that's all there is to it! No point in making a big deal out of something so simple and easy.

Jello

This venerable dessert is an American institution despite the fact that it consists of cheap gelatin, cheap sugar and lots of artificial colors and flavors. You can make your own pure gelatin desserts by adding one package of unflavored gelatin to two cups of fruit juice. An easy way is to sprinkle the gelatin over the juice while heating slowly until the former is dissolved. Add real, genuine sliced fruits and chill to firm mixture. That's all there is to it. There are many variations including the addition of grated vegetables, chopped nuts, and so forth.

Sugar has no B–vitamins of its own, so it steals those in your body. Thus big sugar consumers (and it comprises half the diet of some Americans) suffer from nervousness, depression, fatigue, neuroses, skin problems, digestive upsets, ulcers, alcoholism, and on through a medical chamber of horrors. Sugar may well be the worst nutritional enemy of the people, yet many supermarket foods are loaded with it. Just check the labels.

Salt and Foods Containing Them

Most Americans sprinkle salt on their food without thinking. "The shaker is there, so why not use it?" seems to be the usual response. But the problem is this: excessive salt can rob the body of calcium, disturb the kidneys and act as a poison. (Salt is composed of two poisons: sodium and chlorine.)

If you eat too much salt, the body handles the excess by depositing it in various areas, particularly the legs. To protect itself, the body causes the cells to discharge the saline fluid into the nearby tissues. The body swells, feet and ankles bloat. If you are prone to high blood pressure, a high salt intake will aggravate your condition.

It's easy to avoid salt. Just don't sprinkle it on your food and shun supermarket preparations. For example, one brand of dry soup mix lists its first—and its most abundant ingredient—as salt.

Fat and Fat–Containing Foods

Fat comprises as much as 50 percent or more of the American diet. No wonder we see so many obese people trudging along. Actually, you can get all the fat you need on a vegetarian diet. Even lettuce contains fat!

Excess fat adds unwanted pounds, coats the red blood cells that carry oxygen to our system, and has been found guilty of aggravating coronary artery disease, arteriosclerosis and many other degenerative diseases. Hot dogs at your local supermarket can contain one third fat. Hamburger has been found that contained 90 percent fat stained with blood to make it resemble meat.

A fat you should avoid with diligence is the one that comes with fried foods. Over-heated fats are carcinogenic. So skip those supermarket potato chips.

Additives and Foods Containing Them

The U.S. Food and Drug Administration is charged with guarding our food supply. They have failed us. They permit food processors to use more than five thousand untested additives in preparing our food. The per capita consumption of these strange–looking oily liquids and dull grey powders is *eight pounds annually*. My contention is that these additives are killing us, a little at a time. What a painful and unnecessary way to go!

As an example, FDA–approved "butter yellow" and nitrogen trichloride were permitted for twenty–five years before the dye was found to induce cancer and the bleach to cause convulsions.

The point is this: Read the labels on supermarket foods; then start with a program of obtaining foods from alternative sources.

Your life depends on it!

For More Information

The following are strongly recommended and should be in your local library.

- *Food for People Not for Profit*, Lerza and Jacobson
- *Commercial Foods Exposed*, G. Horsley
- *The Chemical Feast*, James Turner
- *The Poisons in Your Food*, William Longgood
- *Eat Your Heart Out: Profiteering in America*, Jim Hightower
- *Consumer Beware*, Beatrice T. Hunter
- *Keeping Healthy in a Polluted World*, Harold Taub
- *Everything You Wanted to Know About Nutrition*, Dr. David Reuben
- *Let's Get Well*, Adelle Davis
- *The Beverly Hills Medical Diet*, Arnold Fox, M.D.

"Margarine is one atom away from being a plastic.**"**

The Ten *Worst* Foods You Can Eat

Supermarket white bread: It's really not bread at all but a near–plastic concoction made from devitalized flour and a lot of chemicals. Rats die when they eat it and weevils won't touch it. They know something you don't. It won't support life.

Coke and its variations: 99 percent water at an outrageous price. The other ingredients include phosphoric acid and lots of sugar. Without the sugar it would taste like vinegar. Try soaking human teeth in it overnight and see what happens to them. It's shocking.

Cool Whip, Dream Whip, etc: Mainly water, sugar and lots of strange chemicals floating directly into your home on a sea of advertising that is 100 percent lies.

Bacon: Virtually all brands of bacon contain nitrosamines—a medically designated carcinogen. And—in addition to that deadly ingredient—it's mostly fat and water.

Plain white sugar: It's really a drug devoid of any benefit to the body except empty calories. Obesity, diabetes, tooth decay and heart disease are but a few of the results of sugar consumption.

Baby foods: Mostly water and sugar, the latter to get your child hooked on sweet tastes for life. And the cost is prohibitive. Why not make your own baby health foods—for pennies—from your own menu. A blender will make them edible to the little toothless ones.

Sugared cereals: In a fancy box loaded with sugar, these breakfast candies are the most overpriced cereals you can possibly buy. Adorned with synthetic vitamins, this junk is less nutritious than the box it came in.

Breakfast squares and Pop Tarts: Dead flour, drug sugar and dangerous fats, these overpriced cookies will land you in the intensive–care ward sooner or later. And you'll be broke when you get there from paying those extravagant prices.

Prime USDA beef: High in fat, loaded with cholesterol and diethyl stilbestrol (a growth stimulating chemical), our beef is so bad in every way that most countries won't allow its importation. Just ask the Canadians, for example.

Pringles: This canned chip is the final insult to a self–respecting potato. Made from low–grade potato mush, the only good thing you can say for them is that they'll last longer than you will.

Actually, this list could be much longer since it is only representative of how bad food has become in America. There's really just one practical solution: Stay out of su-permarkets and buy your food from sources where purity and freshness are assured.

The Ten *Best* Foods You Can Eat

Here are the ten most health–packed foods you can eat, at any price. (But they cost you only one–tenth the price of the foods you're buying today.)

Sprouts: Fresh, full of enzymes and life, grown in your own home without chemicals, nutritious and vitamin rich, these would be my first choice for vigorous health.

Fresh raw vegetables and fruits: Grown organically or in your own garden, these will build your body and eliminate disease.

Fertile eggs: From chickens that are allowed to live the outdoor life with no chemicals in their feed, these eggs not only taste great, but they provide tremendous nutrition in a small package. Cholesterol is not a problem since these contain lecithin.

Grains seeds and nuts: As long as they are from sources free of dangerous chemicals, both items can ensure good health and maximum nutrition.

Plain yogurt: Make your own and be assured of purity. Bulgarians and many other old–world cultures rely on this to provide all that is needed for longevity.

Raw juices: Made from pure, fresh fruits and vegetables, these have arrested the course of degenerative diseases like MS and diabetes. Try them yourself and see if you don't feel better immediately.

Beans: With many varieties from which to choose, beans provide complementary protein when combined with grains and other foods. Low in cost, high in good–quality protein and other food values, the lowly bean can provide what you need for health.

Potatoes: A basic food that will provide good nutrition in a great many ways. And try all the varieties, including yams and sweet potatoes.

Fish: The staple of many cultures, fresh fish can be prepared in an endless number of delicious ways. High in the food values you need and low in fat.

Poultry: This category would include chicken, ducks, turkeys and other fowl, since they are similar. All possess protein with minimal fat and, *if organically raised*, are free of chemicals.

Build your diet around these foods, and you'll be building a body that can withstand almost any stress. Just make sure that the sources are reliable, or grow and prepare your own.

The Convenience Store

It's hard to believe that many people are somehow surviving on a diet that they purchase from a Quick–Stop or convenience market. If you've been in one lately, try to recall if there was anything *fresh* in the store other than dairy products. From my own explorations, almost everything has a pull–date a year hence. That's not for your convenience but for the profit of those who stock these insidious outlets. In a way you have to think of these stores as sort of *stores for the stomach*.

With an indefinite shelf–life, any food product you would find would have every bit of life and pizzazz squeezed and chemicalized out of it. One might as well eat nails. I have a strong suspicion that the people who make our processed foods intend to purvey all of their products through convenience stores. After all, then they wouldn't have to mess around with all those perishables, like fresh fruits and vegetables.

There's a sure cure for "convenience–store indigestion," when you see one, *step on the gas before you get gas.*

Where To Buy

Pass up all the convenience stores, and find a ranch or farm where they grow natural, organic foods. Alternatively, find a genuine health or natural food store, retail or wholesale. You can buy from the latter by forming a coop with friends and neighbors.

A Summary Of The Dollar–A–Day Concept For Busy People

Why It Is Important To Eat Better For Less

Most food sold in America is processed. That means it has had most of its food value removed and its remainder polluted with chemicals that are cumulatively harmful to humans. There is strong evidence that our one–in–four cancer rate is related to the increasing use of food additives.

Natural, Unprocessed Food Is Available Now

You don't have to wait another day to improve your health with a more natural diet. Go to your local natural food store and buy some basics. We've provided a starter list. Other sources of good natural food include feed and grain stores, neighborhood coops (you can start your own), ranches and farms that use organic methods, and foods that you grow yourself. As the demand increases, more and more outlets will exist.

You Can Make Delicious Meals from Simple Ingredients

You'll never taste a better hot cereal than freshly ground whole–grain wheat simmered slowly and then served with fresh fruit and a little milk or cream. This is just one example of hundreds of basic recipes available in numerous books. We provide a sampling herein. Freshly prepared food always tastes better than canned, frozen or otherwise processed meals. And it's not only less trouble than you think, it's fun!

Fresh, Raw Foods Are Best for Optimum Health

You can save time and energy costs by concentrating your diet around foods that are alive. Cooking kills the enzymes which are essential to assimilation. Therefore, if you eat plenty of fresh fruits and vegetables along with homemade sprouts, you'll regain and maintain your health.

Saving Money Is a Bonus

The best food is the cheapest. Whole grain wheat—which, once it's prepared the quick, easy way I show you below, is one of the most potent natural healing foods on earth—is only $10 per hundred pounds.

Three Proofs

Proof Number One: The average person on this planet lives on food that costs less than twenty–five cents a day. They eat little meat or sugar, and certainly nothing processed. Their health is better than that of most Americans.

Proof Number Two: Basic commodities are cheaper now than in the Great Depression. For example, wheat, oats, corn and rice are at rock bottom. You can buy a year's supply of these items for less than $100.

Proof Number Three: I practice what I preach and often eat well on much less than a dollar a day. I have more energy and strength than when I was half my present age.

A Natural Foods Inventory and Sample Kit

Introduction

Take a walk with me through my food storage area. That big metal can contains organic whole–grain wheat from Idaho. The one next to it has forty pounds or so of whole–kernel white corn. Lined up on the shelves are one–gallon glass jugs full of millet, alfalfa seeds, mung beans, brown rice, barley, split peas, lentils, and sunflower and pumpkin seeds. Well–sealed inside two separate containers is a goodly supply of dry milk powder—skim of course. Next to it is one of my favorites: rolled oats still in its feed store sack. Nearby is a large bag of walnuts, and a smaller one of almonds. Potatoes and onions are stored in a cool, dark drawer. Along a high shelf are jars, bottles and other containers of spices, herbs, blackstrap molasses, kelp, brewers yeast, wheat germ, tamari, dried fruits, carob, vinegar, dry yeast and olive oil. The refrigerator contains my current supply of other oils, ready–to–eat yogurt, fruits and vegetables of all kinds, and a small amount of fresh fish and chicken.

Nowhere will you find white sugar, "enriched" flour, TV dinners, coffee, or anything that has been processed or has any additives.

My conversion to a natural diet didn't happen overnight. Actually it took many years of gradual adaptation. After all, I grew up when there was no information readily available on the subject of processed vs. unprocessed foods. Furthermore, both small and large grocery stores carried just about the same merchandise: white bread, margarine, soft drinks and lots of canned stuff. Lacking other directions and counsel, I presumed that this is what I should eat.

This went on until I was about forty years old. Then, very gradually and almost imperceptibly, I got religion—nutritional religion. Thanks to authors like Kordel and Bieler who advocated healthier foods, I began to add wheat germ and sprouts to my food inventory. At the same time I kicked tobacco and booze. Before I couldn't run around the block without collapsing; on a better diet I began the arduous sport of motorcycle motorcross. Today I'd rather play Russian roulette than eat a Big Mac.

Space Requirements

The surprising thing about using natural foods is that they don't require a lot of room to store. If you know the secrets, natural foods need much less room than packaged junk foods. That's because most natural foods are compact and condensed. A pound of oats takes up much less room than a pound of processed oat cereal in a big, four–color–process package. Also, many processed foods contain water; with most bulk foods there is minimal water being stored.

If you are average in your food consumption, you eat about 2.5 pounds of food per day. That's cooked weight, of course. That's abut 900 pounds per year. Let's say, just for fun, that you "have this thing" for rice. You desire it for breakfast, lunch and dinner. Since rice cooks up to about three times its weight, just *three or four hundred pounds* will provide all the food you need *for an entire year!* You can easily store four 100–pound sacks of rice under your bed.

This raises an important point: You need a lot less space than you may think to store all the food you'll need for an entire year. This is especially true when seeds for sprouting or dry milk for yogurt are concerned. Each of the latter produce a great volume of highly nutritious and delicious food when prepared with water. For example, one pound of dry beans will yield *eight* pounds of healthful sprouts. Thus, a single, 100–pound sack of dry beans will provide almost enough food to meet your nutritional needs for a year! (I've read that a family of seven—who were trapped in their house during a Utah winter—survived by eating nothing but sprouts for those six months. The total cost per meal was a little over seven cents. And they didn't even have a sniffle during the entire six months!)

Where To Store and How

That's easy. Under beds, on shelves in your closet or in the garage. If you have limited space, just don't store so much. Buy more often. Many restaurants will save their food–grade containers for you if you ask. Clean them out, and you have free storage containers. I've found glass gallon jugs used for wine to be ideal. A good way to prevent insect proliferation is to drop a lighted wooden match in the container just before sealing. The flame will use up available oxygen.

Five Basic Foods That You Can Buy For Less Than 50¢ a Pound In Bulk Quantities

While writing this, I am looking at a newly arrived price list from Westlam Foods, with offices in Chino, California Despite inflation, it is encouraging to see that a 100–pound sack of long–grain brown rice still costs only $26.65 and that green peas are less than 20 cents a pound in 100–pound lots. True, you have to buy quantities to get this low price, but we will discuss some ways to do this elsewhere. Even if you bought less than the 100–pound quantities, the price would not be too far above what we've just quoted. For example, 25–pound sacks of that brown rice are only $7.16. Looking through the list, here are my five choices for basics under 50 cents a pound:

	Per Hundred Pounds
long–grain brown rice	$26.65
green peas	19.45
pinto beans	29.95
yellow popcorn	21.95
red lentils	48.12

Let's say that you join with five other people to buy the minimum purchase of two thousand five hundred pounds or five sacks of each item. Your share would cost $146.12. Out of your five–hundred pounds of food, you could make many delicious meals all year long. Averaging an increase in weight of three times for all but the popcorn, you would end up with one thousand five hundred pounds of food, or more than is needed for one person for one year! And all for less than one hundred and fifty dollars. And that doesn't include the popcorn, which would add another one hundred pounds.

Let's assume now that these basic foods would comprise more than half the diet of an average person—the balance being vegetables, fruits, chicken and fish and so forth. The cost–per–person would then be only $73.06 per year, or just about 20 cents per day! With the modest addition of the other items mentioned, it would be possible to live for less than $1 a day!

So there's proof positive and a price list from a typical supplier to boot!

Summary

The more that I investigate the wonderful potential of buying and storing basic bulk foods, the more I'm convinced that this is the best way to ensure good health. Forget, for the moment, cost. After all, even if this were the most expensive way to go, it would be the cheapest in the long run because your health is priceless. But think of it: You not only get the best nutrition but at the lowest cost. It's the antithesis of everything that the food establishment is foisting on a bemused public. But at least you know the truth now. Pass it along!

Cooperative (Coop) Buying

Buying basic bulk foods cooperatively can be as simple as sharing a fifty–pound sack of wheat with a good friend and as complex as organizing two hundred people in your area to buy just about everything they need direct from wholesalers. It's entirely up to you and your needs, as well as the needs of your neighbors and friends. For example, let's say that several of your friends are cheese lovers. OK, find a cheese specialty store or wholesaler and offer to buy a five– or ten–pound block of cheese if they'll provide a discount. One member of the group can volunteer to slice up the cheese in the desired sizes, wrap, and deliver it. The next time around, someone else in the group can perform this service.

From this illustration, it's obvious that coop buying is really not difficult at all, and the benefits are many:

- You will know the quality of your purchased products, since you're buying either from the source or close to the source.

- The price can be lower (in some cases, extremely low) as it would be for quantity prices on large amounts of grain, beans or seeds.

- It's fun to shop at the wholesale level. (For example, you'll love roaming around a large produce market early in the morning, seeing the huge quantities of fruits and vegetables changing hands.

- Coop buying can generate a great sense of community, welding together a diverse group of people: young and old, different races, and various income levels.

- Your group can go direct to the source—the farmer or rancher—even pick or gather foods. Thus, the foods would be freshest and at the lowest possible cost.

These are but a few of the advantages of cooperating in food purchasing. You'll discover many more in your coop adventure experience.

My suggestion is to start small with a few close friends and, if it works out to everyone's satisfaction, then gradually add more members. Once a coop becomes quite large, it can easily be split into two, and these can then expand as needed.

The foods that can be purchased initially with the least difficulty in storing and sharing are bulk grains, beans and seeds. For example, a hundred–pound sack of pinto beans can be divided into ten–pound sacks with ease. All you need are bags and a stapler.

Once started, the list of foods wanted will grow by itself as members of your coop think of more and more items to include. Try cooping. I'm sure you'll enjoy it, save money and eat better all at the same time.

SHIPPERS AND WHOLESALERS OF ORGANIC AND NATURAL FOODS

Arkansas

SHILOH FARMS, INC.
Route 59
Sulphur Springs, AR 72768
(501) 298-3297
(Ship: wholesale; full line)

California

CHICO SAN, INC.
1114 W. First St.
Chico, CA 95926
(Ship: wholesale; organic rice, and various grain products, sea vegetables, condiments)

LEE ANDERSON'S COVALDA DATE CO.
P.O. Box 908, Highway 86
Coachella, CA 92236
(714) 398-3551
(Ship: wholesale; organic dates, date products, low-calorie pecans, grapefruit, oranges, lemons, and grapes)

EREWHON, INC.
8454 Steller Drive
Culver City, CA 90230
(Ship: wholesale for minimum order of $75.00; grains, seeds, butters, cereals, flour, juice, Japanese imports)

RANCHER WALTENSPIEL
Timber Crest Farms
4791 Dry Creek Road
Healdsburg, CA 95448
(707) 433-2800
(Ship or pick-up: wholesale; dried fruit, organic honey-dipped prunes, dates, raisins, figs, peaches, pears, papayas)

WEST VALLEY PRODUCE CO.
712 South Central Avenue
Los Angeles, CA 90021
(Ship: wholesale; organic produce)

AHLER'S ORGANIC DATE CO.
Grapefruit Garden
P.O. Box 726
Mecca, CA 92254
(Ship, world-wide: wholesale to health food stores; dates, grapefruit)

HADLEY YOSEMITE FARMS
P.O. Box 2163
Merced, CA 95340
(Ship: wholesale to health food stores; dried fruit, both sulphured and unsulphured)

VALLEY COVE RANCH
P.O. Box 603
Springfield, CA 93265
(Ship, Parcel Post: 15% discount on 100 pound citrus fruit quantities, wholesale to orders in excess of 25 cartons; Navel and Valencia oranges, Satsuma mandarins, Marsh seedless grapefruit, pomegranates, Lisbon lemons, Kinnow tangerines)

THE FOOD CHAKRA
415 Topanga Canyon Boulevard
Topanga, CA 90290
(Ship or pick-up: wholesale; fruits and vegetables)

JAFFE BROTHERS NATURAL FOODS
28650 Lilac Road
Valley Center, CA 92082
(Ship or pick-up: wholesale)

EL MOLINO MILLS
345 N. Baldwin Park Boulevard
City of Industry, CA 91746
(213) 962-7167
(Ship through distributors; natural carob snacks; grains, flours, seeds)

BARBARA'S BAKERY, INC.
So. San Francisco, CA 94080
(Ship or pick-up: wholesale to distributors only; baked goods, snack products suitable for vending machines)

UNITED NATURALS
David Lippman
Corner of 1 and E St.
P.O. Box 4881
Eureka, CA 95501
(707) 443-4566

PLUS PRODUCTS
Irvine, CA 92705
(Natural snack foods)

ROTO-RICO CO.
490 N. Raleigh Ave.
El Cajon, CA 92020
(714) 442-2202
(Manufacturer of juice machines)

WESTERN ROTO JUICER
15164 Golden West Circle
Westminster, CA 92683
(Manufacturer of juice machines)

SUNBURST ORGANIC FOODS
20 S. Kellogg
Goleta, CA 93107

WIND SPIRIT
11601 Clover Road
Los Angeles, CA 01166

LANDSTROM COMPANY
Ernest C. Miehle
Box 2886
336 Oyster Point Boulevard
So. San Francisco, CA 94080
(415) 873-6240
(Ship: to health food stores only; full line)

JOHNSON FOODS, INC.
610 Rodier Drive
Glendale, CA 91201
(213) 245-3778
(Pick-up only: to Los Angeles organizations; yogurt)

SOKEN TRADING COMPANY
P.O. Box 1705
Sausalito, CA 94965
(415) 332-0633
(Wholesale to distributors only; noodles, crackers, snacks, rice vinegar)

Colorado

CERES NATURAL FOODS
2582 Durango Drive
Colorado Springs, CO 80910
(303) 392-9062/9063
(303) 892-7142 (Denver/Boulder line)
(Ship: Rocky Mountain region; wholesale; full line)

Connecticut

EREWHON NATURAL FOODS
1 Civic Center Plaza
Hartford, CT 06103
(Pick-up only: no wholesale, but 10% discount offered on case lots; organic grains, beans, fruit, bread and pastry, raw milk, yogurt, tofu, miso, cookware, cosmetics)

Florida

LEE'S FRUIT CO.
Box 450
Leesburg, FL 32748
(Ship through Gift Fruit Shippers, Assn., pick-up at Packhouse: wholesale; citrus fruits, watermelons, honey)

BRODERSON GROVES
Route 2, Box 490
Merritt Island, FL 32952
(Ship: no discount; organic oranges, red seedless grapefruit)

TREE OF LIFE
315 Industrial Drive
St. Augustine, FL 32084
(904) 829-3484
(Ship: wholesale distributor to health food stores only; will provide names of local outlets)

GOLDEN FLOWER
1663 11th Street
Sarasota, FL 33522
(813) 366-3019
(Ship: wholesalers and gift fruit shipments to individuals; organic citrus, tropical fruits and vegetables, raw honey)

Illinois

ELAM MILLS
2625 Gardner Road
Broadview, IL 60153
(Ship: wholesale to distributors and retailers — health food stores — only; organic yellow corn meal)

HEALTH FOODS, INC.
155 West Higgins
Des Plaines, IL 60018
(Ship or pick-up: wholesale to health food stores; full line)

SUNRISE FARMS
George M. Wisbrock
17650 Torrence Avenue
Lansing, IL 60438
(Ship: wholesale on several items; organic prunes, juices, yeast, cheese. Vegetables shipped at customer's risk)

FLAVOR TREE FOODS, INC.
2645 N. Rose St.
Franklin Park, IL 60131
(Ship or pick-up: to distributors; snacks and confections suitable for vending machines)

IT'S NATURAL
Norman Coor
502 Main St.
Evanston, IL 60202
(312) 869-2232
(Pick-up only; retail with discount to schools, co-ops, etc.; produce, grains, seeds, dairy, beans, frozen foods)

Maryland

LONDON AND LEVINE, INC.
    Nature's Cupboard of Love
    New Morning Natural Foods
    Powerhouse
5617 Baltimore National Pike
Baltimore, MD 21228
(301) 788-4560
(Ship and pick-up: wholesale; full line)

LAURELBROOK FOODS
Box 47
Bel Air, MD 21014
(301) 879-1717 or (800) 638-7610
(Ship: wholesale; full line. Deliver for minimum orders of $200.00)

Massachusetts

EREWHON, INC.
33 Farnsworth Street
Boston, MA 02210
(Ship, orders delivered free to New England, New York, New Jersey: wholesale; full line)

STEARNS ORGANIC FARM
Penelope Turton
859 Edmands Road
Framingham, MA 01701
(Pick-up only; wholesale on own farm-grown produce only; retail on grocery items)

Michigan

MIDWEST NATURAL FOOD DISTRIBUTORS
170 Aprill Drive
Ann Arbor, MI 48103
(313) 769-8444
(Ship: wholesale to retail stores only; delivery within 300 miles or by common carrier outside delivery route; full line; write for catalog; will direct to local outlet in lieu of direct customer sales)

EDEN FOODS (food manufacturer)
4601 Platt Road
Ann Arbor, MI 48194
(313) 973-9400
(Ship: wholesale to store front co-ops; full line)

Minnesota

SNO-PAC FARMS
Caledonia Cold Storage Co.
Ramon J. Gengler
379 S. Pine Street
Caledonia, MN 55921
(Ship, depending on distance: wholesale; peas, sweet corn, wheat)

Missouri

EARTHWONDER, INC.
Natural Foods Warehouse and Bakery
1735 East Trafficway
Springfield, MO 65802
(417) 831-1565
(Ship: retail, with wholesale available to qualifying groups; full line)

New Hampshire

SALTMARSH CIDER MILL
Central Square
New Boston, NH 03070
(Ship, express charges collect: wholesale; apple cider vinegar)

New Jersey

BALANCED FOODS, INC.
Sam Reiser
2500 83rd St.
North Bergen, NJ 07047

New York

SHADOWFAX WHOLE FOODS, INC.
30 Crandall Street
Binghamton, NY 13905
(607) 723-5446
(Deliver within area or pick-up: wholesale to buying groups and health foods stores; full line)

THOUSAND ISLAND APIARIES
Clayton, NY 13624
(Ship or pick-up: wholesale; liquid honey, crystallized honey, comb honey, beeswax, wax cappings in season)

LANG APIARIES
8448 New York Route 77
Gasport, NY 14067
(Pick-up, preferably, and ship: wholesale to health food stores and co-ops; natural and extracted honey — clover, fallflower, and buckwheat)

NOVA MEGA VITAMINS, INC.
P.O. Box 604
Glen Cove, NY 11542
(Ship: wholesale; vitamins)

MOTTEL HEALTH FOODS
451 Washington St.
New York, NY 10013
(Ship: wholesale to health food stores; full line)

SHERMAN FOODS, INC.
Ernest Fried
276 Jackson Avenue
Bronx, NY 10454
(212) 993-8900
(Ship only: wholesale to health food stores only; foods, vitamins)

THE GENERAL STORE FOR NATURAL FOODS
139 Atlantic Ave.
Brooklyn, NY 11201
(212) 875-9186
(Local delivery or pick-up: retail only; full line)

RAMAPO VALLEY CENTER
Route 17
Slatsburg, NY
(Pick-up only: wholesale to schools, co-ops, etc.; full line)

WELCH FOODS, INC.
Westfield, NY 14787
(716) 326-3131

DANNON MILK PRODUCTS
22-11 38th Avenue
Long Island City, NY 11101
(212) 361-2240
(Delivery in area: wholesale; yogurt)

North Carolina

LAURELBROOK FOODS
330 W. Davis
Raleigh, NC 27601
(Ship, or local delivery: wholesale; whole grains, seeds, beans, juices, kitchen items)

Ohio

GRABER PRODUCE
Glen Graber
13755 Duquette Avenue NE
Harville, OH 44632
(Ship, air freight, UPS in Fall, or pick-up — roadside market: fresh vegetables, grains)

Oklahoma

THE EARTH NATURAL FOOD STORE
309 S. Flood
Norman, OK 73069
(405) 364-3551
        or
1904 S. Harvard
Tulsa, OK 74112
(Ship on minimum orders of $10.00; wholesale to schools, co-ops, etc.; bulk whole grains, beans, mixed nuts, fruits, herbs)

Pennsylvania

PURE AND SIMPLE
Box 13
Boyertown, PA 19512
(Ship and pick-up: wholesale; full line)

PEN ARGYL MILLING CO., INC.
(Millers of Pocono Brand Buckwheat Cereals)
Pen Argyl, PA 18072
(Ship: wholesale for large orders; buckwheat groats, flour, kasha)

NATURALLY
Bill Rakita
226 S. State St.
Newton, PA 18940
(215) 945-3521
(Deliver: wholesale distributor of fresh fruits and vegetables, in season)

WALNUT ACRES
Penns Creek, PA 17862
(Ship UPS, Parcel Post, or commercial truck: wholesale; full line)

SUSTENANCE NATURAL FOODS
Route 162, Marshalton Village
Wdst Chester, PA 19380
(Ship: wholesale; full line)

SHILOH FARMS EASTERN BRANCH
White Oak Road (near New Holland)
Martindale, PA 17549

HOFFMAN PRODUCTS
York, PA 17405
(Candy bars made from peanut butter, carob, honey, and tiger's milk)

NATURAL DEVELOPMENT CO.
Box 215
Bainbridge, PA 17502
(717) 367-1566
(Ship or pick-up: retail; flours, grains, soybeans)

BETTER FOODS FOUNDATION, INC.
200 N. Washington Street
Greencastle, PA 17265
(717) 597-7127
(Ship: wholesale; full line — some organic)

Rhode Island

MEADOWBROOK HERB GARDENS
Wyoming, RI 02898
(Ship and sell in own store: wholesale; herb seasonings, herb teas, herbal cosmetics, herb books. Catalog, 50¢)

Texas

ARROWHEAD MILLS
Box 866
Hereford, TX 79045
(Ship: wholesale to distributors; grains, beans, seeds)

Wisconsin

DIAMOND DAIRY GOAT FARM
Route 2
Portage, WI 53901
(Ship: wholesale; goat cheese and milk)

HONEY BOY FARM, INC.
Route 4, Box 323
Baraboo, WI 53913
(Ship by UPS or commercial truck, or pick-up: wholesale; natural and raw honey in clover, basswood, or wildflower flavors)

Washington, D.C.

HOME RULE NATURAL FOODS
1825 Columbia Road, NW
Washington, DC 10009
(Customer pick-up: varying discounts to approved groups; full retail line)

Canada

FILSINGER'S NATURAL FOODS
R.R. #3
Ayton, Ontario, Canada
(Pick-up at farm store: wholesale; meat, poultry, eggs, fruit, vegetables, stone ground flour, soil minerals and fertilizers, natural spray materials. Canadian orders only)

LIFESTREAM NATURAL FOODS LTD.
12411 Vulcan Way
Richmond, British Columbia
Canada V6V 1J7
(Pick-up, ship via common carrier: wholesale; full line)

BUTTERNUT

A Food Factory In Your Home

The prepared foods that you buy in a supermarket were once basic ingredients—items like wheat, corn, milk, eggs, and so forth. But during processing, these otherwise healthful substances suffered in two ways:

1. They were mauled, beaten, ground, and twirled, and to them were added many strange and indigestible chemicals.

2. The price was upped to an amazing level. Usually just below the point where you would say, "To hell with it."

So when you go to your grocery and buy processed items, you lose in two ways—in nutrition and in economy. But this doesn't have to be. With a few simple pieces of equipment, most of which you probably already have, you can become *your own food processor*. You can make anything the food industry makes—and make it better! Here's proof:

The other day we went on a tour of our local supermarket to see what new horrors were being foisted on the hapless public. A brightly colored package caught my eye: "Frozen Popovers," it said. The price tag was $2.10 for six of them, and they weighed a total of five ounces. Wow!! That appeared to be a lot of "bread" for just a little bread. "Heat in oven until hot," the directions said. With just a little more effort, you could whip up a batch of homemade popovers yourself. After all, they're only a mixture of eggs, milk, and flour. A little work and you'd have enough for a tableful of hungry eaters. No doubt they would taste better, since they'd be fresher and wouldn't contain the BHT and BHA that the store version had, not to mention, by the way, that the flour would not be that deadly "enriched" kind.

So, this thought occurred to us after placing the frozen popover package carefully to rest in its icy coffin: Why doesn't someone figure out how much one is really paying the food industry to make all those processed foods that you so conveniently buy in a market? Or, to put it more directly, how much could you *earn* by making them at home. Naturally, this was a challenging task, and we elected ourselves to find the answers. Here are the results:

Ready–made: They cost thirty–five cents each, and we figured it took about ten seconds to put them in the oven.

Homemade: two eggs, three fourths cup milk and one cup flour yields twelve popovers. This probably could serve a family for less than 65 cents total. The time to make them is about two minutes. The cost is about 5 cents each. In two minutes, you've saved $1.46. This is almost $44.00 an hour—a good wage for pouring some milk, eggs and flour in a blender and then transferring the batter to muffin tins.

Not only are they pure, they are cheap. Far cheaper than any supermarket sale price. Now you'll have an outlet for that sugar craving, without the sugar!

In the following sections, we will show you exactly how to make a veritable cornucopia of delicious foods from natural, bulk ingredients.

Herbs and Spices

What do grocery stores sell? One answer is alleged foods, but their real bag is selling flavor. They take the same basic foods that we've been discussing and doctor them up with various items to make them taste better. A good example would be a Mexican TV dinner. Basically, it consists of corn, beans and a little cheese. Most manufacturers depend heavily on the cheapest seasoning there is—salt—and after that, sugar, since its cost–per–pound is not much more than salt. From here on, things get worse as the producer of this aluminum–tray monster loads the poor, innocent enchiladas with tongue–twisting chemicals. Somewhere amidst all those inorganic molecules one might find a smidgen of chili powder, but don't count on it.

The answer is so simple. You can stock up on the basic herbs and spices listed below and create taste treats that are pure and genuine: real sage in that turkey stuffing, fresh–ground cumin seeds in your Mexican beans, and savory basil in pesto and spaghetti sauce.

Here then are some recommendations for your spice rack and home herb garden.

allspice	cloves	nutmeg	savory
anise	coriander	onion	scallions
basil	cumin	oregano	sesame
bay leaf	curry powder	paprika	shallots
capers	dill	parsley	sorrel
caraway	fennel	pepper	tarragon
cardamom	garlic	pepper pods	thyme
cassia	horseradish	pickling spice	turmeric
cayenne	juniper berries	poppy seed	vanilla
celery seed	leeks	rocket	watercress
chervil	mace	rosemary	woodruff
chili powder	marjoram	roses	
chives	mint	saffron	
cinnamon	mustard	sage	

There are, of course, many other spices, some so exotic they never reach our shores. The list of herbs would be even longer, since these are used for both seasoning and medicinal purposes.

However, those presented can add so much to the basic bulk foods that you'll be amazed. Just check the recipe that follows. Only a trifling amount of five spices make a simple corn dish into ambrosia. Make it, and see for yourself!

Indian Pudding

4 cups skim milk
1 cup yellow corn meal
2 eggs lightly beaten
2/3 cup molasses
1/2 teaspoon cinnamon
1/4 teaspoon ground cloves
1/4 teaspoon ground ginger
1/8 teaspoon allspice
1/8 teaspoon nutmeg

- Preheat oven to 325°. Boil milk and add corn meal gradually, beating well to introduce air. When mixture thickens, set aside to cool. Then stir in other ingredients and mix well.

- Pour into buttered baking dish and bake for two hours. Serve warm with or without a spoonful of chilled yogurt, or with heavy cream.

- This is a classic dessert that is the highlight of many famous restaurants' dessert offerings. It's a prime example of how a few–cents worth of spices can make basic foods sing!

Cheese Straws

1 cup grated sharp cheese
3 tablespoons butter
4 1/2 tablespoons milk
1/2 teaspoon cayenne
1 1/2 cups fine bread crumbs
3/4 cup whole wheat flour

- Preheat oven to 400°. Mix cheese and butter, then add remaining ingredients; knead until smooth.

- Roll out on flowered breadboard to 1/4 inch thickness and cut with knife into strips about 6 inches long and 1/2–inch wide. Place on oiled cookie sheets and bake until browned.

- I've always been amazed at how much flavor a little cayenne imparts—another good example of how inexpensive ingredients become gourmet treats with addition of small amounts of spice or herbs.

Dilly Beans

string beans (at least two pounds)
1 cup vinegar
1 cup water
1 1/2 teaspoons dill seed
5 cloves garlic
3 hot peppers, crushed

- Combine all ingredients in a pot and cook until tender. Remove beans and chill.

- Serve as an appetizer. The marinade can be used again, so try it with carrots, cabbage, and other crisp vegetables.

Savory Navy Beans

2 cups navy beans
1 onion, chopped
1 teaspoon fresh or dried savory
dash cayenne or hot sauce

- Soak beans overnight. Drain and simmer with seasonings until beans are tender—two to three hours.

- If you don't overseason the beans, the subtle flavor emerges.

Rosemary Chicken

1 tablespoon fresh rosemary (can substitute 1 teaspoon dried)
2 teaspoons white wine vinegar
1/4 cup butter
2 tablespoons olive oil

4 onions, chopped fine
2 cloves garlic, crush
1 large organic chicken, cut up
1/2 cup white wine
2 teaspoons minced parsley

- Soak rosemary in vinegar. Melt butter and oil in skillet. Add onions and garlic, and saute until tender. Add chicken pieces and saute until golden brown. Add vinegar, rosemary wine and parsley. Cover and cook until very tender.

- An inexpensive party dish that will go well with crusty French bread and a green salad.

Desert Spuds

3 medium potatoes, unpeeled
1 large red onion
2 tablespoons HVP (hydrolyzed vegetable protein)
1/4 cup olive oil
1 pinch each of the following dried herbs:
   rosemary
   oregano
   paprika
   cumin

- Chop spuds and onions into bite sizes and sprinkle with seasonings. Saute slowly in olive oil until tender. When available, I add some fresh desert sage.

- Potatoes and onions travel well so they were always with me on my nomadic adventures especially in desert areas. Making them in different ways became a challenge, and this was one of the responses. This would make a fine side dish to the Rosemary Chicken.

Tabbouleh

1 cup cracked wheat (buy or make in your blender)
1/2 cup finely chopped fresh mint
1 1/2 cups finely chopped parsley
1 cup finely chopped green onion
3/4 cup chopped tomatoes
1/2 cup olive oil

3 tablespoons lemon juice
freshly ground black pepper

- Cook cracked wheat until tender but still *al dente*. Cool and mix with other ingredients.

- This is a good example of low–cost bulk ingredients becoming a classic international salad. If you've traveled in some of the poorer countries of the world, you may have tried similar dishes. Their existence explains why it's possible to survive on little.

Pesto

1 cup chopped fresh basil leaves
3 cloves garlic, peeled
1/2 cup freshly grated Parmesan or Romano cheese
6 tablespoons olive oil
1/4 cup walnut meats
1/2 cup parsley
1 teaspoon dried marjoram or sprig of fresh marjoram

- In Genoa, Italy, you would use a mortar and pestle to make this sauce. But a blender works fine. Put in everything but the olive oil and blend, adding oil a few drops at a time. Pour this sauce over a pound of freshly cooked noodles or spaghetti and toss. How do you say "yummy" in Italian?

Review of Herbs and Spices

- Herbs and spices are the key to flavorful dishes. Worldwide, cooks have learned how to make the most of any dish by adding judicious amounts. While some are expensive, most are cheap in terms of what they can do to increase the flavors of virtually anything you eat.

- Processed foods bank on your desire for flavor, but you can beat them to the draw by doing it yourself. The examples we've given are but a tiny fraction of herb–and spice–enhanced recipes. There are entire cookbooks that emphasize the use of seasonings.

- Many herbs and spices grow wild, and you can gather your own. I recall, for instance, that the entire facade of the University of Nevada in Las Vegas was festooned with rosemary. And those you can't find, you can grow yourself. An herb garden in a window box is a standard item in Europe. Seeds are available in any garden supply store.

- Don't hesitate to buy spices in quantity if you plan to use a lot. For example, I keep a pound of chili powder and another of cumin in my kitchen all the time. If you use them up within a year, they won't lose their flavor. Also, if you buy in bulk, share with friends on a coop basis.

- In summary, you'll enjoy your food much more if you'll experiment with the world of herbs and spices. Make a few mistakes—it won't really matter because eventually you'll discover new and interesting ways to prepare basic foods. And that will be the payoff.

Those Little Envelopes of Mixes, Soups, Seasonings

Let's start with something simple so you'll see how little effort is involved in running a food factory in your kitchen. At a natural food store, buy a few ounces of:

- dried onion flakes

- garlic powder

- chili powder

- spices (your choice of favorites)

- dehydrated vegetables such as peppers, parsley, carrots and so forth (You can also prepare your own by chopping or grating fresh veggies and drying them in a slow oven.)

- a variety of herbs (such as basil, rosemary, thyme, paprika and so forth)

- whole wheat flour (make your own in your blender)

Now you're prepared to make an array of mixes, soups and seasonings. For example, here's the exact ingredients list from a package of onion soup and dip mix:

dehydrated onions	** partially hydro- genated soybean and cottonseed oil	spices
** dextrose		** corn syrup solids
** salt		* caramel color
** sugar	** soy sauce solids (soy bean, wheat, corn protein ex- tracts, salt, corn syrup, caramel color)	* dextrin
** monosodium glutamate		* citric acid
		lemon juice solids and natural flavor

The items starred can be tossed out with no loss in food value or flavor since our homemade recipe will provide good substitutes. The items double–starred are actually harmful to human beings.

So what does that leave in the recipe for onion soup? Just the dehydrated or dried onions, spices, lemon–juice solids and natural flavor. You just don't need the other junk. Here's your home good–factory recipe that I think you'll like:
dried (dehydrated) onion flakes

- sesame seeds, finally ground and/or powdered kelp (looks like pepper)

- spices (your own selection from your inventory)

- a squeeze of lemon in the final soup or dip

And that's it. That's really all you need for creating a better and cheaper version of the store–bought mix.

Now let's look at costs. The prepared mix we've referred to costs about $1.80 for two 1 1/4–ounce packets. That's 90 cents each or a whopping $11.70 per pound. The same home mix will cost you about one–fifth of that or less, depending on what quantities you buy when you purchase in bulk.

In summary, you have greatly improved the quality of the soup mix while, at the same time, cutting costs drastically. Think about buying the basics in larger quantities, thus saving even more money. As long as they are kept in tightly sealed jars, they should last a year or more. Furthermore, the creation of your own soup mixes and similar items will not only be fun but will spark your creative energies to experiment with other basics. There's really no limit to what you can achieve once you start.

Variety!

Salt has been programmed as the basic seasoning in America, but it doesn't have to be in your home. It may take time to eliminate your craving for salty things, but it's certain to be beneficial in the long–term view of overall health. You'll be getting all the salt you need from the foods you eat.

Also, some experimentation will be required to find that "just right" combination of spices, herbs and other food elements that pleases your particular palate. But once you do, then the craving for salt will surely disappear. A good way to progress is keep a record of the amounts of seasonings you use in your own mixtures. A postage scale is ideal for weighing out small amounts, or you can use measures. Who knows—you may come up with a unique combination that will be as popular as Tabasco or caraway seeds in rye bread!

Some Test Ingredients

Just for fun, mix up one or more of these and apply the taste test:

tahini (a form of soy sauce)	savory
chili sauce	watercress
vinegar	cayenne
cinnamon	basil
cloves	mace
cumin	saffron
marjoram	black and white pepper
scallions	dill
chervil	sage

Some Suggested Applications

Garlic: rub on chicken parts before roasting, insert in lamb, rub on salad bowl.

Nutmeg: sprinkle on asparagus, beans, and especially steamed or baked squash.

Bay leaf: use in stews, soups, or with braised meats; remove before serving.

Paprika: lends a delightful color to omelettes, soups, hash–brown spuds.

Onions: wonderful with almost everything!

Parsley: ditto!

Rosemary: perks up lamb dishes, stew, and goulash.

Caraway: add to boiled potatoes, cheese dishes, breads, and rolls.

Specific Food Suggestions

Eggs: curry powder, mustard (dry), green pepper, mushrooms, onion, paprika, parsley.

Fish: bay leaf, lemon juice, marjoram, mushrooms, parsley, paprika, tomato.

Potatoes: onion, mace, green pepper, parsley, paprika.

Tomatoes: basil, marjoram, onion, chilis.

Green beans: marjoram, lemon juice, nutmeg, dill seed, French dressing (homemade).

Old Fashion Apple Peeler
Pares, Slices, and Cores in Seconds

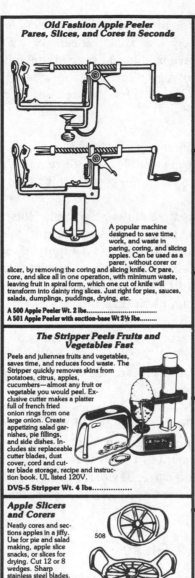

A popular machine designed to save time, work, and waste in paring, coring, and slicing apples. Can be used as a parer, without corer or slicer, by removing the coring and slicing knife. Or pare, core, and slice all in one operation, with minimum waste, leaving fruit in spiral form, which one cut of knife will transform into dainty ring slices. Just right for pies, sauces, salads, dumplings, puddings, drying, etc.

A 500 Apple Peeler Wt. 2 lbs............................
A 501 Apple Peeler with suction-base Wt 2½ lbs........

The Stripper Peels Fruits and Vegetables Fast

Peels and juliennes fruits and vegetables, saves time, and reduces food waste. The Stripper quickly removes skins from potatoes, citrus, apples, cucumbers—almost any fruit or vegetable you would peel. Exclusive cutter makes a platter full of french fried onion rings from one large onion. Create appetizing salad garnishes, pie fillings, and side dishes. Includes six replaceable cutter blades, dust cover, cord and cutter blade storage, recipe and instruction book. UL listed 120V.

DVS-5 Stripper Wt. 4 lbs................

Apple Slicers and Corers

Neatly cores and sections apples in a jiffy. Use for pie and salad making, apple slice snacks, or slices for drying. Cut 12 or 8 wedges. Sharp stainless steel blades.

508

512

508 Standard Apple Slicer Wt. ¼ lb............
512 Deluxe Apple Slicer Wt. ⅓ lb..............

Stainless Steel Corn Cutter and Creamer

The easiest way to remove tender, fresh corn from the cob. Five easy strokes finish an ear in less than 10 seconds. No mess, no splatter. Adjustable for just the right consistency of corn you desire from cream style to whole kernel. Fits all size ears. Easily cleaned.
202 B Corn Cutter Wt. ½ lb..........................

Kernel Kutter

Cuts all kernels from an ear of sweet corn with one quick stroke. None mashed or crushed. Cutter expands to fit all size ears. Perfect for freezing, canning, or fresh table use. Sharp stainless blade.

KK Kernel Kutter Wt. ½ lb...................

Stainless Pear Corer

The quick, easy way to core pears and eliminate excessive waste. Starting at stem end, insert small cutter scoop under stem and slide toward center of pear, dipping gently to allow larger part of scoop to remove core. Finish in one continuous motion by sloping up and out. Simple, fast.

278 Pear Corer Wt. ½ lb...................

French Bean Slicer

Slices beans lengthwise or French-style. Great for freezing or canning beans. Save hours by slicing beans the easy way. Tenderizes and makes delicious frozen beans. Heavy cast iron, with six steel cutting blades.

296 French Bean Slicer Wt. 2½ lbs...........

Bean Cutter

Turn the handle and out come perfectly cut string beans—sliced quickly and evenly by 3 revolving cutter blades. Ideal for canning and freezing. Heavy cast iron, with stainless steel cutting blades. 9" high

299 Bean Cutter Wt. 2½ lb..........................

Food Processing Equipment: *Do it yourself with items from this well—stocked, mail—order company. Back to Basics, Sandy, Ut 84070. Their catalog is a trip through time that's well worth taking.*

Herb Teas for the Time It Takes To Gather Them

Many people have discovered that caffeine in coffee and tannic acid in regular tea are harmful. Healthful, fragrant and *free* herb teas that you can gather in the wilds are marvelous alternatives. If you already live in the country, you have it made. And even city dwellers have an occasional opportunity to roam the wild woods. Either way, with a little luck you should be able to find herbs to provide the makings for homemade tea.

Chamomile: This little shrub grows wild in many parts of the world. Nip off the flowers, dry them, and pour boiling water over a tablespoon or two in the bottom of your teapot. Steep for a few minutes, and you'll have Peter Rabbit's favorite brew.

Mint: The other day while strolling up a stream bed near San Luis Obispo, I found a wild garden of genuine mint. There was enough there to start a mint–tea business! I selected some young stalks, dried them in the sun, and had a supply of tea to last the rest of the year. They are best stored in an airtight container. Incidentally, this is an easy one to grow. Just break off a stalk, put in a glass of water until roots form near the base, and then plant near some shade and plentiful water.

Rosehips: Wild roses are common in many states. The round seed pods, or rosehips as they are called, are a good source of vitamin C. Gather and dry them; then crumble them into your tea caddy for a comforting, nutritious drink.

Other possibilities: The leaves of blueberries and blackberries make a good addition to other wild teas. Blend them with dried flowers such as hibiscus, orange blossoms or passion flowers and throw in some lemon grass, hawthorn berries or a little rosemary. Some of the other popular ingredients in herb tea blends include ginger, anise, dried orange or lemon peel, fennel and clove. Try dried alfalfa with mint for a stimulating brew. And don't hesitate to make your own original combinations.

A Meal In A Glass

Grocer's shelves are loaded with packages of powdered drink mixes. There's just one problem. While the content may be reasonably palatable, the price is completely out of line. Usually, the main ingredients in these diet and breakfast drinks is skim milk powder. You may get 20 cents worth of dry milk and a few flavorings in a package costing two dollars or more.

The solution to this problem is simple: Make your own. Without further ado, here's how.

Your Own Drink Factory at Home

First, acquire bulk supplies of the following ingredients:

dry, non–instant, non–fat milk powder

edible (brewers) yeast, also called nutritional yeast

lecithin

molasses

honey

carob powder

wheat germ (be sure it's fresh)

soy protein

nuts and seeds of all kinds

With these items near your blender, you're ready to make almost any kind of drink. Start with something simple and basic such as:

Banana Bash

1 ripe banana
1/4 cup dry milk
1 cup pure water
1 tablespoon edible yeast
1 teaspoon honey or molasses

• Blend in your blender and drink immediately.

Orange Julian (Wild Bill's version of a famous chain's orange drink)

2 sectioned oranges
1/4 cup milk powder
1 teaspoon honey
1 cup pure water

• Blend and enjoy!

Carob Shake

1 tablespoon carob powder
1 cup pure water, chilled
1/4 cup dry milk powder
1 ripe banana
1 tablespoon edible yeast
small amount of honey

• Blend.

Almost everyone likes chocolate flavor, and here's a way to satisfy that craving without chocolate (which has caffeine and other harmful constituents). See if this isn't more satisfying than the ice cream version. One thing certain, it's far healthier.

Powerhouse Beverage

1 tablespoon each:
lecithin
edible yeast
wheat germ
soy protein
sunflower seeds
almonds
1 cup pure water
1/2 cup dry milk powder
1 teaspoon honey or molasses
1/2 cup pineapple or orange juice (or equivalent fresh fruit)

• Blend and see if this doesn't give you instant energy.

Obviously, there's no limit to the variety you can make on your own with basic ingredients plus fresh fruits or other healthful additions. And don't limit yourself to sweet drinks. Here's one that is a good alternative to expensive "V–8" type vegetable drinks.

V–12 Go Juice

1 fresh tomato
1/2 green pepper
handful spinach, watercress, butter lettuce

1 large stalk celery
1 tablespoon kelp powder
dash of hot sauce if desired
1/2 cup cold water

• Cut veggies into small pieces before blending.

The cost of this full meal in a glass would be dependent on the ingredients. As little as twenty cents—for the same smooth, complete, quick nutrition that costs up to $2 in a health bar. If you work in an office or a factory, I suggest that you carry it along in a thermos.

Milk from Seeds, Nuts, and Beans

If you love milk—and what it does for your emotions and your health—but if you just can't digest it any more, this is the answer to your prayer.

Some people are allergic to regular milk, whether from a cow or goat. Others simply can't digest it, especially when they get older. But milk seems to be a drink that appeals to many, and it's certainly useful to perk up cereal and such.

To make nut milks, just blend desired nuts with a small amount of pure water in your blender. You can regulate thickness by adding or reducing water. Seeds can be made into milk in the same way. For beans, see the section on soy.

Use your nut, seed and bean milks in any way that you would use regular milk. Pour over your hot oatmeal, combine in blender drinks, and even make your own ice cream recipes.

Keep in refrigerator as you would milk, or make up fresh as needed. The great thing about keeping regular milk cold when you can easily make a nut milk from freshly shelled walnuts, almonds, cashews or other nuts and use almost any kind of seeds from sunflower to sesame.

Yogurt

Imagine millions of workers preparing food for you while you sleep. That's just what happens when you make your own yogurt at home. Tiny yeast cells convert ordinary, dry skim milk into a wonderful, smooth, custard–like dish that can be used in hundreds of different ways.

The cost is so low you'll never want to pay the exorbitant prices for store yogurt. Another plus is that you won't be getting all those strange additives that food processors toss in their products. And furthermore, you can make it fresh anytime you want, in any quantity. It keeps well, so make a big batch and coast.

Healthwise, yogurt has some noteworthy benefits, the best of which is life extension. Bulgarians, who eat a lot of yogurt, claim that it is the best life insurance around!

And remember, yogurt is very easy to digest, which is a boon for seniors. The calcium it contains is readily absorbed. The protein is predigested—which is again a great advantage to older folks whose digestion is weak.

So here's how to make it:

Basic Yogurt Recipe

Mix one cup non–instant, skim milk powder with two cups warm water and a couple of tablespoons of pure yogurt from your health food store. You can also buy dry starter (which keeps indefinitely); use amount directed. Pour mixture into glass jar and keep in warm place:

- Unlit oven (the pilot light may keep it warm enough)

- On top of your water–heater

- In warm sunlight

- On a food warmer or "hot tray"

- Any other place where the temperature will be around 110F

The process takes from three to eight hours or until the mixture is quite firm. Then eat immediately or refrigerate. Yield is one pint, and you can make as much as you wish using the same proportions. If you like a thicker yogurt, add more milk powder. A teaspoon of honey added to your mixture will often speed up the process.

Flavor your yogurt with freshly chopped fruit, carob powder, molasses or honey. For variety, try topping with chopped dried fruits, nuts or sunflower seeds. Use it like mayonnaise in salad dressing recipes. Add chopped chives for a wonderful baked potato topping. The more you play around with your homemade yogurt, the more uses you'll find for it.

Kefir is a cultured milk product similar to yogurt except that it's thinner. Make in the same way using kefir starter from your health food store. Kefir is usually blended with fresh fruit purees for added flavor and color.

Note: Some kitchen appliance stores carry a unit that is especially designed to make your own yogurt. It consists of a small warming tray and four or more containers. The unit uses very little electricity since the temperature need not be above 120F.

Yogurt Smoothie

- Whirl a cup of homemade yogurt in your blender with:

  Sliced bananas
  Fresh peaches
  Wheat germ
  Brewer's yeast
  Lecithin
  A little honey or molasses

Or any variations of the above. That will give you a health drink far superior to any you could buy in a store. And the cost will be far less.

As one gets older, a juicer could be a beneficial investment. But if your teeth are in good shape, you don't really need one.

Cheese

If you like the factory version of cheese known as American process cheese spread, you can make your own. Just take a pound of old, dried—up cheese with a dubious reputation, (returns from stores would be just dandy), grind it up and add two packages of dissolved gelatin and two cups of water. Whirl in blender, and pour into mold to set up. That's exactly what the cheese people do, so you might as well beat them at their own game. However, if you don't like the idea of your cheese being made from old scraps and a lot of gelatin and water, you can make your own real cheese.

The Sinclairs, John and Judy, of Little River, California, enjoy virtual autonomy on their fifteen acres of verdant Mendocino County land. Along with gardens and orchards, they have a large herd of goats. One afternoon I learned the secret of having a cheese factory in your own kitchen. All you need for starters are the following:

- 1 quart whole milk (cow or goat are both fine)
- 2 tablespoons lemon juice

Heat the milk just to scalding; don't boil. Remove from heat and stir in lemon juice. Cover and let stand for several hours. Pour the mixture through a strainer or colander lined with cheesecloth (or other loose–mesh cloth) placed over a large bowl. Save the liquid that drops through; it's called the whey and can be used with skim milk powder to make yogurt. Allow the cheese mixture to drain for several hours or until it's dry.

And that's it—fresh, sweet, homemade cottage cheese to use in many ways. No additives, no high cost, just pure food you've made yourself.

If you want to go a step further, you can make a simple cheese by placing the cottage cheese wrapped in cheese cloth between two boards and applying pressure. Something heavy such as a pail of water or some bricks will do fine. The combination of squeezing and drying will produce a cheese that resembles the many peasant cheeses made in such countries as Greece and Mexico.

For variety, add chopped green onions to the cottage cheese before eating or making cheese. Pimientos, green chilis and olives may be used singly or in combination. And don't forget your sprouts. Now, there's a wonderful symbiosis: Homemade cheese with homegrown sprouts!!!

Mix Your Own Recipes

Herb Tea Blends

You won't have to pay those premium prices for a small box when you mix your own from bulk ingredients purchased from your local wholesale spice and herb dealer. The amounts are left to your own taste. Experiment with small quantities.

Cinnamon spice: Black tea, cassia, cinnamon extract or powder

Fruit blend: Hibiscus, lemon grass, rose hips, orange peel, peppermint

Jasmine spice: Jasmine tea, orange peel, cloves, cardamom

Orange mint: Black tea, orange peel, cinnamon, licorice root, peppermint

Spearmint spice: Spearmint, cinnamon, orange peel, cassia, cardamom, vanilla (pure)

Spice Blends

Chili blend: Chili peppers, cumin, garlic powder, oregano, coriander, allspice

Italian seasoning: Rosemary, oregano, thyme, basil, anise, cumin, garlic powder

Lemon pepper: Black pepper, garlic powder, dehydrated honey, wheat germ, citric acid, onion powder, lemon juice powder

Pickling spice: Bay leaf, coriander, chili peppers, dill seed, yellow mustard seed, cassia, ginger, caraway seed

Natural Food Snacks

Energy mix: Raisins, Spanish peanuts, sunflower kernels, Virginia peanuts, almonds, cashews

Deluxe trail mix: Blanched peanuts, date bits, golden seedless raisins, sunflower kernels, Thompson seedless raisins, almonds, cashews, Brazil nuts

Oriental mix: Corn nuts, rice crackers, Virginia peanuts, cashew pieces, almonds

Nutritious nuggets: Sunflower kernels, toasted whole wheat kernels, Spanish peanuts, soya nuts, corn nuts, pumpkin seeds

Dehydrated Vegetables and Fruits

Vegetable blend for soup: Dried puffed carrots, tomato flakes, celery stalk and leaf, cabbage diced, chopped onion, spinach flakes, parsley flakes red and green diced peppers

Blend for stew: Diced potatoes, sliced white onion, diced carrots, diced cabbage, celery stalks and leaves, diced red and green peppers, tomato flakes

Fruit galaxy mix: Dried peaches, apples, grapes, apricots and chopped dates

Note: To rehydrate fruits and vegetables, use about three parts water to one part dried ingredients.

Finally, experiment on your own. Once you have the basic ingredients in your kitchen inventory, you can let your imagination roam. But, to get your started, here are some of my standard combinations:

First, obtain a variety of storage jars or other containers such as No. 10 cans with plastic lids. They can range in size from 1/2–pint on up to a gallon or larger. Now, drawing from your inventory of bulk foods, you're ready to make any number of what the stores call "convenience foods."

Trail Mix: Combine 1 cup each of peanuts, raisins, chopped dried fruit, sunflower seeds, sesame seeds, chopped almonds and 2 cups toasted oatmeal in a larger glass jar. Shake vigorously. Keep tightly sealed. This is the perfect snack anytime and costs a fraction of prepared mixes. It's high in protein and other food values, so add it to simple foods like whole wheat cereal or rice pudding. I usually carry a container on my long auto trips thus avoiding fast–food restaurant fare completely.

Pudding Mix: No cornstarch in this. The secret is rice flour, which makes puddings smoother and certainly more nutritional. And there's no mixing. Just keep a jar of rice flour on your shelf. When you want to make a pudding, do this: Mix 6 tablespoons rice flour with 2 1/2 cups milk and cook over low heat, stirring constantly until mixture thickens. Then add 1 1/2 teaspoons vanilla flavor (pure), 2 tablespoons honey and a dash of cinnamon. Stir until blended; then pour into pudding or sherbet glasses and chill. Top with sliced fresh fruit. Try variations with other flavors, such as almond, carob, and flavorings made from fruit syrup like strawberries and raspberries.

Your own Bake and Shake Mix: The main ingredient of this costly convenience food is flour. So outwit the grocer and mix the following in your handy seasonings jar: 1 cup whole wheat flour, 1 tablespoon each of paprika, dry mustard, freshly ground pepper, cumin and 1/4 cup of HVP. To use, just put this mix in a paper bag and shake with moistened chicken, or other shake–and–bake foods. Dry remaining mixture in oven for re–use. Be creative; mix up various combinations of your own. Personally I like a flour, HVP and chili–powder mix since it has great flavor and lively color!

Cornbread Mix: Mix 2 cups of corn meal with 1 cup whole wheat flour. Add 1 teaspoon baking soda, 1 cup dry skim milk powder. Shake well. Use as the basis for your favorite cornbread recipe using buttermilk to activate the soda for leavening.

Pancake Mix: Blend 6 cups whole wheat flour, 1 cup buckwheat flour, 3/4 teaspoon baking soda, 1 cup dry milk powder. Add eggs, oil and buttermilk in the usual proportions and fry on a buttered griddle.

Cake Mix: This type of concoction didn't exist before World War II, but now it's on every grocer's shelf. Beat the system by creating your own mixes. Just mix all dry ingredients of your favorite cake recipes in larger quantities than you would ordinarily: flour, dry milk powder, baking powder (see below) and so forth. Store in large jar; when you want a cake, just add the liquid components, eggs and flavorings and bake. After all, you always have to add the expensive ingredients yourself when you buy the prepackaged mix.

Baking Powder: The commercial versions contain the usual weird chemicals including aluminum. Therefore mix 4 teaspoons of pure cream of tartar (derived from grape seeds) and 2 teaspoon plain bicarbonate of soda. This will leaven 2 cups of flour. It is advisable to mix this fresh for each use. Incidentally, there are other ways of making baked products light and toothsome. Try buttermilk and soda, yeast, egg whites. Plain charged water or soda water. The latter can be used in all quick breads and cookies. Another leavening is sourdough, which is made by mixing flour and water and letting the mixture sour through the action of wild yeasts. Only a small amount need be used to leaven bread or other baked goods, and you can continue to add wheat flour, water and a bit of honey for food to keep your sourdough going indefinitely.

"Chocolate" Shake (using carob, of course): Mix 1 cup carob powder with 2 cups dry skim milk powder, non–instant. Add 2 tablespoons granular lecithin and shake well. To use, add desired amount to cold or hot water and whirl in blender. Add honey or fruit syrups as sweetener.

Salad Dressing Mixes: One famous brand of salad dressing consists mainly of salt and MSG (monosodium glutamate, which plays evil games with your insides). You're supposed to mix it with a quart of mayonnaise and a quart of buttermilk. Why not start with the latter and just add a few of your favorite spices and a dash of tamari if you crave salt.

Here's a combination you can store and add to vinegar and oil. Mix 1 tablespoon dry mustard, 1 teaspoon each garlic powder and basil, 3 tablespoons grated Parmesan cheese. This will make enough seasoning for an Italian dressing consisting of 1/4 cup olive oil and 1/8 cup wine vinegar. You can make up a larger quantity of the spices and cheese and store in refrigerator in a tightly sealed jar. For French Dressing, mix 1 teaspoon dry mustard, 1 teaspoon garlic powder, 1/2 teaspoon each of pepper and paprika. Add to 1/2 cup wine vinegar and 1 1/2 cups oil. This improves with age.

Mustard Mix: Grind together 1 cup mustard seeds, 8 tablespoons whole wheat flour, 1 teaspoon each celery seeds, turmeric, nutmeg in a blender and add enough vinegar to make smooth paste.

Soup Mixes: Blend dehydrated onions, carrots, celery, potatoes, and green peppers in approximately equal proportions along with HVP to taste. (Add to soup while simmering.) You'll beat any packaged mix on the market in both taste and purity, not to mention cost.

Coffee You Make in Your Own Oven from Cheap Grains

1. Caffeine makes people nervous.

2. Decaf coffee retains chemicals used to decaf it. Recent revelations indicate that there are pesticides and herbicides in much coffee. It seems that our American chemical industry has been pushing chemicals on foreign growers. As a result, American consumers are getting high levels of these chemicals in coffee and other imported food products.

3. Coffee has been statistically linked with heart disease.

4. One cup of coffee is equivalent to .01 roentgens of radiation. Thus, it may be a precursor to cancer.

A switch to herb tea would instantly solve all these problems, but, if you still love that coffee taste, there are options.

Barley, a Coffee Alternative: Roast a half pound of pearled barley in the oven at 350° F for about thirty minutes or until deep brown. Grind and mix with an equal amount of chicory (available at many natural food stores). Brew just like coffee in any way you wish.

With barley at thirty cents a pound and coffee at several dollars a pound, this makes a lot of sense budgetwise, not to mention the health cautions above. Incidentally, you can also use corn, wheat or rice as the roasted grain. Shouldn't you experiment until you find the brew that satisfies you?

Sprouts

Most people already know sprouts, since they are the main ingredient in many Chinese dishes. But did you know that:

- Sprouts are the world's most nutritious and most inexpensive foods.

- Sprouts can be grown in your kitchen—even if you live in a studio apartment.

- Sprouts are so nutritious that they alone could keep your stomach full and your body healthy.

- Sprouts are so economical that—by using them as a staple—you could live for much less than a dollar a day.

- Sprouts require no fancy equipment to grow. A container and some water is all that is necessary.

- And they're so versatile that you can use them in hundreds of different ways in your diet.

There is no other food that provides so much nutrition per penny. And the variety will amaze you. Almost any seed can be sprouted, and a list would include alfalfa, mung bean, lentil, corn, wheat, sunflower, radish, soybeans, cabbage, garbanzo beans (chickpeas), peanuts, and many others.

How to Sprout Your Own Seeds

First, make sure that the seeds you buy are not chemically treated. Most natural food stores can provide seeds especially marketed for sprouting. Next soak the seeds overnight in a glass container—a mayonnaise jar is fine. Put a cheese cloth or nylon–mesh cover on with a rubber band to prevent the seeds from escaping when you pour off the soak water. Then, all you have to do is rinse them once or twice a day with fresh, clean, tepid water. The seeds will do the rest.

After a few days, the hulls will separate from the sprouts and will rinse away. You can continue to rinse until the sprouts have grown to the desired size. Now they're ready to use in any number of ways. Here are some suggestions.

About Sprouts

Ever heard of fenugreek or chia seeds? There are many exotic, little known seeds that are highly nutritious and easy to sprout. These cheap–as–dirt seeds were used by Indians to provide energy on long, overland journeys.

Did you know that alfalfa sprouts contain more protein than meat—about 35 percent more. Or that one pound of alfalfa seeds will fill a ten–gallon container when sprouted! That means that the cost of a gallon of alfalfa sprouts would be only 22 cents. Many sprouts are even less costly than this. And don't forget that their nutritional value is much higher than the original seed or bean.

Sprout Recipes

Alfalfa Sprout Sandwich

• Spread homemade mayonnaise on two slices of whole wheat bread. Then add a thick layer of alfalfa sprouts, tomato and avocado slices and some sweet red onion slivers. Sprinkle on a few fresh sunflower seeds and you'll have a delicious meal that will keep you energized for hours.

Your Favorite Sprout Quiche

1 cup sliced mushrooms
1/2 sliced onion
1/4 cup oil
3/4 cup of your favorite sprouts
9–inch whole wheat pie shell
2 eggs beaten with 1 cup milk
1/2 cup grated cheese
sea salt to taste and herbs, if desired

• Preheat oven to 350°F. Saute the mushrooms and onion in oil. Add sprouts and spread mixture into pie shell. Blend eggs with milk, salt and herbs and pour over mixture. Bake for about 30 minutes. Serves 4 to 6.

Hong Kong Chop Suey

6 cups mung bean sprouts
2 large onions, chopped
1 stalk celery, sliced
3 mushrooms, sliced
6 cloves garlic, minced
soy sauce
cooked Chinese noodles
optional: chicken slivers

• Stir fry everything except the sprouts in a wok or large cast iron frying pan. When tender, add sprouts and cook only until barely warm. The secret of sprouts is to eat them as close to raw as possible. Serve over noodles and add soy to taste.

This is a low–cost dish that we make often. No matter what kind of appetite you have, it would be difficult to eat more than 50 cents worth of this dish.

Sprout Medley Salad

- Combine one cup each of alfalfa, lentil and mung–bean sprouts with your favorite lettuce–tomato salad recipe. You'll be amazed at how delicious and how cheap this giant salad will be. Top with yogurt dressing (see yogurt section). Thus the cost per pound of the healing food would be around 50 cents...enough for a salad that would serve about eight people. Cost per serving—about six cents. Compare that to some of the expensive salad makings and also consider that this salad is far more nutritious per unit weight than say, iceberg lettuce.

Wheat Sprouts

Making whole grain wheat into sprouts is one of the best things you can do nutritionally and the cost is so low, it's ridiculous! Use the jar method as for other sprouts or place them in a clean flower pot with a piece of netting on the bottom. Then rinse two or three times a day until the roots are about 1/2 inch long. Here are some things you can do with wheat sprouts:

- Add wheat sprouts to the liquid in your blender when you make pancakes or waffles

- Sprinkle the sprouts into your scrambled eggs just before they set

- Add fresh sprouts to your hot cereal just before serving it

- Grind them and add to your bread recipe

- Toss into your blender when you make a date shake or smoothy.

Sprouted Wheat Biscuits

1 cup wheat sprouts, ground
2 cups whole wheat flour
3 tsp natural baking powder (from your natural food store)
dash of sea salt
1/4 cup sesame or safflower oil
1 cup milk (from powder)

- Preheat oven to 400°F. Sift dry ingredients, then add liquids to barely mix everything. Place dough on floured surface and pat to about 1 inch thickness. Punch out rounds with cutter or small glass. Bake until lightly browned.

Tip: If you ever make too many sprouts and can't use them fresh, dry them in the oven, grind in your blender, and keep on hand to add to any recipe that uses flour.

This makes problem health foods far easier to digest—and at the same time completely eliminates the gas problem. Also, they cook much faster this way—an important saving in this era of high fuel costs.

Price Information For Sprouting Seeds, Beans And Grains

	Price per pound
Seeds	
Alfalfa seed	$2.26
Poppy seed	1.74
Sesame seed	.84
Grains	
Rice	.34
Barley	.32
Millet	.55
Wheat	.10
Beans	
Lentils	.78
Mung	1.33
Adzuki	1.67
Soy	.47
Garbanzo	.74
Black	.57
Pinto	.46

Note: While the cost of some items is high, remember that many seeds, beans and grains double, triple, quadruple or more in size, bulk and weight. Thus, a few teaspoons of expensive alfalfa seeds becomes an entire quart jar of delicious, highly nutritious salad sprouts. And keep in mind also that what is really the key factor with any food is the good it does to your body. Even if sprouts cost ten times what they do, they would still be the *least* expensive foods you could eat in terms of your overall health.

❝There's no doubt that fresh, whole foods are more trouble to prepare. It is convenience that has made the market for processed foods so enormous. But remember, if you ever come down with a fatal disease because of the chemicals in convenience foods, you will then learn what trouble really is.❞

—Harold Taub

Savings

Here are some typical savings that can be realized by using the new–old techniques.

Whole Wheat Cereal

8 ounces of typical sugared cereal	$1.36
8 ounces of whole–wheat cereal, freshly ground	.02
Savings per day	$1.34
Savings per year	$496.40

Think of it—almost $500 savings a year on just one item. I'm certain that you see the picture. Naturally, you wouldn't eat the same cereal every day, but the savings are there no matter how long it takes to consume.

Review

- The world's largest users of sprouts are the Chinese, who have had eight thousand years to develop a low–cost, high–quality cuisine.

- When seeds, grains, nuts and beans are sprouted, their food value increases phenomenally. For example, the vitamin C in oats increases about 600 percent after sprouting!

- Sprouts are fresh, pure food, untroubled by profit–hungry processors. You make them any day of the year in your own home for a few pennies a serving.

- With only a jar, a rubber band, and a piece of nylon, you can have a garden in a rented room! You don't even need a kitchen. Just a supply of water.

- You can store the dry seeds anywhere and sprout as many as you need when you need them. The time involved totals from two to seven days.

- Wheat, which now costs only about 12 cents a pound in 100–pound sacks, can become your sprouting mainstay. Its vitamins are greatly increased during the sprouting process. Furthermore, one cup of wheat makes 4 cups of sprouts.

- If you don't have room for a vegetable garden, just sprout the seeds in your handy jar. Use any seeds: cabbage cauliflower, broccoli, mustard, radish (especially tasty), chard or lettuce.

- Sunflower seeds are especially valuable, plain or sprouted. After all, parrots live to be a hundred or more on a diet of sunflower seeds and water.

- Cut down or cut out the high cost of meat with soy sprouts. It costs pennies and contains 40 percent protein. This is far more protein than any meat and has none of the chemical additives that turns modern meat into slow arsenic.

- Pumpkin seeds, sprouted or plain, are a folk remedy for many ailments, including prostate trouble and urinary disorders. They are about 30 percent protein, rich in unsaturated fatty acids, iron and phosphorus.

- You can even create a business. Many restaurants will buy these (fresh healing foods that you can grow in your own kitchen) on a regular basis. So will natural food stores.

- Check your local library for sprout cookbooks; a good one is *The Complete Sprouting Cookbook*, Troubador Press.

    Happy Sprouting!

Beautiful Beans

Ever wonder why the people of Mexico survive revolutions, tourist invasions and the catastrophic devaluation of the peso? My own theory has it that they just keep on eating lots of beans—beans with tortillas, beans with rice, beans with chili and their famous refried beans.

Francis Lappe has pointed out that, when certain vegetables, grains or legumes are combined with others, they complement one another and produce a complete protein—one that is every bit as valuable to the body as meat. And that's the case in the bean tostada recipe below, a joining of beans with corn.

Also, as John Steinbeck described in *Tortilla Flat*, a sack or two of beans in the house gives one a great sense of security. The cost by the sack is still quite low, despite inflation. In areas of large Mexican population throughout the West and Southwest, you'll always find markets stocking beans by the 100–pound sack. They store well and can be made into hundreds of tasty dishes from salads to main courses. So what are you waiting for?

Savory Bean Tostadas

12 tortillas (corn)
1 1/2 cups mashed red kidney beans
1 cup shredded cooked chicken or turkey
1 head lettuce
1 cup diced boiled potatoes
oil and vinegar dressing
1 avocado in slices
1 cup salsa (tomato, chilis and onions chopped and mixed)
grated cheese
Mexican hot sauce

• Heat tortillas in a little oil until they retain their shape. Spread with layer of beans and chicken or turkey. Meanwhile, shred lettuce and toss with potato and dressing. Add layer of this mixture over beans. Then garnish with avocado, salsa and hot sauce.

• There are infinite variations to this recipe. Shrimp or crab instead of chicken for example. And almost any kind of soft, well–cooked beans can be used as the base.

Economy Note: One pound of raw beans equals about six cups cooked. And one cup of cooked beans provides more than a fourth of the protein need of an adult—thus generous amounts of vitamins and minerals. Few foods offer so much food value per penny invested.

Hot–As–You–Like Chili Beans

2 cups dried pinto or kidney beans
1/4 cup soy sauce
1 teaspoon cumin powder
chili powder to taste

• Cover the beans with water and soak overnight. Drain and add enough water to keep them from sticking while they simmer for about two hours or until tender. During last half hour, stir in remaining ingredients. Top with chopped red onion and grated cheese.

Bravo Bean Salad

4 cups cooked, drained red kidney beans
1 cup sharp French dressing
1 cup sliced celery
1/2 cup sliced red onion
minced garlic and freshly ground pepper to taste
Garnish: onion rings and radish slices

- Toss the first four ingredients gently, cover and refrigerate. At serving time, drain off excess dressing. Heap the mixture into a serving bowl and sprinkle with minced garlic and pepper. Garnish with onion and radish. Serves 4.

Bean Dip

2 cups cooked pinto beans
1/4 cup butter
1 cup shredded cheddar cheese
1/2 teaspoon cumin powder
1/2 teaspoon garlic powder or minced garlic

- Melt butter in skillet and add beans. Mash with potato masher or large spoon. Heat for one minute while adding seasonings. Add water to make desired dip consistency. Stir in cheese and serve warm with corn chips.

Bean Soup

4 cups navy beans, dry
4 qts water
2 large onions, chopped
butter
2 tablespoons Tamari (soy sauce)

- Rinse beans. Simmer for about 3 hours. Braise chopped onion in a little butter and add to soup along with Tamari just before serving. This is a subtle soup that really tastes like beans instead of strongly flavored smoked meats.

Beans Italiano

2 cups dry navy beans
1 bay leaf
2 medium onions, grated
2 cloves garlic, mashed
2 tablespoons parsley, chopped
1 teaspoon chopped dill
1/2 cup olive oil
2 cups freshly stewed tomatoes
1/2 cup olives, chopped
1 cup celery, chopped
grated cheese

- Soak beans overnight. Put beans and liquid into pot, adding more water if needed to barely cover. Add bay leaf, onion, garlic, parsley and dill. Boil slowly until beans are tender but not too soft; about 1 1/2 hours. Separately, cook tomato, olives and celery in oil until tender. Pour over beans and then transfer mixture into casserole or large pot. Cover and bake at 275° for about 2 hours. Uncover and sprinkle with cheese. Continue baking until cheese is browned.

Review of Beans

- Beans have been a staple in the human diet since the Bronze Age.

- High in fiber, they make a welcome addition to the usual diet of refined foods.

- Beans vary in price during the year, with the lowest being around September when the harvest comes in. Buy all you can afford and store in a cool, dry place. Clean gallon wine jugs are great.

- Try all varieties; here are some samples: Black, great northern whites, fava, haricot, lima, kidney, navy, pinto, red and Windsor, adzuki, soy, garbanzo and mung.

- When you are thinking of your weekly menu, include beans in appetizers and dips, soups, main dishes, sandwiches, and salads, as well as in many international recipes—falafel, pasta fazooli (beans and macaroni), and minestrone.

Falafels

What is the hamburger of the Middle East? It's the widely popular *falafel* (accent on second syllable), a tasty concoction of nonmeat ingredients that you will enjoy making as much as eating.

Falafels are labor intensive and are the most fun when prepared by a family or social group as the prelude to a party or other gathering. With low cost ingredients, you can make a lot of them and freeze or share. Falafel is good as a snack or a main meal, healthful, and above all interesting and different. Try them once, and you'll want them again and again.

Here's a three–part recipe: the falafel balls, the bread to serve them in, and the wonderful sauce, tahini.

Falafel Balls

2 cups dried garbanzo beans
1/2 cup water
1 clove garlic
2 tablespoons parsley
1/4 teaspoon cumin
dash of soy sauce

- Soak garbanzos overnight. Then grind in blender or meat grinder. Add other ingredients and form into balls about the size of an English walnut. Place on ungreased baking pan, cover with foil and bake at 350° F for 15 minutes. Then turn them over and bake uncovered for 10 more minutes. Keep warm.

Pita Bread

1 tablespoon dry yeast
1/4 cup warm water
2 1/2 cups whole wheat flour
3/4 cup warm water

- Dissolve yeast in 1/4 cup water and then add additional water and flour. Turn dough onto a floured board and knead until smooth and elastic. Let rise until double and then turn out on floured board and form into 12 balls. Roll each ball into a circle 1–inch thick. Place on greased baking sheet and let them rise in a warm place for 15 minutes. Bake at 500° F for 10 minutes. Don't let them get too brown.

Tahini Sauce

1 cup sesame seeds
2 tablespoons oil
1/2 cup water
dash soy sauce
1/4 cup lemon juice

• Put all ingredients into a blender and whirl until seeds are ground fine. Makes about one cup.

Assembly of Falafel

Cut pita bread in half and open the pocket. Place three or four falafel balls inside and top with chopped cucumbers, tomato, lettuce, and green or red onion. Then drizzle Tahini sauce over the contents. The combination of warm falafel balls, the chopped salad and delectable Tahini is a most unusual taste treat. Furthermore, the cost is so low that you can serve them often and save money every time.

BLACK WALNUT

So-called primitive cultures understand how to make simple ingredients taste wonderful!

Make–It–Yourself Survival Foods

Familia is a Swiss–origin fruit, nut, and grain combination that is easy to make, relatively low in cost and highly nutritious. It's handy to take with you on trips or hikes, stores well in a sealed container and is light weight in comparison to foods that contain lots of water. It's really a perfect survival food and contains most everything your body needs to stay healthy. Supplemented with fresh veggies and fruits, you can live indefinitely on Familia. Eat it as is, cooked, or use it to make cookies, breads and other baked goods.

I like to make a lot at one time since it allows me to buy in quantity and save. Also, as mentioned, it keeps well in glass, metal or plastic containers. This will make a 15 pound batch:

1 lb oats

2 lbs wheat flakes

2 lb rye flakes

1/3 lb soy flour

1 lb wheat germ (if you add this, be sure and refrigerate the stored Familia, because wheat germ deteriorates rapidly at room temperature)

1 oz rice polish (available at most good health food stores)

1 lb soy lecithin

1 lb sunflower seeds

1/2 lb pumpkin seeds

1 lb sesame seeds

1 package sesame seeds or chia seeds

2 lbs raisins

1 lb dried fruit, chopped

1 lb nuts, whole and chopped as desired

• Mix in large container then transfer to smaller containers and jars.

Millet Candy: Slowly cook millet and honey until it thickens. Then pour into buttered pans. When chilled, cut into bars and wrap in aluminum foil. The best and healthiest no–additive candy you can find!

Carob Energy Balls: Combine 1/2 cup each of carob powder, honey, peanut butter, sunflower seeds and sesame seeds with 1/4 cup each of wheat germ and sifted soy flour, heating slightly over double boiler to blend. When cool, form into balls and roll in chopped peanuts.

The Unknown Grain

The irony never escapes me. There goes the harried housewife with her shopping cart loaded with packaged junk right past the bags of "wild bird seed," usually stacked just outside the checkstands. There is little if any food value in the woman's high–cost purchases, but in the millet (the bird seed) there's a rich supply of vitamins, minerals, quality carbohydrates and every amino acid needed for health except lysine. And that is abundant in many foods that you can combine with millet such as seafood, legumes and most vegetables.

I'm sure you've seen those five, ten, and twenty–pound sacks of millet which are almost always labeled "for the birds." The cost is so low as to be absurd—often 20 cents a pound. Millet is one of the most widely consumed grains on this planet, especially in Africa. Easy to grow and an abundant crop—in terms of return per acre—millet is the rice and wheat of millions of healthy people.

Incidentally, you can find it in bulk in many natural food stores. That way you won't have to pick out the few sunflower seeds that are placed in millet packages to give it that bird–seed look. (Clever, aren't they?)

Here is a recipe that will allow you to phase into millet in accompaniment with better–known ingredients. A favorite in Russia, variations on this theme are eaten in many other countries including China and India. It feeds a veritable army of people for a few cents each.

Kasha

1 cup wheat kernels
1 cup millet
5 cups water
1 chopped large onion
1 cup diced green pepper
1 cup sliced celery
2 cloves garlic, crushed
1/2 cup chopped fresh mushrooms
2 tablespoons sesame oil
dash or two of tamari

- Cook wheat until tender after overnight soaking. Cook millet separately since it takes less time, after 30 minutes in an uncovered pan. Drain and set aside. Brown vegetables in the sesame oil and add to cooked grains. Mix well and add tamari as desired. Can be served as a main or side dish, hot or cold.

Morning Millet

- Brown a cup of millet in a little oil and combine with 1 cup of sesame seeds that have been ground in your blender. Add to about five cups of boiling water and stir well. Cook until thick, stirring often. Eat with skim milk and molasses or honey as a breakfast porridge. Any remaining can be poured into a pan, chilled until firm, and then sliced and crisped in a little butter as a unique scrapple. Great with your morning eggs or topped with melted cheese for a snack.

This can be made with millet alone if desired.

Millet Souffle

4 cups boiling water
2 tablespoons oil
1 cup millet, ground in blender
4 eggs, separated
1/4 cup skim milk powder
1 cup water
3 tablespoons minced chives or green onion tops
1/2 teaspoon dill seeds, crushed
1 cup grated cheddar cheese

- Bring water to boil and add oil. Gradually add millet stirring with wire whisk. Place mixture in top of double boiler over boiling water and cook for 20 to 30 minutes. Remove from heat. Beat egg yolks and add skim milk powder and water. Combine with millet and add the chives, dill seeds and cheese. Beat egg whites until stiff and gently fold them into millet mixture. Pour into oiled 2–quart casserole and bake for 35 to 45 minutes at 350° F.

An unusually tasty dish for a group. They'll get a tasty introduction to millet.

Millet Pudding

1/4 cup millet
2 cups skim milk
2 eggs beaten
4 tablespoons molasses
1/4 cup sesame seeds

• Soak millet in 1/2 cup milk. Heat rest of milk in top of double boiler. Stir in millet and cook for about 45 minutes, stirring occasionally. Remove from heat and cool. Blend in eggs, molasses and sesame seeds. Cook for another five minutes. You may add chopped dates or raisins or fresh fruit. Pour into dessert glasses and eat warm or chilled, topped with a bit of cinnamon.

I guarantee that your children will love this and begin throwing rocks at all those junk puddings that are being peddled under the guise of food.

Review of Millet

• Almost ignored by Americans, millet is a delicately flavored grain which can be used in hundreds of ways.

• It's inexpensive and can be purchased anywhere as "bird seed." Also available from feed stores, wholesalers and natural food outlets in any quantity.

• It stores well in cool, dry places. Use glass or metal containers.

• Well worth experimentation. Keep a supply of cooked millet handy to add to soups, stews, to make desserts and add to cold salads.

• Very high in nutritional values, you could virtually live on millet and vegetables—as many people do worldwide.

Add a measure of ground millet to your next cookie recipe.

Up With Oats!

Turn to the stock market page of your local newspaper and look for the commodities listings. They are usually listed under the heading, "Chicago Board Of Trade.". The most common items listed are wheat, corn, oats and soybeans. Check the price of oats—it will probably be under two dollars a bushel.

Surprised?

Isn't it a jolt to discover that oats sell for around *four dollars per hundred pounds.* (A bushel of oats weighs less than forty–five pounds usually.) That's the same ingredient of those expensive cookies in your local supermarket and also the same stuff that is made into all those high–priced cereals. A hundred pounds of oats should cost you less that twenty dollars, even in these inflationary days. Shop around and get the best buy. Then make your own cookies and cereal, and it will be better, by far, than any you buy in a store.

Granola

1/2 cup honey or molasses
1/2 cup oil
1 teaspoon vanilla (pure stuff)
1/2 cup sesame seeds
1 cup soy grits
1/2 cup wheat germ
7 cups rolled oats (non–instant)
1/2 cup sunflower seeds (fresh)

• Heat honey, oil and vanilla in a large cast–iron pan. Turn off heat and stir in remaining ingredients in the order given. Bake in oven set at 350° F until oats begin to turn brown (about 15 minutes). Then stir every 5 to 10 minutes for a total of 30 minutes or so. Be sure and scrape up the bottom. Add raisins and nuts later after mixture is cooled. Store in large jars with tight lids. Makes about 3 quarts.

Once you try homemade granola, you'll never want to pay exorbitant prices for any kind of cold cereal, or buy store versions of granola either.

Hearty Oatmeal Cookies

3 eggs
3/4 cup honey or molasses
3/4 cup oil
1 teaspoon vanilla (pure stuff)
1/4 cup milk
2 cups whole wheat flour
2 cups oatmeal

1 cup chopped dried fruit, raisins, dates, prunes, apricots
1 cup chopped walnuts
1/2 cup sesame seeds
1/2 cup sunflower seeds

- Mix ingredients in order given and drop by spoonful on an oiled cookie sheet. Bake at 350° F for 15 minutes or until light brown.

Everyone has a recipe for oatmeal cookies that uses white sugar and "enriched" flour. Once you eat one of these hearty cookies, you'll toss that old recipe in the trash where it belongs.

Personally, I enjoy a big bowl of steaming, fresh oatmeal almost every day of the year. It's one of those tasty grains that seldom tires the palate. Besides, you can add anything you have available to embellish it—chopped fresh fruit, walnuts, almonds, peanuts—even a spoonful of raspberry jam. With milk or fruit juice, it's an ambrosial dish that never fails to make your day an energetic and fruitful one.

A friend of mine is a fine baker and this is his best bread recipe:

Honey Oatmeal Bread

2 cups boiling water
1/2 cup honey
2 tablespoons oil
1 cup rolled oats
1 cake yeast
1/2 cup lukewarm water
4 1/2 to 5 cups whole wheat flour

- In a large mixing bowl, stir together the boiling water, honey, oil and oats. Let cool to lukewarm. In a small dish, dissolve the yeast in the lukewarm water and add it to the first mixture. Stir in 4 1/2 cups of flour and beat well. Cover and let rise until double in bulk. Add more flour if necessary and knead until elastic. Shape into two loaves and place in two oiled pans. Let rise again. Bake for 50 minutes at 350° F. Remove from pans and cool loaves on wire rack.

- If you want these loaves to look especially attractive, brush tops with honey and sprinkle with uncooked oats.

Trail Cakes

2 cups rolled oats
1/4 cup bran
1/4 cup wheat germ
1/4 cup honey
milk to moisten

- Mix ingredients, except milk, and then add the latter to moisten. Form into 1/2–inch thick cakes and bake until slightly brown in moderate oven. Or place in iron skillet and cook slowly until brown on each side.

Muesli

This cereal dish is mainly oats and was invented in Germany several decades back. Used as a food to rehabilitate sick people, it's even more efficacious when used as a preventive of illness. There's nothing to it—just mix raw oatmeal with chopped fruits and nuts. For even greater nutrition, add sesame and sunflower seeds. Serve with skim milk.

Review of Oats

- Oats have the highest protein content of any cereal grain.

- Oats have five times the fat content of wheat.

- Always buy regular oats, not the quick–cook kind. To cook for cereal, just soak in the pan overnight, then gently simmer for a few minutes. Oats need not be overcooked.

Chop dried apricots fine and add to your homemade muesli recipe.

Potatoes

The finest meals in the world are often the simplest. Remember when you used a stick to dig baked potatoes out of the coals of a campfire? Crisp on the outside but sweet and fluffy within, they could be eaten plain and still taste like a gourmet chef's presentation. With butter and chives or finely chopped red onion, outdoor baked potatoes are gustatory heaven. And they're close to that even when you use your oven.

In the following paragraphs, we'll prove that a basic food like a potato can become a star performer at any meal. And best of all, potatoes provide high-quality nutrition at a consistently low price.

Twice-baked Spuds

One large potato for each guest
For each potato:
1/4 cup cottage cheese, homemade
1/8 cup milk or buttermilk
1 tablespoon finely chopped onion
paprika and chopped parsley as garnish

- Bake potatoes until tender. Be sure and pierce with fork before baking to prevent bursting. Cut in half lengthwise and scoop out inside, keeping skins intact. Whip potato with cheese, milk and onion and replace in skin. Sprinkle with paprika and parsley, then bake again until tops are golden.

- There are many variations to this basic recipe. Mix chili powder with the potato for a Mexican flavor. Or use oregano and some cubed mozzarella for Spuds Italiano.

Variations on a Baked Potato Theme: Whenever you have the oven going for any other purpose, put in some spuds and let them ride along for free. Slow-baked at low temperatures are just as good if not better than those done in a hot oven. With a bowl of baked potatoes in the fridge, there's no way you can go hungry or without a flavorsome snack:

- Dice or slice for a quick saute with onions, garlic and/or cheese.

- Slice and put in marinade of olive oil, vinegar and herbs along with finely sliced onion, celery, chives and garlic.

- Cut lengthwise, sprinkle with: sesame seeds, slivered pimiento or green pepper, whipped butter and coarsely ground pepper, sauteed mushrooms, yogurt seasoned with herbs and HVP (hydrolyzed vegetable protein). Then heat in oven and serve with green salad. This is faster than the twice–baked recipe but no less delicious.

Red Onion Potato Salad

- Scrub 6 medium potatoes and boil with skins on. Then slice and mix with the following:

1 cup sliced celery
1 cup thinly sliced red onion
1/3 cup chopped parsley
1/4 cup olive oil
3 tablespoons wine vinegar
sprinkle of oregano
splash or two of Tabasco or similar hot pepper sauce

This one is delicious whether you eat it warm or chilled. This is the type of low–cost, high quality dish that can be the anchor of your food budget. Keep some around for that inevitable snacking that's become our new eating format.

Eating well on a low–cost food budget need never be dull. In fact, recipes like the following prove that simple, home–prepared dishes can easily outshine anything in the frozen food section of a market.

Potato Puff

2 cups mashed potatoes
3 tablespoons hot milk
1 egg separated
2 tablespoons butter or olive oil
1 teaspoon grated onion
2 tablespoons chopped parsley
1/2 teaspoon soy sauce
pepper to taste

- Preheat oven to 375° F. Add hot milk to potato. Then stir in beaten egg yolk, butter or olive oil, onion, parsley, soy sauce and pepper. Beat egg white until stiff and fold into potato mixture. Pile lightly into greased baking dish and bake for about 35 minutes or until brown. If you want a deeper brown, put dish under broiler. Serve immediately.

Low–Fat French Fries

- Everyone likes French fried potatoes but with all that hot fat they can kill you. Here's a better–tasting alternative that's bursting with health. Cut four medium potatoes into strips and toss with a couple of tablespoons of high–quality salad oil until coated. Sprinkle with paprika for a delightful color. Spread strips in one layer in a cookie sheet and bake in hot (450° F) oven until golden brown and tender, about 30 to 40 minutes. Now that's proof you don't have to sacrifice tasty treats! For a gourmet flavor, use sesame oil. While expensive, it lends a unique flavor to almost anything it touches.

New England Clam Chowder

1 cup chopped onion
1 tablespoon butter
2 cups cubed potatoes
1 pound minced clams, fresh preferred but canned if you must
1 cup skim milk makes it richer than usual
Tabasco if desired

- In an iron kettle, saute onions in butter until *al dente*; then add potatoes with one cup water and cook until spuds are tender. Add remaining ingredients and simmer a few minutes to blend flavors. Add hot sauce if desired.

Potatoes lend themselves to many fine soup recipes. Potatoes and leeks make a superb combination.

Review of Potatoes

- Potatoes have remained relatively low in price and are often a bargain when purchased in fairly large quantities.

- They store well as long as they are in a cool ventilated place, preferably dark.

- Buy firm, smooth, well–shaped spuds free from cuts, blemishes, green patches and decay or sprouts.

- Why spend a fortune for vitamin and mineral supplements?

- One medium–sized potato yields great nutrition in the form of vitamins B and C—plus minerals—including iron and potassium—all for less than 100 calories. Sauces, butter and gravy make the potato an offender for those who must watch their waistlines.

- Don't peel potatoes; the best nutrition is in or near the skin. If you must peel, then use the peelings in another dish, such as soup or stew.

- Potatoes are one of the best stretchers of other foods. If you're into meat, you can extend a small quantity by adding lots of cubed, sliced or mashed potatoes. Spuds are the rice of America.

- If some of your stored potatoes happened to sprout while you weren't looking, cut them in pieces with an eye on each piece and plant in your garden. Nothing like new potatoes boiled and served with parsley butter.

- There aren't many foods that can compare with potatoes in nutritional value, flavor and versatility and still cost so little.

Brown Rice

One of the most versatile foods I know is rice—brown rice. It can and is eaten three times a day by countless people. I've never heard anyone complain that they were bored with rice dishes; it's one of those unusual foods that has such a good flavor, blends so well with other dishes and is so satisfying that it's ever–new.

Rice is the most widely consumed grain on this planet and the absolute foundation of Chinese cuisine. Rice is an excellent source of protein, although it must be supplemented by other foods to make up for a deficiency in two of the essential amino acids. It's an important source of iron, calcium and B–complex vitamins. At the same time, it's low in fat, sodium and cholesterol.

Buy brown rice since white rice is greatly diminished in important nutritional values. For example, brown rice has .34 mg of thiamine per 100 gm, while white rice has only .7 mg.

In bulk, rice is cheap, and it stores well almost anywhere that's cool and dry. Cooked rice is easy to store in your refrigerator and is always ready to make a main dish or an unlimited number of side dishes that can be enjoyed anytime. Here's our basic recipe that always works if you follow the directions exactly.

Basic Brown Rice

• Measure one cup of rinsed brown rice and three cups of water. Pour the two into a saucepan with a tight–fitting lid. Set over very low heat and cook without stirring or removing the lid for about 40 minutes. After that time, check to see if the rice is tender. If not, add a little water if necessary and cook for about 5 or 10 minutes longer. This makes about three cups of rice, which should serve four.

Here are a few of the things you can do with cooked brown rice:

1. Add milk or cream, chopped almonds or raisins, and eat as a breakfast cereal.

2. Stir–fry some vegetables, pour over rice and add soy sauce for a quick lunch.

3. Add rice to almost any kind of soup, tomato rice is especially good.

4. Use to stretch other ingredients such as chicken in an enchilada or meat in stuffed peppers.

5. Add eggs, milk and honey for a baked dessert.

Keeping cooked rice in your refrigerator ensures that you're never without the stalwart base for something really good and nutritious to eat. How much better this is than opening some dumb can or reaching for snack crackers loaded with hydrogenated oil and salt.

Starting from scratch, here are a few good ways to incorporate rice into your diet for nutrition and economy:

Spanish Rice

1 large onion, chopped
1 green pepper, chopped
2 large stalks celery, chopped
6 tablespoons oil
8 large tomatoes, chopped and whirled in blender with water to mix
1 heaping tablespoon chili powder
1 cup of cooked brown rice

• Saute vegetables in oil, add tomatoes, seasoning and rice. Add water as needed. Simmer slowly or place in casserole, dot with cheese or olives, and bake for 20 minutes.

This is a quickly–made dish that almost everyone loves. Your budget will never feel it and it can be infinitely varied. It's so compatible with virtually every other food that it's tough to make a mistake. For example, you can add chopped leftover chicken or turkey, fish or beans. And Spanish rice serves well as either a main or side dish. When thickened by cooking or with a little cornstarch, it makes a fine filling for im-promptu enchiladas. And try warmed Spanish rice as a dip with corn chips.

Chinese Pilaf

2 cups raw brown rice
1/4 cup oil
tops from two stalks celery, chopped
1 bunch green onions, chopped
1/2 cup low–salt soy sauce
4 cups water
1/4 pound mushrooms, sliced

- Saute the rice in oil for a few minutes, stirring constantly. Add the celery, onions, soy sauce and water, and bring to a boil. Stir and lower heat, cover and simmer for about 40 minutes or until rice is tender. Add mushrooms the last 10 minutes. Serves 8.

Finished with a turkey? Then place all bones and scraps into a large kettle with water to cover and one cup brown rice. Add any seasonings you wish. Result? A fine kettle of soup!

Soybeans

Do you know what the largest crop is in the U.S.? Wheat? Corn? No, it's soybeans! America is the largest producer of this fantastic food which provides a myriad of good things to eat. Most people are only familiar with the peripheral products; soy sauce or perhaps soybean curd or tofu. Here are some other ways in which soybeans are used worldwide: fresh or frozen beans, soybean sprouts, soy flour, grits, milk powder, with the latter producing cheese, ice cream, drinks and on and on.

For centuries, oriental cultures have depended on the soybean as their basic staple food and have invented an incredible number of ways to use this versatile bean. There's a good reason for this effort: soybeans are the only vegetable that yields a complete protein comparable in quality to that of milk, eggs or meat. Soybeans also consist of about 20 percent unsaturated fats, the most important of these being lecithin. This has the ability to break up cholesterol and other fatty substances in the body so they don't form plaques on the artery walls.

Now if all of the above wasn't enough to convince you, take a look at this chart. It is based on the fact that you can buy at least five times as many pounds of soybeans as you can beef *for the same amount of money*.

	Beef (4.5 lb)	Soybeans (25 lb)
Days Protein	13	180
Total Protein, GM	355	4,540
Calories	5,659	37,569
Servings	6	150

To reiterate, you get twenty–five times more servings, thirteen time more protein and seven times the calories, plus equivalent increases in vitamins and minerals. And, as a bonus, soybeans have no dangerous additives. The list of horror–house chemicals that appear in American meat is virtually infinite. It includes—as a beginning—DES, herbicides and pesticide residues. The latter have made every country on earth forbid the importation of our meat products!

To summarize, you can boost your family's and your own health by including soybeans in their many forms in your daily diet. Just wait until you taste this typical recipe: soy burgers. Make up a big batch the next time you host a barbecue. We guarantee two results: your guests will love them, and they'll tell you how much better they felt the next day.

Soy Burgers

• Soak one cup dry soybeans overnight and cook covered over low heat for two to three hours or until tender. Drain off liquid (stock can be used for soup), mash and add any of the following, experimenting with varying amounts and combinations: chopped green pepper, cooked brown rice or bulgur, chopped parsley. Make into patties, and broil until brown and crisp. Serve on whole wheat buns with all the usual hamburger trimmings, but don't forget the alfalfa sprouts.

The cost of soyburgers can be under twenty–five cents each depending on what you add to the finished product.

Mexican Chili

2 cups cooked soybeans
2 tablespoons chili powder or 1 chopped fresh chili pepper
1/4 cup tomato puree or ketchup
1 onion chopped
1/2 cup grated cheese

- Mix ingredients and simmer until flavors are well–blended. Pour into individual bowls and top with grated cheese and red onion slices if desired.

You can buy soy grits in your health food store or make your own by coarsely grinding whole or split soybeans. Here's one way to use them:

Peppers Stuffed With Soy Grits

4 large bell peppers
1 small onion, minced
2 cloves garlic, minced
2 tablespoons oil
1 cup soy grits
1 teaspoon summer savory
1/2 teaspoon basil
1/2 cup cooked brown rice

- Top peppers and remove seeds. Blanch in boiling water. Saute onion and garlic in oil. Precook grits for 1/2 hour in stock, then add other ingredients and cook until grits are tender. Fill peppers, place in casserole, and bake at 350° F for 40 minutes.

The following is similar to a Middle Eastern dish know as hummus.

Savory Soybean Spread

1 cup well cooked soybeans
1/4 cup each minced onion, green pepper, parsley
1/2 teaspoon each cumin, oregano garlic (grated)
1/2 cup yogurt

- Blend ingredients thoroughly and spread on homemade crackers or celery. Try dill, caraway, paprika, or other seasonings for variety.

More Soy Tips

Soy Flour: This is available in many health food stores. Add to your favorite recipes for bread, pancakes, biscuits and other baked goods to increase protein content.

Soy Protein: Obtainable in bulk and best used in health drinks. Many of the packaged drink mixes use this but you can make your own much cheaper.

Sprouting Soybeans: Soak beans overnight in the refrigerator (they ferment easily), then drain thoroughly and keep in warm, dark place. Flood with warm water at least four or five times a day, draining well each time. In four to six days, the sprouts should be two to three inches long. Store in cool place and use like other sprouts. Note that soybeans are often difficult to sprout, and this may be due to the variety. Try to obtain soybeans that are recommended for sprouting. Uncoated seed beans are a good bet.

Soy Grits: Toss these in cereals, soups, stews, grain dishes, casseroles and other places where increased nutrition is needed.

Soy Coffee: Roast soybeans in the oven until quite dark. Then grind like coffee beans in your grinder or blender. Use exactly like coffee. Look, Ma, no caffeine!

Soy Miso: This is a dark paste that is obtainable in many oriental food stores and is a fine flavoring aid. Add to soups, stews and similar dishes.

Soybean Dairy

Heard of Tofutti, the newest alternative ice cream? It's the latest in uses for soy milk, which you can make yourself. Few people are aware that they can easily make a variety of soy dairy products and none require a cow.

Soy Milk: Soak a cup of soybeans overnight (in the refrigerator remember). Liquefy in your blender with three cups of water. Heat the mixture to a boil (oil the top of pot so it won't boil over). Simmer for twenty minutes. Strain through a clean cloth (cheesecloth is ideal) placed in a colander or strainer. That's it! Soy milk can be used like regular milk for drinks, cream sauces, puddings, chowders and so forth. Frozen with the usual ice cream flavorings, you have your own tofutti! (Use remaining pulp in mashed soybean recipes.)

Tofu: This soybean–based food is becoming very popular as people realize that it can be substituted for meat in many dishes. Also knows as bean curd or bean cake, tofu has been called soy cheese. Look for it in natural–foods and Chinese markets. It resembles a firm custard with a creamy white color and a very delicate flavor. Tofu can be used in many ways: Cubed into soups and stews, made into tofuburgers, used like cheese in cheesecake recipes, and so on. You can save even more money by making it at home yourself like this: Boil desired quantity of soy milk for five minutes and add sufficient lemon juice or vinegar to curdle the milk. Ladle the curds into a cloth–lined strainer or perforated box and press out moisture with a weighted lid. In a few minutes the remainder will become firm and ready to use. Now wasn't that simple and easy? For added firmness, chill in cold water or the refrigerator. Then slice and use. There's an even easier way using soy flour:

Easy Tofu

1 1/2 cups soy flour
cold water as needed
4 1/2 cups boiling water
6 tablespoons lemon juice

- Add enough cold water to soy flour to make a paste. Beat until airy. Add boiling water and cook five minutes. Remove mixture from heat, and add lemon juice. Curds will form as it cools. Strain through cloth and refrigerate in plastic bag.

Tofu and Eggs: Slice tofu like bacon and saute in butter. Serve with scrambled eggs garnished with parsley. A great breakfast without all the bacon chemicals.

Vegetable Soup and Tofu: Make your favorite recipe and add slices or cubes of homemade tofu during the last 10 minutes. Tofu goes well with any soup or stew adding protein and other food values.

Tofuburgers: Even more delicious and tender than the soyburgers, you will serve these often, especially to children who have grown up with hamburgers. Combine desired quantity of tofu with grated carrot, chopped onion, green peppers and minced garlic. Form into patties and saute them in soy oil until they are crisp on the outside and tender on the inside. Decorate whole wheat buns with all the usual trimmings, toss in a tofuburger, and enjoy!

Some Advantages of Tofu

- Low in cost, especially when you make at home.

- High in protein, as much as chicken or steak without a trace of the fats or chemicals.

- Eight delicious ounces yield only 150 calories. So you can lose tons of weight with it, and never gain an ounce back when you're slender.

Review of Soybeans

- Soybeans are the Wonder Bean!

- The only vegetable on earth that yields a complete protein comparable in quality to that of meat, milk and eggs.

- I have been to the famous Farm at Summertown, Tennessee, a 3,000–member commune that virtually lives on soybeans and its many variations.

- Think of this! Soybeans give you thirteen times more protein for your food dollar. And they do it without the heavy doses of fats and chemicals you get with meat.

- Soybeans prepared in special ways can take the place of meat and taste as good or better. For example, enjoy a soyburger!

- With several sacks of soybeans on hand, you never need fear a food shortage. You can even plant them and grow more.

• Here are a few things you can make from soybeans: soy flour, soy grits, soy milk, soy sprouts, soy cheese, soy bread, soy ice cream, soy tofu, soy sauce, soy oil, soy mayonnaise, soy pancakes and waffles, soy noodles and spaghetti, soy dips and spreads, ad infinitum!

• From the basic soy staples, you can make an endless variety of dishes, including custard, puddings, desserts, cakes, pies, casseroles, sauces, salad dressings, dumplings, muffins, biscuits, pizza, soups, foreign recipes, main dishes and some of the specific names include:

Soy Raisin Bread

Soy Carob Carrot Cake

Potato Bake with Soy Cheese

Tofu Casserole Al Italiano

Soy Chili Con Tofu

Quiche with Tofu

Banana Almond Pie

• With the current cost of soybeans, you can feast like a king, never get fat, avoid additives and be a gourmet all at once.

• *Soybeans and their many variations are healthful, easily digested, low calorie, high nutrition and inexpensive. You can live better for less when they have a prominent place in your kitchen.*

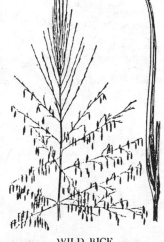

WILD RICE
Left: stalk; *Right:* leaf and stem.

The Soyfoods Center

SOYFOODS

PROTEIN SOURCE OF THE FUTURE... NOW.

The Soyfoods Center was founded in August 1976 by William Shurtleff and Akiko Aoyagi Shurtleff. Our basic activities are:

Soyfoods: Our center is, above all, a source of information and materials related to soyfoods.

World Hunger: Presently more than 15,000,000 people die each year of starvation and malnutrition-caused diseases; three fourths of these are children. This urgent and growing problem is at the very heart of all our work. Each of our basic books contains an analysis of the causes of world hunger and suggests practical solutions. We are developing creative, low-cost, village-level methods for soyfoods production using appropriate technology. We have traveled and lectured extensively in Third World countries and have many contacts there with soyfoods producers and researchers.

Meatless Diets: Over half of all agricultural land in the U.S. is now used to grow crops (such as corn, soybeans, and wheat) that are fed to animals via the feedlot system. Since, in the case of a feedlot steer, it takes 16 to 21 pounds of soy or grain input to make 1 pound of beef protein, this wasteful system transforms the earth's abundance into scarcity. Furthermore, the affluent American-style diet is emerging as a major cause of world hunger as well as of degenerative diseases such as heart disease, cancer, diabetes, and obesity. We encourage the adoption of meatless or vegetarian diets using soyfoods as a basic protein source. Current medical research shows conclusively that vegetarians in the U.S. are healthier and slimmer than meat eaters and that they live significantly longer. Moreover a meatless diet is more economical and ecologically sound, is kinder to animals, and helps make best use of the planet's precious food resources.

Commercial Soyfood Production: We actively encourage and aid soyfoods producers around the world as they start and run new plants on any scale from small village or community shops up to modern factories. We support appropriate technology and Right Livelihood. We serve as consultants for many soyfoods businesses.

THE SOYFOODS CENTER
P.O. BOX 234
LAFAYETTE, CA 94549
(Phone: 415-283-2991)

Like a growing number of scientists, experts on world food supplies, agricultural economists, and nutritionists, we feel that soybeans will be one of the key protein sources for the future on Planet Earth. One of the world's great renewable resources, soy holds great promise to meet great needs. Here are ten good reasons why:

1. Lowest Cost: Soybeans are presently the least expensive source of protein in virtually every country of the world.

2. Optimum Land Utilization: A given area of land planted in soybeans can produce much more usable protein than if planted in any other conventional farm crop and twenty times as much as if the land were used to raise beef cattle or grow their fodder.

3. High Nutritional Value: Soyfoods are a rich source of high-quality complete protein, with a protein quality equal to that found in chicken or beef. They are low in calories and saturated fats, and completely free of cholesterol.

4. Time Tested: For over two thousand years, soyfoods have served as a key protein source for more than one fourth of the world's population.

5. Remarkably Versatile: The soybean yields a cornucopia of delicious foods including tofu (the world's most popular soyfood), tempeh, soymilk, miso, shoyu or soy sauce, soy flour, soy nuts, fresh green soybeans, textured soy protein (TVP) and various meat analogues.

6. Appropriate Technology: Most of these foods can be produced in cottage industries using appropriate technology as well as in modern factories.

7. New Dairylike Products: Soybeans yield an array of high-quality, low-cost, healthful dairylike products: soymilk, yogurt, ice cream, cheese, etc.

8. Hardy and Adaptive: Soybeans can be grown under a wide range of climatic conditions and are quite resistant to pests, diseases, and drought.

9. Free Nitrogen Fertilizer: A legume, the soybean enriches the soil with free nitrogen fertilizer, a key fact, since the price of chemical fertilizers has quadrupled since 1973.

10. Great Productivity Potential: Worldwide production of soybeans continues to skyrocket, having more than doubled in the past decade. Soybeans could now provide 25 percent of the yearly protein needs of every person in the world.

Thus, soyfoods can serve as an ideal protein backbone of the diet for health-minded, cost-conscious people who love fine foods.

This organization is bringing a new era in good food to the United States. Write for their handsome brochure, listing books and other data.

Corn: The Aztec Staple

The Aztecs thought so much of corn that they cast it in solid gold. It is said that many Aztec youths ate nothing but corn and water until they reached maturity. Present–day Aztec land is peopled with Mexicans who thrive on a diet that is mainly corn.

Corn is a highly nutritious food, some varieties being more than 12 percent protein. It's economical to buy and easy to store. The kind I like best is large–kerneled white corn that costs only a little more than the standard yellow variety. I have noticed that this is the type that is used by tortilla makers, and I assume they know the best one to use.

Parched Corn: Easy to make, this one will start you out on the right track with little effort. Just pour some whole–kernel dry corn on a cookie sheet and toast in the oven until it turns slightly brown. It is now roasted or "parched" and can be eaten as a snack anytime. Shake in a bag with finely ground herbs for even more flavor. Incidentally, parched corn can be used in any recipe calling for whole–kernel corn.

Popcorn: No need to explain how this is made, although I would like to mention that the new oil–less electric poppers are great since you can eliminate fats.

- Try grinding fresh popcorn into a highly nutritious cold cereal. Use your meat grinder or food chopper.

- Sprinkle hot popcorn with Parmesan cheese for Poppacorna, an Italian treat.

- Mexicorn is made by shaking freshly–popped corn with a little chili powder or cumin.

- Other international flavors can be made by using a country's favorite herbs.

- Make your own crackerjacks by mixing corn with peanuts and covering both with a carmelized honey coating.

- While salt and butter are standard for popcorn, try adding molasses, maple syrup, or date sugar to a hot batch.

- Popcorn makes one of the best croutons for soup.

- A delicious snack can be made by simply sprinkling HVP (hydrolized vegetable protein) over freshly popped corn. No salt needed!

- For an interesting texture, add ground popcorn to your next pancake batter.

Homemade Corn Chips: Put fresh corn tortillas in a 300° F oven and bake until crisp. Cool, break into pieces and store in an airtight jar. For a fraction of what you pay for the oil–fried kind, you have a healthy dip chip or snack.

Corn Crackers

- Place 1/4 cup of whole–kernel white or yellow corn into your blender or grinder at one time and make yourself some fresh corn meal. Now proceed:

    1 1/2 cups corn meal
    1 cup whole wheat flour
    1/2 cup wheat germ
    1 teaspoon honey or molasses
    1/2 cup water
    1/3 cup oil

- Mix dry ingredients. Beat honey, oil and water together and add them slowly to the dry mixture. Mix and knead lightly. Roll out dough with a rolling pin as thinly as possible. Sprinkle with sesame seeds, caraway or herbs. Paprika is a nice touch. Cut dough into any shapes you wish, place on well–oiled cookie sheet, and bake one minute at 400° F. Then turn down heat to 300° F and bake for 25 minutes more. If you serve them warm there may never by any to cool but that's life.

Corn Crunchies

Once you make these, you'll be free of those high–priced, heavily sugared, over advertised and nutritionally worthless cold cereals.

    1 cup water
    1 cup corn meal, freshly ground from parched corn
    1/4 cup safflower oil
    1 cup brown rice ground into flour in your blender or grinder
    1/2 cup soy flour
    1/2 cup wheat germ

- Heat water to a boil and add corn meal all at once. Remove from fire and stir until mixed. Add safflower oil, rice flour, soy flour and wheat germ. Knead lightly. The dough will be a little crumbly. Spread it out on a lightly oiled cookie sheet and bake until lightly browned in a moderate (325° F) oven stirring occasionally. Eat plain with milk or drizzle honey or molasses or other natural sweeteners over it.

• Substitute freshly ground wheat for the corn in this recipe and have Wheat Crunchies! Once you acquire the knack and expertise of making your own homemade snacks, your enthusiasm will create the spirit to do more!

Hot Cornbread with Wild Blackberries

2 cups whole wheat flour
2 cups freshly ground corn meal
2 tablespoons homemade baking powder
1/2 cup safflower or soy oil
1/2 cup honey
skim milk

• Sift dry ingredients together. Blend oil and honey and add to flours. Add enough skim milk to make a fairly thick batter. Pour into an oiled pan and bake in hot (400° F) oven for about 25 minutes or until toothpick comes out clean. Cool slightly, slice thickly and spoon crushed berries over top.

If you live in the country where there are wild blackberries, this is the recipe for you.

BLACKBERRY

Spoonbread

1/2 cup corn meal, fresh ground
2 cups milk, skim
2 eggs separated
1 tablespoon oil
1 1/2 teaspoons baking powder

- Cook the corn meal in the milk until thick. Remove from heat. Beat egg yolks, and add them to corn meal along with oil and baking powder. Beat egg whites until stiff, and fold them in. Pour batter into buttered casserole and bake at 375(198 F for 30 minutes. Serve warm.

This is one of those unique, early–American hot breads that defy description. You must try it yourself.

Polenta

This is one of those great recipes from Italy that could change the eating habits of millions of Americans if it were better known. So we're doing our bit to publicize what is, to our way of thinking, a simple yet nutritiously delicious way to live better for less.

1 quart water
1 cup yellow corn meal, fresh ground

- Bring water to a boil and slowly add corn meal, beating with a wire whisk to break up lumps and introduce air. Turn heat low and cook for about 20 minutes stirring frequently. Turn out on large platter and top with your favorite spaghetti sauce.

Naturally, there are infinite variations to basic polenta. The freshly cooked, hot corn meal dish lends itself to almost any sauce, from marinara to pesto. It can also be topped with stewed fruits and raisins as a dessert!

Another variation is to place layers of polenta in a casserole, alternating with sauteed onions, mushrooms, shredded fish or chicken. Then top with grated cheese and bake until the latter melts. Serve with a green salad for a bountiful meal at a cost that's truly ridiculously low.

Bradford Island Corn Cakes: This was the most popular dish aboard our boat tied to Bradford Island. Grind some dried corn in your blender or mill, and mix with milk or water to form a thin batter. Pour on a hot oiled griddle. Flip the cakes as soon as set and cook on other side until crisp. Serve immediately with honey heated with chopped walnuts or chopped fruit, such as apricots or peaches.

Hot Corn Meal Mush: Grind some dried corn in your blender or grinder. Cover with water, and soak it overnight. Simmer until done adding more water as needed and stirring occasionally. Serve it piping hot with honey and skim milk. Add sunflower or sesame seeds for added taste and nutrition.

Old Fashioned Scrapple: This is a follow–on dish of the above. Follow instructions for mush and add any tidbits you like from chopped dates to freshly sliced figs. Pour mixture into a rectangular pan and chill. When firm slice and dip in corn meal. Saute in butter or other oil. Serve with maple syrup, honey or top with fruit. This can be a main dish or breakfast, depending on the item added to the scrapple. For example, you can add bits of chicken, turkey or other meats or cheese and then pour over a hot Italian sauce ala polenta. Either way the cost is low, nutritional values high purity established!

Double Corn Cakes

1 cup freshly ground corn meal
1 cup whole wheat flour
1 cup fresh corn kernels
2 teaspoons baking powder
2 tablespoons oil
1 egg
1 cup milk (You can use buttermilk and substitute 1 teaspoon soda
    for the baking powder.)

• Blend all ingredients and drop by spoonfuls onto heated oiled griddle. Turn when light brown and serve with molasses.

This is one of those unique treats that combines fresh and dried corn and extracts the best flavors of each.

Homemade Tortillas: Grind 2 cups of dried corn and make stiff dough with cold water. Roll into balls about the size of a walnut and then press flat with dinner plate or use tortilla press (available in Mexican–food stores). Cook until lightly brown on heated, unoiled griddle. A basic staple you can use in hundreds of ways. Freeze and store excess tortillas.

Review of Corn

- A staple in societies that have survived for 10,000 years. This tells you that it's worthwhile from every standpoint—economy, nutrition, ease of preparation and variety of dishes.

- Corn in its whole–kernel state has all of its nutritional values intact. If you merely grind it, cook it promptly and eat it, you'll derive *all* the benefits from the vital nutritional core (corn germ) to the fiber in the bran. Compare that to one of those overprocessed, beat–to–death, chemicalized cold cereals at two dollars per box!

- Once you touch and smell the freshly ground corn meal, you'll get your own ideas on what to do with it. There are few baked recipes that can't benefit from the addition of fresh corn meal.

- Popcorn is really a sleeper. We think of it as a fun food but it's much more than that. Make it yourself at home, skip all the junk that's added to commercial popcorn, and you'll have a highly nutritious food that's good anytime, morning 'til night.

- Corn stores well. Just keep it cool and dry, and it will be there when you need it—this year or next. It's safe in metal or glass containers, but I've stored it for long periods in the original feedstore sack.

- Corn is often more available than wheat in a feed store. This is because whole–kernel corn is a basic foodstuff for chickens and other animals. Usually comes in two styles, whole kernel and cracked. Since you can grind your own, I would recommend the whole kernel, which would have the corn germ intact.

- Atoli, a drink of slightly cooked corn meal and water, is a staple energy–builder in Central America. It can be flavored with fruit juice, molasses, or honey. Try it in lieu of one of those chemical shakes the fast–food places sell at high prices.

- In summary, whole–kernel corn at its current low price is one of the best storable commodities for your home kitchen. Easy to grind and use in many recipes, it not only saves you lots of money, it will build your health account.

All About Wheat

An experiment in Texas proved that rats living on a diet of white bread and water expired within sixty days. The bread was made from what may be laughingly termed "enriched" flour.

Let's take a look at this substance that won't support life. Grains are ground in cylinder or hammer mills that create such high temperatures that the flour created lacks any significant nutrients or enzymes. The process causes almost *instantaneous rancidity of the important oils.* If this weren't sufficiently devitalizing, the nearly dead flour is subjected to an aging process which can use such chemicals as mercurials, nitrogen trichloride, chlorine dioxide, alum, chalk, plus bleaches and whiteners

The milling process removes about ninety nutrients; the law requires only four to be replaced and these are in a chemicalized, nonfood form. Enrichment indeed!

It's no wonder the rats died. What is surprising is that they lived as long as they did.

What's the solution to this problem? It's easy! Just bypass the giant food processors and go to their sources. This way, you'll get top nutrition for every food dollar.

Wheat contains almost everything a person needs to be healthy. John Muir once roamed the Sierras for months carrying only a goodly supply of whole wheat bread. That and pure water gave him the strength and enthusiasm to create a wonderful philosophy based on close proximity to nature. And did you know that whole–grain wheat contains one of the richest natural sources of B– an E–vitamins, plus valuable proteins, carbohydrates, iron and fat. In all, it contains thirty nutrients which are vital to your good health. That's why we strongly advocate that you make this marvelous food one of your good–health, low–cost building blocks.

Acquiring Wheat And Other Bulk Foods

Years ago my daughter Jill had her own horse, Pixie, a quarter horse mare. Along with hay, I often bought a sack of whole–grain wheat, a treat that Pixie loved. One day, I took a close look at the wheat, lovely golden kernels, and thought to myself:

I took some home and ran it through my meat grinder with the fine blade installed. What came out was something that closely resembled popular hot cereals. It was a propitious moment in my life. I realized that it was possible to buy food in its basic, natural, unprocessed form. Not only would the cost be far less than its packaged counterparts, there would be no unwelcome additives.

So I began to buy 100–pound sacks of whole–grain wheat and before long added bulk quantities of oats, rice, corn, millet, barley and all kinds of seeds (sunflower and alfalfa), plus wheat germ and bran. I began saving so much money on food bills, I thought there must be a Catch–22 somewhere. I asked the feed–store manager about purity—were the grains and seeds I was buying as pure as for human use? He explained that, as far as he know, his products had never hurt an animal and conjectured that many of the race horses he provided feed for were insured for lots more than people.

I got the message. I also found out that there were grains that were "recleaned" for human consumption. This meant that there was less chaff or other foreign matter in the grain. But no matter what I bought, it has apparently never harmed me or anyone else who ate it.

Thus, my first selection for a place to buy bulk grains would be a feed store. If they don't have what you want, they'll order it for you. After all, they are in the business and know exactly where to get just about any grain, seed or bean.

As this is written, I can get a 100–pound sack of whole–grain wheat for just twelve dollars. I don't see why you can't buy wheat in your area for about the same price, and, if you live anywhere that produces wheat, it will probably sell for less. A natural–food store that sells bulk grains and seeds would be my second choice for acquiring these products.

Grind Your Own

Unground wheat will keep for a long time, especially if you store it in a cool, dry place. My favorite location is in a glass jug, tightly sealed in a dark storeroom. In that way it's always available when I need it, and it can be ground fresh in minutes. Hand and electric grinders are available from many sources, and you can even use a kitchen blender. Just be sure you don't put in more than about one cup, otherwise the upper layers won't be ground. Grinding times vary with the hardness of the wheat, but you can always sift the results, saving the larger particles for cereal. Incidentally, it will closely resemble Wheatena or Roman Meal, packaged cereals that not only cost eight or ten times as much, but will have gone stale on the grocer's shelves.

Here are some ways that you can use your home–ground flour and cereals:

Wild Bill's Favorite Whole Wheat Cereal: Grind four ounces of whole grain wheat in your meat grinder or blender, and then pour in a pint of rapidly boiling water. Stir to eliminate lumps, then turn down to simmer. Add raisins, dates, nuts or anything else you'd like, and cook for thirty minutes. Pour into a bowl, add milk or fruit juice and enjoy. This is the best tasting, most nutritious cereal you've ever eaten. All the food values are there—including the important elements like bran and vitamin E. Nothing added. Nothing taken away. Wheat, just the way nature intended!

Incidentally, you can soak the ground grain overnight, and it will require less cooking.

Bulgur, Kasha, Cous–cous: With slight variations, these are all healing foods you can make yourself! In your grinder, blender or even by hand. Then parboil (partially cook). Dry in the oven or in the sun. That's all there is to it!

This can be used in many ways; like rice in dishes that involve stir fried vegetables or like pasta or polenta in sauced recipes. It can be browned in oil and, when stock is added, becomes a base for soup, or it can simply be boiled with herbs and spices as a side dish to chicken or fish. Whatever you do with this Middle—eastern dish, one thing is certain—you're enjoying good taste at low cost in a pure, homemade food!

Creative Pizza

It's obvious why pizza places have proliferated in the United States. People enjoy something tasty and hot. However, if you were to investigate commercial pizza as I have, you'd never buy it. The flour is the same, devitalized, chemicalized cement that we talked about earlier. The tomato is a red—tinted mixture of bizarre synthetics. So is the cheese—only this time they add orange dye and something weird called "cheese flavor." What you end up eating is unadulterated junk.

Here's an alternative that will not only make your taste buds dance for joy, but it will cost you a mere fraction of commercial pizza: Start with two cups of your whole wheat and mix it with two cups of freshly ground corn meal. In a bowl, mix an envelope of dry yeast with 1/3 cup oil, a teaspoon of honey and two cups of warm water. Add the flour and mix with vigor; this is the fun part when you develop your arms and your appetite simultaneously. Put the dough in a warm place, and let it double in size. Roll it thin or thick, as you prefer, and place on large round cookie sheets. Then spoon on your homemade tomato sauce and any toppings you like, including chopped mushrooms, seasoned garbanzo beans, anchovies or chopped veggies. Bake in a hot oven (500° F) until the crust is browned. Serve immediately.

From this same basic dough recipe you can make bread, rolls or coffee cakes. Add raisins, nuts, spices and honey to suit your taste and bake in fanciful shapes. Experiment, be creative, use your imagination in your home bakery. I'll guarantee that you'll not only enjoy the experience, you'll never want to buy anything storebought again!

Before the review, here's our special Pioneer Pancakes recipe that you are sure to enjoy:

Pioneer Pancakes

1/2 cup each of whole wheat flour, corn meal and rye flour
1/4 cup each, wheat germs and soy flour
4 eggs
1 1/2 cup buttermilk plus 1 tsp soda

1/3 cup safflower or other good oil
1 tablespoon honey or molasses

- Blend all ingredients and pour on hot greased griddle. More liquid may be added if you like thinner pancakes. Use this batter in your waffle iron. Top with pure maple syrup or honey and real butter. Mmmmm!

Review

- For the sake of profit and their own convenience, American grain millers have almost completely destroyed the nutritional values of wheat and other grain products.

- Your most precious possession, your health is at stake. Thus any effort you make to acquire and use natural grains is worth it.

- Historically, bread made from pure, natural, fresh–ground wheat flour was the staff of life. And it still is in countries where real flour is used (just try some Canadian or French bakeries).

- Feed and seed stores often carry a wide variety of grains in their totally natural form. And if they don't have them, they have the capability to get them for you. Natural–food stores selling bulk grains are another source.

- Why not buy 100 pounds of whole wheat for less money than two dozen boxes of sugared cereal!

- The average person eats about one thousand pounds of food per year. Thus, about three 100–pound sacks of whole–kernel wheat in cooked form could provide all the food for one person, since one pound becomes three when cooked. The cost would be less than *fifty dollars or about fourteen cents a day*. (Of course, no one would live on wheat alone, although they could. The point is that pure natural food from the source is not only the best, it's the cheapest!)

- Wheat can be prepared in the home with simple equipment. Most homes have a blender or grinder, and these can be used to make flour, cracked wheat or bulgur.

- As a hot cereal, wheat doesn't even need to be precessed—just boiled.

- Sprouting is another way of increasing food value—turning the wheat into a hundred delicious dishes at virtually no cost whatsoever and, best of all, with trifling labor.

- Many of the most–costly items in a food store are flour–based—but every single one of them can be made in the home. Then these become gourmet meals at beggar prices. And the process can be fun and enlightening, a group activity that yields better health for all.

- Stored, whole–grain wheat kernels are a great insurance policy against any disaster—physical or economic. Some Mormons store a year's supply.

- Whole–grain wheat stores easily with little deterioration. Glass jugs with tight lids make inexpensive, effective containers.

- Wheat, along with other storable grains, can be the foundation for a good diet for you and your family. Grains can always be available to provide nourishing, delicious meals with minimal effort and at a cost so low as to be almost unbelievable—even with today's inflation.

Fish and Chicken Instead of Red Meat

As you may have noticed, there's no use of beef or other red meats anywhere in this book, and for good reason. Canada and most other countries won't import our beef because it's so loaded with dangerous chemicals. So take their advice, and don't import any into your stomach!

There are lots of alternatives, and two good ones are fish and chicken. Fish can be caught by you personally, and you can even raise your own chickens. The other options include making sure that the fish and chicken you buy are as free from harmful chemicals as is possible in this era of rampant pollution. Assuming that you do encounter one or both that you feel won't make you glow in the dark, there are some ways to prepare them.

Country Catfish

2 eggs beaten
1/4 cup milk
1/4 teaspoon pepper
2 cups whole wheat flour
2 cups bread crumbs
oil for frying
25 catfish, skinned

- Combine eggs, milk and pepper. Combine flour and bread crumbs. Dip fish in egg mixture, and roll it in flour and crumbs. Fry in oil until fish flakes easily with fork. Drain on absorbent paper.

- Serves 25 moderately hungry people; 12 1/2 ravenous ones. Great accompaniment would be spoon bread or other corn recipe.

The reason we cite catfish is that they are easily caught in many areas. Be alert, however, to regions where water contamination may have harmed the fish.

You probably won't catch these next little critters yourself, but they are quite reasonable in most fresh fish markets. And don't be squeamish about squid, just think of it as calamari. It's been a favorite in the Mediterranean area for many centuries and with good reason.

Squid with Rice

3 tablespoons minced green onion
2 cloves garlic, minced
1/4 cup parsley, minced
2 tablespoons butter
2 pounds cleaned squid cut in rings
grated Parmesan cheese

- Saute the vegetables in butter until soft. Raise heat and saute squid for 5 minutes. Excellent when served over rice and sprinkled with the grated cheese.

Note: Values of seafood are quite uniform regardless of how much you pay. Thus, squid is both good and a bargain.

Here's a good way to finish off the rest of that large baked fish in the fridge.

Fish Cakes

2 slices whole wheat bread
1 cup milk
3 cups cooked fish, flaked
1 egg beaten
1/4 cup parsley
1/4 teaspoon pepper
3 tablespoons butter
3 tablespoons oil
dash tamari or hot sauce

- Soak bread in milk until soft. Combine with fish, egg, parsley and seasonings. Form into fairly thin cakes and brown them on each side in butter and oil mixture.

One Pot Clam and Corn Chowder

1 large onion, sliced
2 medium carrots, sliced
2 celery stalks, chopped
1 green pepper, diced
1 cup fresh tomatoes, chopped
1 cup fresh corn kernels
1 cup raw potato, diced
3 tablespoons oil
3 cups water
1/4 teaspoon fresh ground pepper
1/2 teaspoon thyme
1/2 teaspoon oregano
1 can (6 1/2 oz) minced clams or same amount fresh clams

- Saute veggies in oil until just tender. Add tomatoes potatoes, water and seasonings. Bring to boil, stirring frequently. Reduce heat and simmer until potatoes are tender. Add clams and their juice and simmer a few minutes longer.

- Serve with crusty French bread and a crisp green salad. Delicious and economical!

Western Chicken

2 chickens cut into serving pieces
1 cup whole wheat flour
1/4 teaspoon each of marjoram, oregano, rosemary and thyme
2 tablespoons oil
1 onion sliced
1/2 pound mushrooms
1/2 green pepper, chopped
3 stalks celery, diced
2 cups stewed tomatoes
1 bay leaf

- Wash and dry chicken pieces and shake in bag with flour and herbs. Heat oil in heavy iron skillet and brown chicken in it. Remove and set aside.

- To the drippings in the pan, add the sliced onion and mushrooms and saute them until soft. Add pepper, celery, tomatoes and bay leaf. Arrange the chicken pieces on top of the vegetables, cover pan and simmer gently until chicken is tender.

Sage Hens are a little tough, but this recipe will handle the situation adequately. Sage Hen Saute: (I got this recipe from an old prospector in Central Nevada). Clean and pluck hen and soak for 48 hours in salt water. Boil for three days. Then fry in oil for two days. Throw away sage hen and eat the pan.

The Chinese make a single chicken serve a platoon of diners. They have learned how to use precious and expensive foods as a condiment rather than a main dish.

Chicken with Bean Sprouts

2 cups mung bean sprouts
1 cup celery, sliced
1 large onion, chopped
1/2 cup bamboo shoots, sliced fresh or canned but preferably fresh
3 tablespoons sesame oil
1/2 cup cooked shredded chicken
soy or tamari sauce
2 cups cooked Chinese noodles

- This dish is best prepared in a Chinese wok, but a large iron skillet will work as well. Saute onions and celery in oil until tender. Then add bamboo shoots and chicken just long enough to heat through. At the last minute toss in the sprouts on top and steam them briefly. They should remain crisp. Serve over noodles and pass the soy or tamari.

This is a dish that was served often on my old houseboat when we were between royalty checks.

I can guarantee that it allowed a very small amount of money to serve a lot of hungry houseboaters.

Review of Fish and Chicken

- Fish and chicken are expensive items except, of course, if you either catch or raise them yourself. If you have them in abundance, there's no question that they will provide lots of high–quality protein. If not plentiful, use as a condiment, as the Chinese do.

- Cooked fish and chicken can be added to large dishes of other foods: pasta, rice or veggies to enhance their appeal, flavor and protein content.

- A great stretcher of fish or chicken is the soup route. Clam chowder takes very few clams but produces lots of flavorful and nutritious soup. The carcass of a chicken or turkey can make gallons of soup when plenty of rice and celery are added.

- Creole cooking introduced the concept of mixing seafood and chicken, as in their marvelous and tasty gumbos. Again, a small amount of the high–cost ingredients can lend much flavor to otherwise bland items like potatoes and rice.

- In summary, think of fish and chicken as flavoring material rather than as main dish candidates. That way you'll have gourmet meals at beggar prices.

Desserts for Those with the Sweet Tooth

It's a tradition, worldwide...something sort of sweet and delicious to top off a meal. The Chinese like their almond cookies; the Greeks, baklava; the Austrians, their fabulously ornate pastry; the French, their fresh fruit and cheese; the English, their trifles; Americans, their apple pie and ice cream.

All can be well and good if certain basic rules of health are observed. The sweet part should be as natural as possible—no white sugar and the fats minimized and also au natural.

Here then are some suggestions of how to keep health up, costs down, but after–dinner delight at a peak.

Peach Crisp

6 cups fresh peaches
1/3 cup whole wheat flour
1 cup rolled oats
1/4 cup honey (if peaches are really sweet and ripe, this may be omitted)
1/3 cup melted butter

- Preheat oven to 375° F. Place peaches in baking dish. Combine dry ingredients, add melted butter, mixing until crumbly. Sprinkle on top of peaches. Bake for 30 minutes or until peaches are tender. Drizzle honey over top. Serve warm or cold with or without milk or cream. Apples can be substituted for peaches.

Spiced Fruit Rice Pudding

1 1/2 cups of raw brown rice
3 cups milk (skim)
1/2 cup honey
1/2 teaspoon powdered ginger
2 cups fruit (apples, apricots or oranges, coarsely chopped)
1 egg beaten
1/2 teaspoon cinnamon
1/2 teaspoon nutmeg
1 cup yogurt

- Preheat oven to 350° F. Cook rice until tender in milk instead of water. Stir in honey, egg and spices. Oil a 1–quart casserole and spread half of rice mixture over bottom. Gently place half of the fruit on top of rice. Repeat the two layers and place in oven. Bake for 25 minutes. Remove and chill, placing yogurt over top just before serving.

This is one of those healthy, low–cost desserts that are actually a beneficial part of a regular meal. Also, this dessert can be served as part of a substantial breakfast. (One portion yields about 25 percent of your daily protein need.)

Alternative Food Sources

There are many books that discuss doomsday and what might be done to prevent one's personal doom. Some advocate hoarding gold, others silver, still others old coins, antiques, classic cars and so forth ad infinitum. I have to chuckle at these indirect methods of assuring continuation of one's life. I don't have a single Krugerrand or silver coin, and the only antique I own is a twenty–year–old pickup camper. However, I never lose one moment's sleep worrying about doomsday—since what I have is a stored–up encyclopedia of survival secrets. I'd like to share some of this with you, and I'll guarantee that, if doomsday does, indeed, arrive in our lifetimes, this information will be worth much more than gold.

Wild Foods

Cattails: Did you know that a common plant that grows in all parts of the world can provide all the food for everyone on this planet. You've seen it many times growing in marshy areas and know it by the name cattail. Few people are aware that this plant was and is a staple foodstuff for native populations. Almost the entire plant is edible, from the potato–like roots to the pollen which can be used like flour in baking. The tender new shoots taste like the best asparagus you have ever eaten, while the tendrils from the roots make a fine celery substitute. Try them sometime; then you can quit being concerned about what you'd eat if the stores all closed next Tuesday!

CATTAIL

Acorns: The Chumash Indians of Southern California had no grocery stores. Instead, they lived off the land, enjoying such free foods as white–oak acorns, which they ground into flour for porridge and bread. Oaks are indigenous to many parts of the United States, so it's not hard to find this source of free food. Gather the acorns, shell and grind the nuts in your blender. Then pour boiling water through the meal to leach out the bitter tannin. Once this is done, the dried meal can be used in place of flour in any recipe. Acorns contain almost everything one needs for health—vitamins, minerals a complex carbohydrate, and fat. No wonder the Chumash were healthy until the supermarkets came into their lives.

Cactus: If any region looks inhospitable from a nutritional standpoint, it has to be the desert. Despite its appearance, deserts often contain everything needed not only for survival, but for good health. For example, the common broad–leafed cactus that is native to most deserts is eaten with relish by thousands of people daily. Usually, the young, tender leaves are selected, held under water while the spines are removed with a paring knife (they float to the surface and can be skimmed off). Then the leaves can be cubed, cooked in oil or water, and eaten with the usual condiments.

If there are leftovers, chill and add to salads or make them into pickles. Any way you prepare them, they're good, and certainly the price is right!

Blackberries: Of all the wild plants that grow in America, the ubiquitous blackberry is one of the most popular. I've seen acres of blackberry thickets containing tons of the juicy, sweet berries and, often, no one picking them! Besides enjoying them fresh off the bush, it's possible to make any number of delicious dishes from blackberry pie to jams and syrups. Frozen, they'll keep for a long time, and it's also possible to dry them as the Indians did.

Volunteer Fruit and Nut Trees: Ever since I was a small boy, I've had a built–in "radar" receiver for the ripe fruits and nuts that grow in the wilds. Sprouted from a discarded seed, these trees usually don't have the elegant harvest of commercial orchards. But what they lack in looks they make up for in unique flavor and the fun of gathering them. I've practically lived on the loquat, which grows wild in many parts of the West. Once I found an abandoned orchard of walnuts still yielding a bountiful crop that kept us in shelled walnut meats for months. Then I've found dozens of wild apple trees, from the Canadian border to Mexico, and each was a pleasant surprise in flavor and texture. Black–walnut trees abound nationwide, and, even though the meats are hard to extract, it's worth the effort. All it takes to be a gatherer of this free largess is a sack. Keep one with you during harvest season, and keep your eyes open. Opportunities abound, as you'll see.

Nettles: These wild weeds yield tender tops that the French make into many gourmet dishes. Wear gloves when gathering to avoid the stinging hairs. As soon as they are cooked, the leaves become tender and edible. Nettles can be used in almost any way that one would use chard or other greens.

Wild Oats: There is no way that anyone could starve with millions of pounds of these hardy grass seeds available all over the United States. Indians made a porridge from them, first singeing off the hairs and grinding them between stones. Oats have a high protein and fat content and thus are valuable as a basic staple item.

Ferns: Wild ferns yield young, tender fronds, called fiddleheads, that can be cooked as a typical green. Also, the roots can be boiled to produce a starchy, potato–like food.

Watercress: I once parked my trailer for a month near a brook which yielded a bountiful crop of fresh, crisp green watercress. Mixed with chopped cabbage and topped with a homemade dressing, many visitors called it the best salad they'd ever tasted.

Manzanita: Deer love the leaves and berries, and you'll like the latter. Eat them right from the bush or make into pies, cobblers and jelly. If you have too many, dry and grind to make a porridge down the road. You can make a fine drink by scaling the berries, crushing them to a pulp and adding water. Let stand for an hour or so; them enjoy this manzanita cider. You can also make wine from the berries in the usual way.

Milkweed: One of the tastiest wild items I've ever had was the young and tender pods of common milkweed. Try them and see if they don't out–taste fresh asparagus. The pods can be steamed and served as a vegetable with a little butter and pepper.

Willow: These streamside trees are common in many places. The inner bark can be removed, dried and ground into a flour usable in the usual ways. Imagine worrying about food when there are millions of willows? Many other trees also yield edible barks. Some are so sweet that they can be eaten on the spot. Many a flier has survived the wilderness by just knowing this one fact.

Fennel: A common vegetable in Italy, fennel grows wild even in arid, rugged terrain. Leaf stalks can be eaten raw in salads or cooked like spinach. The seeds are quite sweet and tasty, similar to anise. Dry them and use for tea.

Miner's Lettuce: This light green tender wild vegetable grows in shady, moist areas. Pick the youngest leaves for one of the best salad greens you've ever had.

MINER'S LETTUCE

Pine Nuts: If you can beat the squirrels to these tasty little nuts, you'll enjoy a delicate flavor and benefit from top nutritional values. Many species of pine contain these small nuts in their cones. Gather in the fall, beat with sticks to release nuts. Carry a little solvent with you to remove sap from hands.

Myrtle or Laurel (Bay Laurel): The nuts of these giant trees can be shelled and eaten or ground into flour and baked with other grain flours to make bread. Dry a handful of leaves (bay) for seasoning stews and soups.

Summary

We could go on for quite a number of pages since, out of the three hundred thousand plant species in the world, about one hundred thousand are edible. There are books in your local library that picture and describe edible wild plants in your area. One word of caution: Be sure you check any unknown plant with an expert to make sure it's not poisonous.

Grow Your Own

Once you roam the wilds and see how much good is grown by Mother Nature without plows, pesticides or people effort, it becomes quite clear that anyone can be a first–time farmer. All you have to do is relax and let the plant do her thing.

In a famous breakthrough book by Ruth Stout, she tells of discovering that since nature doesn't do any plowing, there's no need for anyone to break up the soil. All one needs is mulch (straw, hay, or other grasses) to cover the ground and keep it moist and friable. Nature does this by sowing the next year's crop into the debris of the last one.

To try this method, dig up your garden area just once and mix in compost or fertilizer. Then sprinkle your seeds and cover with a layer of mulch a few inches thick. Keep damp and soon you'll find the little green plants climbing their way up through the mulch. What could be simpler?

There are lots of books on home gardens, and your local library doubtless has many. So we won't clutter up this book with more than a primer on the subject of growing your own.

What to Grow: This depends on what you like. If salads are your thing, then concentrate on veggies like butter lettuce and tomatoes, parsley and radishes. If you love root veggies, then carrots and beets should have lots of space. Also, one should consider the local climate and frost season. If you have a short growing period, then go for the crops that mature within a short time. If you're lucky to be in a sub–tropical region, then you can count on having garden–fresh foodstuffs practically all year.

Space: Did you know that by using an intensive gardening program (planting constantly as foods are harvested) a space 100 x 200 feet can provide all the vegetables and small fruits that a large family can eat all year, with plenty left over for canning and even sales. So by extrapolating up or down from that size, it's easy to calculate how much space you need for your garden produce requirements.

In Europe, almost everyone has a garden and they grow an enormous amount of food in a small space by succession gardening and plentiful fertilization. All trimmings from harvest go right back into the soil.

Seeds: There are many American seed companies and we have a list in the Resources section of this book. They love to send out their catalogs, and you'll love to peruse them. It's such a joy to plan on what you'll grow in the next time period—and also to outdo the catalog in the size and opulence of your plant production.

You don't need to buy much to plant a lot. For example, 1/4 ounce of bronze lettuce seed will plant a 100–foot row, while an ounce of Danvers carrot will seed a row 300–feet long!

Growing: This is taken care of by the plants themselves, so just keep them watered, the weeds down and the dogs away. The best pest remover I know of is a high–pressure water spray followed by a chicken. If you can encourage birds, toads and other insect lovers to spend time in your garden, you won't need chemicals.

Summary

Except for harvesting, which is the fun part, that's really all there is to it basically. Again, remember that nature grows millions of tons of edible foodstuffs without the hand of man to interfere. No pesticides, no herbicides, nothing that is damaging to health is used in the wilderness, and yet plants are bountiful. You can do the same in your backyard.

Here are a few tips that may be helpful.

1. Start with simple veggies like loose–leaf lettuce. Once you grow a few heads, you'll have the confidence to tackle other varieties of veggies.

2. Limited space? Just plant in tubs, pots, Number 10 cans, plastic jugs with the tops cut off, window boxes and raised beds. If you keep them small enough, you can move them around to take advantage of sun and the best growing conditions.

3. There's a simple spray: just mix cayenne pepper with water and use a hand sprayer. Rotenone and pyrethrum are also natural pest removers. Saucers filled with beer will make snails so drunk they'll wander off to somewhere else.

4. That book by Ruth Stout is *How to Have a Green Thumb Without an Aching Back: A New Method of Mulch Gardening*, Exposition Press, New York.

5. Try your local county farm agency for tips on gardening in your area.

6. Remember, only plant 1/2 of a zucchini plant and it will supply you, and the neighbors, with plenty left over for pickles.

7. Benefits of home gardening include:

   • Savings in money

   • Fresher food, higher food value

   • No chemicals added

   • A great way to get outdoors

   • The children love to participate

   • Surplus can be sold, traded, dried, canned or frozen

   • Add a row of herbs to season your output

   • Great way to exercise

   • You become independent of supermarkets

   • It's fun and connects you with the earth

The Kaysing Method of Growing Your Own Vegetables and Small Fruits

Here is a simple method of gardening that costs little and yet produces an abundance of food per square foot:

1. Build a wooden frame measuring 4 feet x 12 feet, 8–inches deep. Redwood is the best, but you can use almost any kind of wood, including scraps. Or use concrete blocks to form the frame. It can be placed on ground of any description.

2. Find a source of rich soil; river–bottom land is best, but you can create your own by mixing natural fertilizer with ordinary sand, adding peat moss, leaves, and sawdust to make the mixture light and easily worked. Fill the box with this soil mixture and add enough water so that the entire plot is quite moist.

3. Now plant your seeds or seedlings using the guidelines given on the package for spacing, time of year, and so forth.

4. As soon as plants sprout, place soaker hoses between them and keep ground moist but not wet by turning on water periodically. The key is to let the water drip–irrigate the plants rather than drown them one day and let them parch the next. The Israelis have proven that plants need moisture constantly and when deprived, they simply stop growing. They've increased yields of tomatoes, for example, by several hundred percent using this simple, work–free method.

5. Because the plants are above ground, you shouldn't have trouble with pests. However, if you do, then mix cayenne pepper with water and spray with a hand sprayer. The hot–pepper mixture will drive away any unwanted insects. Running your chickens or ducks through the veggies after a hard water spray works fine, since the poultry consume the insects on the ground.

6. By now you have noticed that this is a completely chemical–free way of gardening using only natural materials. Your vegetables and small fruits will appreciate your organic treatment and respond by producing great–tasting harvests.

And that's all there is to it! Most books on gardening are so complex that they have a tendency to dissuade the amateurs before they begin. But I guarantee that the above method works. In a few wooden frames, Ruth and I grow a tremendous supply of delicious, fresh vegetables all–year long.

A few more tips:

• Have a compost heap in a smaller frame where you toss trimmings, leaves and anything else that's biodegradable. Use the compost to fertilize your garden between plantings.

• To grow all year, cover the frames with plastic film supported on 2 x 2's.

• As soon as you harvest a plant, drop in another seed or seedling.

Here's How to Grow Just About Anything from Seed
(from a 1930's *Sunset Magazine*)

It is economical to buy quality seed. Carefully read and follow the cultural directions printed on the packet to get the best results, for each plant has its own requirements.

For soil drainage, break up old flower pots and cover the bottom of the seed box, in addition to boring holes in the bottom boards provided they are set with no space between.

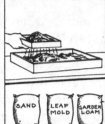

Sift well-prepared soil composed of sand, leaf mold and good garden loam on top of drainage material through a fine-meshed sieve, filling box to about 1 inch of the top.

Firm the soil so it will not settle after water is applied by pressing down heavily on entire surface with a block of wood, making the surface perfectly level at the same time.

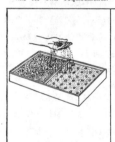

Scatter fine seed thinly over soil surface. Set large seeds down into the soil ¼ to ½ inch deep. Sift enough soil over the top of the seed box to lightly cover the seed.

Gently sprinkle seed flat by means of a fine spray so as not to dislodge the seed. Water thoroughly, then do not water again until soil surface shows indications of drying out.

Cover seed flat with glass slightly tilted to provide plenty of ventilation. To aid germination a couple of thicknesses of newspaper can be put under glass till seed sprouts.

Set seed box where protected from direct sunlight, winds or downpour—in lath house, cold frame or under a tree. If set in the open, shade with burlap, muslin or lath screen.

After the seeds sprout, keep the flat free from weeds. Also, thin out the little plants just as soon as they begin to touch so they do not grow up tall and spindly.

When fourth leaf appears lift out the plants with a fork and transplant into pots or box, using a little richer soil. Harden off plants by gradual exposure to sun and air.

In about two weeks set plants out into a garden spot prepared in advance by removal of stones and replacement of some of the subsoil with good garden loam and fertilizer.

After planting, carefully water the plants, so soil packs about the roots, then shade them for a few days by means of plant caps, improvised cardboard shields or inverted berry boxes.

This method is just about foolproof, since you protect the plants at the early stages when they are most vulnerable. Pay attention to the soil where the plants will be grown. Make it rich and friable with sand, mulch, straw, vegetable trimmings, and fertilizer. But don't use chemicals!

Shelter Now: A Variety of Ways to Put a Roof Over Your Head without Going Bankrupt

Introduction

Do you know what the *number one* subject of conversation is at assemblies of Americans? Over dinner, at golf, in subways and especially in downtown skid rows, the topic is *housing*!

There's good reason for this interest. With respect to affordable housing, most Americans are poor. Millions of people are no longer qualified to buy a house, nor is it likely that they ever will be. Still other millions have shelter but are hanging on by the tips of their fingers. Every available dollar goes to pay that gigantic mortgage or those high rents. If you know these ingenious little strategies, that can be corrected. Here's how.

What we will be presenting in this section is a comprehensive review of what we call "alternative architecture" or "shelter now." While most books on the subject refer to the building of a single–family dwelling on a lot, we will go much further. We will examine many unconventional opportunities to provide oneself with an affordable roof. (The roof could be the top of a cabin cruiser, but that's just part of the fun.) We won't forget the 3,000,000 Americans who are totally homeless. In fact, we'll start with some ideas for them.

Move In Now

Out of work? No money in your jeans? No place to live? Not even a bed for tonight? Cheer up. Wild Bill has some practical ideas that can produce instant shelter for everyone with a modicum of gumption.

Live–in Jobs

Go to your local library, and get the daily papers. Look for ads that look like this:

LIVE–IN AIDE positions (2), flexible schedules, care for elderly couple. Room & board plus $400/mo. Call _____ .

DECK HANDS. Extensive travel. Train aboard ship. Good pay & benefits. Ages 17–33. U.S. citizenship required. Call toll free: _____ .

Resident manager for 30 unit apt. bldg. Salary + apt. Send resumé including phone no. to _____ .

There are millions of people who are elderly, handicapped, convalescent or otherwise in need of full–time or part–time live–in care. You would get a room of your own, all you can eat, and a salary. Some jobs pay so much you would net more money than a person who had to commute to work and pay all those miscellaneous expenses that occur in routine eight–to–five jobs.

To explore this avenue, I recently assumed the daycare of a young man who was badly injured in a motorcycle accident. He was barely able to walk and needed someone around full–time to ensure that he did not fall and injure himself. Often we went to a local park where he would practice walking on the grass. I sat nearby busily working on my book projects. So everyone benefited. I was paid, and the young man had his guardian. At the same time, I was able to pursue my own goals without neglecting my responsibilities. A true symbiosis!

Another way of seeking this type of employment/shelter is to check the yellow pages of your phone directory under the headings:

Health Service

Nurses and Nurses Registries

All you need do is register. They'll put you to work, often right away since needs are great with so many people getting older every day. There's a great side benefit to this type of work—you'll be helping someone cope with a difficult situation. Nothing is more rewarding in life than that!

Few people think of looking for a place to live under the classification "Domestics" in the daily papers. We have a foolish stigma attached to servant work in America. But innumerable people enjoy being proficient housekeepers or a gentleman's gentleman. See any city daily for samples. Note the number that mention "live–in"! Keep in mind that nothing is forever. Work as a live–in helper for as long as it takes to put yourself back on your feet again. Then you can reach out for other opportunities.

My father, Charles Kaysing, was, at one time in his life, the chauffeur and body-guard for Marshall Field, the Chicago department store owner. He never had an accident and was a trusted and reliable employee for many years. When he retired, the Fields voluntarily gave him a pension, and he was able to live comfortably for the rest of his life.

I've often thought of my dad when people put down service work for others. What's wrong with doing something right? I've always believed that Kazantzakis was most profound when he had his character, Zorba, say, "I've got hands and feet, what does it matter what I do."

And I would add, do it with all one's heart.

In 1974 I received a contract to write a book titled *Eat Well on a Dollar a Day* for Chronicle Books of San Francisco. I wanted to escape the wet winters of the Bay Area, so I selected sunny Las Vegas as my writing locale. My advance was not too large, so I was looking for an inexpensive place to live when I ran into an old friend, a charming lady who was public–relations director for Circus Circus. She mentioned that she had just lost her gardener. Jokingly, I suggested that she hire me. After all, didn't I have the original black thumb? As it turned out, I *did* become her gardener on the following terms: I would tend her garden and lawns for an hour or so a day in ex-change for a large room in her spacious home. It worked out beautifully; I had a chance to do some outdoor work to balance my hours at the typewriter, and my friend had her gardener for free.

Hotels and Motels

Where can you find a lot of rooms? You're right—at any facility providing lodging. So it's supremely logical to look for instant shelter on a live–in job basis. The most common variety is that of desk clerk at a hotel or motel. People willing to work nights are often hard to find, and the turnover is great. So if you need a place to stay right now, just put on your best suit or dress and amble on over to the nearest lodging place. Often you can get relief work, which means you would work a few days at several facilities. In any event, you'll be warm and dry and earning a stake to ad-vance to other possibilities.

Lodging places need maids, security guards and maintenance people. So even if there are no desk jobs available, you can probably make a connection and take a room as part of your pay.

I met a retired sheriff who acquired a place to live, a job that suited him perfectly and a salary that allowed him to bank his social security check. He became the chief of security for a modern re–creation of a Western mining town. He had his choice of parking his motorhome in the area surrounding the town or taking a room at one of the hotels. Actually, he enjoyed trading off between the two.

Dressed in his authentic Levi's, a ten–gallon hat on his head and a real six shooter on his belt, he became a colorful addition to the rip roaring tourist attraction. Incidentally, although we're discussing instant shelter, think about how much more rewarding retirement can be in a situation we've described rather than vegetating in some Sun City.

Old Nevada

A man with a great love for the early West has built an authentic reproduction of an old Nevada mining town in a picturesque location about ten miles south of Las Vegas. I visited several times and was intrigued by the charm of the false–front buildings, the staged "gun fights" and the fact that it was actually being lived in by the staff. In front was a small but usable railroad that ran for a quarter mile or so to a parking lot.

I still don't know how it happened, but I began running the miniature locomotive, to my great delight and amazement. One of my childhood dreams came true unexpectedly! I chugged back and forth wearing an engineer's cap and rang the bell and blew the whistle for the entertainment of tourists, especially the children.

Later, when a store became available, I started a self–service used book shop, *Wild Bill's Literary Bar*. Osmotically, I began to become a part of the entire mining–

town scene: eating at the *Miner's Saloon*, sleeping in one of the unused hotel rooms and even participating in the hourly gun battles as the kindly combination parson and undertaker. As each cowboy "bit the dust," I would take out my tape and measure him for his coffin. I hadn't had so much fun since the days when I watched Ken Maynard and Hoot Gibson on the screen at the Rialto Theater in my hometown of South Pasadena, California.

My point is clear, I believe. A person can live almost any kind of life he wishes. It's just a matter of retaining one's health, being free to cast about for opportunities, and then taking them as they appear.

There are many variations on the theme described above. For example, near Willits, there's the station for the Skunk Railway system that goes from that town to Fort Bragg on the coast. Near Santa Cruz, California is the Roaring Camp Railway. Others are scattered across many states. What's to prevent you from adding to the fun of high–timber railroading by staging a "robbery" or "Indian attack."

Caretaking

Even If They're Closed

My friend Terry put in some hard times in Vietnam and needed a place to get his head together. Fortunately, he was able to become the caretaker of a defunct brothel in southern Nevada. All he had to do was keep the diesel generators running and the vandals away. Room, board and a small salary were his basic compensations. But there were other rewards: long walks in the desert with the rag–tag collection of stray dogs that called the old cathouse home, views of the sun setting over the Sheep Range, and the stillness one can only find in places that remote.

One's pay, it seems, doesn't always have to be in coin.

Adaven

Spelled backwards it's "Nevada," and that's where this remote ranch is located. You'd never find it without exact directions, and then there's the possibility you couldn't even get there. Desert roads have a way of washing out in cloudbursts. However, if you did finally arrive you'd find one of those storybook western ranches tucked away beneath some towering snowclad peaks. The ranch buildings are traditional; a flock of healthy, outdoor–type chickens run here and there. A solid stream of spring water keeps everything green, including a garden and a productive fruit orchard.

Like to live there at no cost and help yourself to fresh eggs and veggies? That's the offer that was made to me some time back and I almost took it. Some other lucky person(s) seized this opportunity and may still be there, for all I know.

The reason for outlining Adaven is that it is representative of many chances to live in peace and quiet for just the simple chore of caretaking. There are ranches, farms, boats, resorts, unused factories, hotels, and just plain old property that welcome someone to "just watch" in exchange for the use of the facility or space to park a trailer or camper. Here are some others, both specific and general.

We'll start with possibilities for you to live in scenic, adventurous locales on a live–in basis. This means that you'd have a full–or part time job accompanied by room and board. The bottom line would be everything you need in the way of food and shelter, a paycheck, and an opportunity to enjoy the surroundings on your time off.

Resorts: Travel is booming. Worldwide, tens–of–thousands of resorts have opened to provide services for millions of tourists who are now streaming by air, ship and bus all over this fascinating planet. If you've ever wanted to enjoy a particular place—the Grand Canyon, the coast of Maine, La Paz, Mexico, Venice, Italy—now is your chance. There are nearly always some provisions for live–in help, and all you have to do is ask. Incidentally, many years ago I decided that as long as you had to live somewhere, it might as well be a resort area. I concluded correctly that there were as many opportunities at, say, Lake Tahoe, as there were in downtown Smogville.

In the past forty years, I've had the pleasure of living—for pennies—in some of the finest resort areas in the world. This includes Tahoe, the fabulous Napa Valley (delightful wine country), the Bay Area, the California Delta, Santa Barbara (for seven years), Sun Valley, Idaho, Las Vegas, British Columbia and even at a castle in Austria (Stainach). Of course most of my time was spent writing, but I had plenty of leisure to really enjoy the various resorts. I am convinced that I could have had some means of employment, including room and board, at any of these world–famous places.

How would I go about it? Simple: Either write the place of my choice, offering my experience and services, or just go there and take pot luck. Remember that, at any given moment, about fifteen percent of all positions are available or are becoming available, virtually everywhere. That's because people quit, are fired, get sick or just move on. I've heard that some hotel casinos in the Vegas–Reno–Tahoe circuit replace thirty people a day. Even if you couldn't get full–time work, you could work part–time temporarily. And there's always the opportunity to work on your own.

Vacation Camps and Schools: There are thousands of recreational and educational facilities in desirable locations all over the world. I recall a 160–acre ranch in the backcountry of Santa Barbara along the Santa Ynez River. Owned and managed by a couple, it was everything anyone would want. They offered horseback tours by day or week, camping by tent or trailer, and month–long summer camps for children featuring a spectrum of studies from botany to computers and activities befitting a working western ranch. Obviously, an enterprise of this magnitude offered a myriad of live–in possibilities, from wrangler to teacher, from swimming instructor to kitchen help. And what a wonderful place to work and enjoy—in the company of people having fun. And unlike the guests, you are paid instead of paying!

Dude Ranches: There are so many of these, there's a catalog published to list them. The mystique of the Old West persists to this day and has captured the imagination of practically everyone on this planet. Recently I was in a small town in France (Bedoin) and happened to strike up a conversation in halting French with some children. What did they want to hear? All about cowboys and why was I wearing western boots and were there really Indians running around with tomahawks, ad infinitum. So it's obvious that dude ranches will attract a large clientele for a long time to come. As with any other resort or vacation place, just pick your favorite and make your inquiry. If one doesn't have what you want, there are plenty more from which to choose.

One of the great advantages of living and working at a dude ranch is that you'll meet people with similar tastes and preferences, the major attraction being, of course, the outdoors and its delights. Furthermore, I can't think of a better place to slim down, get all that smog out of your lungs, and sweep the urban cobwebs from your mind and spirit.

Cruise Ships: Ever since my good friend, talented and beautiful Jerry Saunders, wrote *The Love Boat*, there has been an avalanche of interest in touring the world aboard cruise ships. Jerry was once a tour and entertainment director aboard these ships, and I highly recommend her book for an introduction to how much fun one can have while being paid for traveling. Just think, instead of being cooped up in a tiny cubicle in some noisy polluted city, you can be sailing serenely through the Greek islands. Even though you would have shipboard duties, there's always the possibility of taking the same shore leaves as the passengers.

Cruise ships advertise in all travel magazines, and you can make contact in this way. Every type of live–in job is available afloat, just as they would be at a first–class hotel.

Hot Springs: These are so important to low–budget lifestyles that we have a separate section about them. However, it's appropriate to mention them in the context of diversified living opportunities. With more than 1700 known thermal springs in the eleven western states, you have a bountiful spectrum of choices. Many are developed and can be approached on a live–in basis. Still more are undeveloped and primitive and welcome the weary, way–worn traveler.

A particularly successful hot springs is Harbin, north of San Francisco, where anyone who wants to live and work is welcome. It's a New Age center for advancing the consciousness level of human beings everywhere. All that *and* warm–water pools. What could be nicer?

Travel Trailers: In the spring of last year, I decided to enjoy a little ocean frontage. Costs of a house along the beach would have bankrupted me ten times over. So I towed my faithful old 18–foot Kenskill to a lovely wide beach overlooking the vast, blue Pacific. There weren't any hookups but that didn't matter. The trailer is self–contained and there was a source of water nearby. For bathing, the warm Carmel River was only about a half–mile away. I stayed at this location for about two months with only two minor problems: traffic noise during the day and occasional hassles by the police. But I stayed until it was time to examine some of the other scenic locations in the Carmel region.

The many plus aspects included fishing (including free fish from friendly fishermen), beachcombing, swimming (cold in ocean, warm in river), hiking in nearby hills, and some great cooking on the sand.

The pictures show: (1) my rig, its tow vehicle and runabout cycle plus friend just back from a beach saunter; (2) (next page) a view from across the bay showing trailer location (white arrow)—Carmel River outlet is in the center of this shot; and (3) a view which reveals the scene we could see from the picture window or from the beach itself.

You just cannot beat a recreational vehicle for ease of locating in a desirable place. And with the turn of the ignition key, you can change the scene out your window as easily as other people change a TV station.

Industrial and shipping point areas in large cities make ideal places to park a big rig like this. Police seldom hassle you, since they are accustomed to having big trucks

and similar units park for long periods of time. And if they do object, just turn the key!

The owner of this unusual trailer truck rig was a traveling technical writer who simply parked near his current employer—in this case not far from San Francisco.

The converted bus contained a large living room, handy kitchen and even a complete bath with shower and tub!

When you have a rig this size, you lack for little in the way of home comforts. Of course, it costs more to get around, but then one doesn't need to travel all the time anyway.

Are You A Novice Tire Tramp?: If so, then acquire a copy of *Secrets of Successful RVing*. All about how to buy, rent, maintain and use any RV, trailer, camper, motorhone or whatever. Write *Trailer Life*, P.O. Box 4500, Agoura, CA 91301. The cost is twelve dollars. If you write, ask about the Good Sam Club.

Can You Live in a Small Space?: Probably yes if the space will take you to faraway places in comfort. Here's a typical floor plan for an Xplorer motorhome:

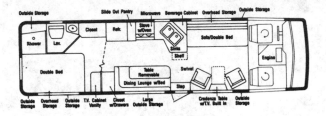

No Home: Then consider living aboard one of these large powerboats. Just look at those prices—less for the entire boat than a down payment on a ticky–tacky track house!

HUNTER, WOOD, dual inboard V8s, needs work, but nothing major; liveaboard slip available. In San Pedro. $12,000.	31' 1953 FAIRLINER sedan cruiser, FWC Chrysler Crown, refurbished, very clean and sound, ready to cruise; includes inexpensive Seattle moorage. $7,500.

66The friendly cow all red and white
I love with all my heart
She gives me cream with all her might
To eat with apple tart.99

R.L. Stevenson

Nomadics

We've found many people living full time in fifth wheel trailers. They offer as much space as many small apartments and houses plus the wonderful attribute of becoming an Arabian Nights magic carpet whenever you choose to press the starter!

Fifth Wheels

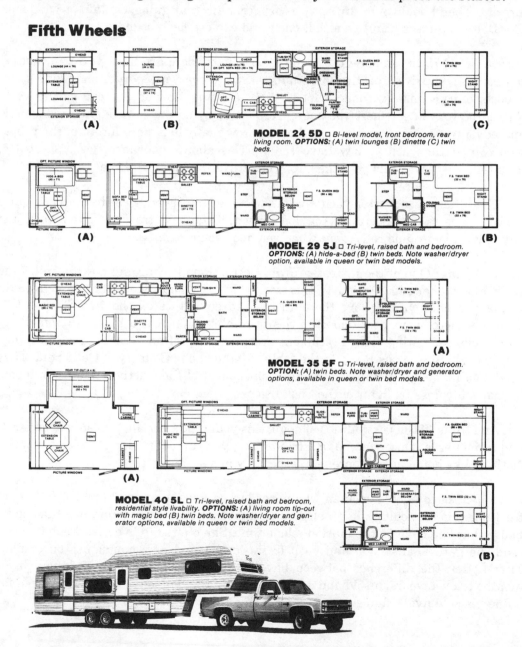

MODEL 24 5D □ *Bi-level model, front bedroom, rear living room.* **OPTIONS:** *(A) twin lounges (B) dinette (C) twin beds.*

MODEL 29 5J □ *Tri-level, raised bath and bedroom.* **OPTIONS:** *(A) hide-a-bed (B) twin beds. Note washer/dryer option, available in queen or twin bed models.*

MODEL 35 5F □ *Tri-level, raised bath and bedroom.* **OPTION:** *(A) twin beds. Note washer/dryer and generator options, available in queen or twin bed models.*

MODEL 40 5L □ *Tri-level, raised bath and bedroom, residential style livability.* **OPTIONS:** *(A) living room tip-out with magic bed (B) twin beds. Note washer/dryer and generator options, available in queen or twin bed models.*

Houseboat: On a smaller scale, one finds houseboats worldwide, and all need tender loving care to keep them ready and mobile. In my own favorite waterway, the California Delta, there are hundreds of them, and they are available all year. My own fantasy would be to have a small, live–aboard boat moored alongside the houseboats for rent. Then I could offer my services as mechanic, tour guide, captain or whatever. The Delta is a fascinating area that one could explore for lifetimes.

Yachts: Wow! Here the potential is mind–boggling. There are huge yachts owned by companies and private parties. All require crews in every category from engine–room experts to captains. I've done a lot of yacht crewing, and no one can call it work. Furthermore, you go where the passengers go, enjoying the same sights and sounds and adventures. I've often thought that the crew really had more fun than the people who owned the yacht. They have the worries about insurance, loss, passports, maintenance costs while you, the happy crew, can live it up carefree.

Then there are charter yachts in every one of the seven seas that often require maintenance as well as crews. And don't forget, if you have the capital to invest, just buy a live–aboard and rent it out when you need some cash.

River Rafting: One of the fastest–growing recreations is charging down a rollicking river on a rubber raft. Obviously, this is a world–wide sport since there are rivers in virtually every country. Love the outdoors and adventure on the water? Then this could be one of your best opportunities to combine a place to live with something absolutely fascinating to do. I recall one group of river rafters that lived on the banks of the lovely Stanislaus River in the fabled Mother Lode Country of California. They used small trailers, mainly for sleeping, since most of their activities were outdoors in that matchless fresh air of the Sierra slopes.

And think of the possibilities of doing this yourself. After all, you only need a raft and some nerve. Once you make a trip or two, you can offer your services to others. Nothing like being an entrepreneur, especially in a scenic setting.

For Sale: I once know a woman who never lacked for a mansion in which to live for free! She phoned realtors in an elegant neighborhood until she found one that had a house that had been on the market a long time. She offered to live in it, keep it clean, tend the garden and lawn and keep fresh flowers and new magazines on display. That's often the difference between having a house sell promptly or languish for months or even years unsold and deteriorating. In her entire life she never lacked for a fine place to live. Often she received a bonus from the selling realtor.

The Heaviest Front Door in the World: If you would like a far–out place to live, apply to the federal government for listings on obsolete missile sites. A friend of mine bought an old Atlas ICBM site complete with the land, silo and all equipment. It's air conditioned, has diesel generators and, since it is one of the "hardened" bases, it has the gigantic steel door to protect it. Fortunately, there are other ways into the site, because lifting that door would cost a fortune each time it was done!

Opportunities to buy obsolete military facilities are bound to increase as the star–wars era takes over defense. Just write Defense Surplus, Federal Center, 50 Washington Avenue, Battlecreek, MI49017 for details on what is available.

Fixer–Upper: I know of a group of young people who have the free use of a large old Victorian house in exchange for repairing it. The contract is long–term, since the house is in need of much work. So these people enjoy two rewards: a good place to live and a chance to learn how to repair old houses. And of course they have no rent to worry about each month.

Universities and Colleges: Thousands of educational institutions dot the landscape worldwide. I recall that education is the second largest industry in many states. Further, a goodly number of universities and colleges are located in areas that are conducive to the good life: mountains (University of California at Santa Cruz) and seashore (UC Santa Barbara). Needs for live–in staff are constant. Housemothers and resident managers enjoy the company of students, availability of large libraries, room, board and a paycheck. Now *that* should beat any lonely room in a retirement hotel, don't you think?

Wagons Ho!: It seems that no one wants to stay home anymore. Increasing in popularity every year are trips through the western United States in old–fashioned covered wagons, pioneer style. Some even feature an Indian "attack" and visits by a mountain man. All allow you to relive the days of emigrants on the trail West.

Where do you fit in? Obviously, these adventures need staff: cooks, wranglers, entertainers and such. What a great way to have a vacation, earn your room, board and a salary. (And someday, think about your own wagon!)

In Summary

Obviously, an entire book could be written on the subject of ready–made opportunities to live where you want to low cost, or as we have cited, to live and get *paid* for any type of work you desire. We've suggested a few likely possibilities just to trigger your imagination. Pick up almost any book on travel or related subjects (boating, skiing, trailering), and you'll encounter many more opportunities.

Build It Yourself

The Backyard Bedroom

A unique solution to the housing shortage is the small, detached playhouse/bedroom that any person handy with a hammer and saw can construct in a weekend or two. It can be almost any size, ranging from a tiny 6 feet x 8 feet to a larger 8 x 12. Construction is straightforward: 2 x 4s and plywood panels, so it goes together quickly. Designs are flexible so that you can create a simple bunkhouse or an elaborate backyard studio complete with lights and music!

The best thing about the backyard bedroom is that, in most areas, no permit is required. It falls under the classification of a playhouse or shed, and usually anything under about 125 square feet is exempt from bureaucratic meddling.

By placing it on pier blocks or cement bricks, there's no permanent connection with the property; thus it can be moved readily. In fact, the smaller ones are light enough to move with the aid of a dozen husky friends. Otherwise a forklift would do the job.

Normally, one would not put plumbing in these units; a transportable toilet such as a Portapotty would suffice. Wiring can be included, especially the new low–voltage type using a transformer to step down 110–volts AC to 12–volts DC just as is used in cars and recreational vehicles. Many appliances are now available that operate on this low voltage, including blenders, irons, small pumps and so forth, not to mention the car–type music equipment such as stereos and tape decks.

Interiors can be designed to suit the needs of the occupants. For example, an overhead bunk bed can allow a large desk below. The bed can be double or even king size and still permit sitting headroom beneath. Beds can also fold up or be dual purpose—a bed in the evening and a slanted drafting table during the day. A studio couch that makes into a bed would permit the room to function as a living room during the day and still provide sleeping accommodations at night. Book cases, office equipment, a small workshop, a sewing machine, typewriters or even a computer setup can be readily accommodated in the larger units. With a hot plate or microwave and one of the portable RV sinks, light meals can be prepared. It's obvious that there really are no limits to the uses of the backyard bedroom.

Best of all, the cost is low both in materials and labor.

Minigrannies

History

After many years of diligent effort, California State Senator Henry Mello was able to obtain legislation that created the *Granny house*. It may be defined as a second unit for use by older people. The two major stipulations are that it be occupied by at least one person over 60, and that it be less than 640 square feet. Other than that, anyone who owns an R–1 lot with an existing home can now act as though his or her lot was an R–2. In short, all over California, every homeowner has the privilege and right to build his or her own granny house.

Events to date have been slow regarding this otherwise startling development. Few people have taken advantage of the Mello Act, and even fewer seem to know about it. So to correct this situation, the members of the Holy Terra Church obtained a modest advance from Lee Simpson of Moss Landing Boat Works and built a model—the one that is illustrated here. It sold promptly at a fair price—under $1,000 as a matter of fact. Currently, the Holy Terra people are busy arranging to build several more of this style as well as several other models.

HOW TO HELP THE HOMELESS AND SIMULTANEOUSLY HAVE AN INCOME FROM YOUR OWN BACKYARD!

If you don't have the money to build a minigranny, then just charge the lumber at a nearby lumber yard have the homeless person build his own minigranny, and then pay it off with the rent!

Water systems can be simple: a connection to the nearby home, a drilled well, or simply having the water brought in by containers. Rooftop water–collection devices would be practical in rainy areas worldwide.

Heating is no problem, since the space is tiny. A small wood stove such as those used in Mexico would be adequate to not only heat, but cook also! In the more elaborate units, a gas or electric burner or two can be installed. Solar cooking is also a proven possibility.

Refrigeration can be as basic as an evaporative cooler or as sophisticated as a 12–volt DC "fridge" powered by the aforementioned low–voltage systems. Home–cooling would be accommodated in the same way.

So with lights, water, power and heat easy to provide, living in a minigranny would be just as relaxed and comfortable as in any well–furnished standard–size dwelling.

And don't forget that all of the deluxe appliances such as stereo, video and VCR can become built–in's! With a microwave and blender in the compact kitchen, phone and computer in the den, hot and cold water in the bath, thermostatically–controlled heat in the main living area, who needs to pay exorbitant rents and mortgages!

Minigrannies in the Year 2000

Visualize an untra–lightweight unit blow molded like a giant PVC waterbottle. Handsome, sturdy, colorful, the *minigranny 2000* can have every conceivable creature comfort, from touchplate interior controls to self–cleaning windows and rugs. Meals can be cooked or prepared automatically; temperature monitored inside and out for the best and most economical use of energy, while the latest entertainment can be piped in from a rooftop satellite antenna. The original charge of water would be recycled so that no sewage line is needed. All power is from the highly efficient solar voltaics, and the cost is negligible.

Since the hightech minigranny is totally self–contained and self–sufficient, it can be transported by helicopter to mountain eyries, desert hideouts and remote beaches. Anyplace on earth is home with a minigranny!

❝Be it ever so humble, there's no place like home.❞

Uses of Minigrannies

Foremost, of course, they can be used for emergency or permanent shelter, depending on the environment and circumstances. The Church hopes to obtain the support and backing of county welfare agencies to provide minigrannies for the thousands of new homeless now suffering on the streets of many cities. Later, minigrannies can be used for:

- Senior settlements.

- Mini–motels or resorts.

- Portable housing for farm workers.

- Small shops or stores in locations where permanent dwellings would be impractical.

- Minifactories providing both shelter and work space for unemployed.

- Housing for disasters such as earthquakes or floods.

- Temporary shelter for those who have lost their homes by fire. The minigranny can be placed on the back of the lot while the main house is rebuilt.

- Summer cabanas on beaches. They can be removed to protect them from winter storms. The same would apply to river resorts and lakes with variable depths.

- Entire villages in new areas such as at hot springs.

And in many other ways both in America and overseas. Don't forget that most of the world lives in mud huts and would welcome even the tiniest minigranny with great warmth and affection.

Minigranny Models

The models shown are but a sampling. The Holy Terra architectural staff is busy designing a multitude of new concepts. These include minigrannies structured especially for use on the water, modular minigrannies that can be stacked several stories high or arranged in geometric designs with connecting breezeway, and so on. Actually there is no limit to what can be done with the basic concept of a miniature home. Nor is there any constraint on materials or methods of construction. The Holy Terraists plan to make minigrannies from adobe, concrete, clay, rammed earth, lightweight materials of all kinds, recycled wood, plastics, and from some newly developed composites from France that won't burn and never need painting!

Prices

Like any item that can be mass–produced, the cost of minigrannies will go down as the number increases. It's like bringing the old Model–T Ford into being as a home! Obviously, minigrannies can be built on an assembly line by relatively un-skilled workers worldwide. This means that labor costs can be quite low while still retaining high quality. Imagine, for example, the electrical components being manu-factured in Japan while Mexico contributes their famous and practical clay stove/heater unit. With an expanded vinyl shell complete with foam insulation and carpeting, the minigranny becomes an international cooperative housing effort!

I recently checked with a minister who is living in one of the minigrannies. He is delighted with it and commented on how little energy is needed to keep it warm.

The potential of housing the staff members of various facilities is unlimited. As long as there are more sanitation facilities available, then a minigranny can provide all the rest.

Now here's the plan. If you own a home or are making payments on one, why not put a minigranny in your backyard and rent it to a homeless person or two. Sure, one of them has to be over 60, but you'll find many people in that age group without a de-cent place to sleep.

Second Units and Prefabs

There are about 600 small homes built in Bolinas, a small seaside village north of San Francisco. Until recently, they were in limbo since they had been built on the back of lots which already contained a house. Fortunately, many other cities are rec-ognizing that second units make sense. With utilities already on the property, it's far less expensive to hook up the additional residences. Furthermore, the homes are small and require less in the way of services.

Prefabs make excellent second units as they are quite inexpensive, look good and are easy to assemble. Many firms offer prefabs including: Lindal Cedar Homes, 9004 South 19th St., Tacoma, WA 98466; Redecut Log Industries, 327 22nd St., Oakland, CA 94612; and Techbuilt, 127 Mt. Auburn St., Cambridge, MA 02122.

Buildability

As shown here, the early model minigrannies are super simple. Just 16 sheets of plywood form the basic structure along with some dimension lumber like 2 x 4s and 2 x 6s. Windows are standard new or used wood or aluminum. (They've obtained used wood sash for prices as low as fifty cents each!) Doors can be standard items or built yourself. Interiors are "to order." Holy Terra plans to build the shells and permit the resident to add all finishing touches to suit his or her personal preferences in carpeting, drapes, and interior furnishings. Since the space is so small, it takes very little of everything to make a minigranny a cozy and comfortable home. Almost anyone with even basic building skills can either do the entire job or complete a shell that has been delivered to the premises.

Floor joists are placed in Simpson hangers.

Plywood floor consists of three pieces. Each one meets the joist at its center.

First frame is erected on floor.

Rafters are also hung in hangers.

Framing complete.

Insulation and roof are
now in place.

Roofing is roll–type with
tar and flashing to finish.

Plywood exterior is
placed over entire
front area.

Then door and window cutouts are made. This assures a good fit. Install windows and door, and you are done!

The finished minigranny.

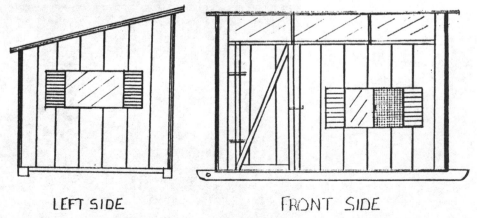

LEFT SIDE   FRONT SIDE

Minigranny Bill of Materials

(8' x 12' = 96 sq. ft.)

Qty.	Description
2	4x6x14 DF
18	2x4x16 DF S/B
15	2x4x12 DF S/B
1	2x4x12 DF S/B diagonal cut
22	1x2x8 DF S/B R/S
10	1x2x12 DF S/B R/S
8	1x4x8 DF S/B R/S
3	4'x8'x1/2 w/face sound board
4	4'x8'x1/2 OSB S/C
3	4'x8'x5/8 OSB T&G
10	4'x8'x5/8 T111 D/F 8" OC.
2	90 lb. roll roofing (white)
5	1x2x10 gal. metal roof flashing
4 lbs.	#16 vinyl sinker nails
2 lbs.	#4 smooth coat nails
3 lbs.	2" drive screw vinyl nails
1/2 lb.	1/2" roofing nails
1/4 lb.	#6x1" sheet rock screws
6	pier blocks
1 qt.	lap cement
2	4" tee strap hinges
1/2 pt.	Elmers carpenters glue
2	12x28x3/4 pine shutters
4	10x28x3/4 pine shutters
1	tube window calk
1	4" ronko 93s hasp
30	Simpson F-24 hangers
1	23-3/4x46-1/4 D/S glass
2	13-1/4x4 4-00 S/S glass
1	13-1/4x42-1/4 S/S glass
2	3020 slider windows

Minigranny Features

Thanks to some recent advances in various technologies, the minigranny can become a self–sufficient entity. If desired, there would be no utility connections other than possibly water. Even that could be supplied by the owner/tenant in alternative ways.

Electricity can be low–voltage—usually 12 volts direct current just like most boats and cars. This can be provided by batteries charged with your own car generator or photovoltaics or perhaps a wind or hydrogenerator.

Waste water can be accommodated in two ways: grey water to be directed to a nearby garden while black water can be piped to an existing sewer connection, a minigranny septic tank system, or one of the new self–contained dehydrating or composting toilets.

The Philosophy of Minigranny Houses

A home is the most expensive item that anyone usually buys in the United States. Often, it takes an entire lifetime to pay for even a modest house. This means that the person must commit himself or herself to a particular location and an established line of work—in short, nose to the old grindstone for decades. While it's always possible to sell one's home and buy another in a different area, it's not always that easy to make a change. Children dislike being uprooted, good jobs are not as easy to get as they once were, and other factors make frequent moves difficult.

However, imagine a lifestyle revolving about the minigranny concept. Since they can be fabricated in modular form—one a kitchen, another a bath, still another a bedroom or living room—it's possible to assemble them like children's blocks and create exactly what is needed at the time. They can grow with the family and, when the family's needs diminish, so can the assembled structure.

Another aspect, the use of marginal or even impossible land areas, becomes feasible with minigrannies. Since they can be trucked in or even transported by helicopter, any site can become a minigranny homesite.

In summary, low cost, portability, utility, assembly possibilities, infinite interior design potential, mass–production feasibility and other parameters make the minigranny a choice for our expanding populations.

Minigranny or Microhouse Futurist View

- The floating microhouse, comfort at low cost with no land taxes to pay. Enjoy a different harbor every day.

- Custom–designed microhouse interiors can reflect both good taste and modern technology.

- An unbeatable combination is the microhouse with a large garden—healthful living at the lowest cost.

- Combining microhouses and hot springs locations, the ultimate symbiosis.

The *microhouse village*…it's a possibility now. Combining cooperative and communal living with the best in small shelter.

> **"**If this life is not a real fight in which something is eternally gained for the universe by success, it is no better than a game of private theatricals from which one may withdraw at will. But it *feels* like a real fight!**"**

Minigranny Sites

Where can you put your minigranny or microhouse? Here's an inventory:

- In your backyard or that of a friend.

- On a float on any river or lake (no taxes!).

- On rural or farm land as a core dwelling, labor–camp element, shop or whatever.

- In the woods! No one will ever find it! (Mendocino and Humboldt counties are great for this hideout concept; the land is still cheap, or you can rent or lease some.)

- On top of an old but sturdy truck. That way you have a gypsy wagon. Paint it multi–colored and hang a lantern from the back.

- Out in the Nevada desert near a spring. There are many hot and cold springs in that vast state; find out for yourself soon. You'll love the fresh air, and it is possible to live there for a few bucks a day.

- As a caretaker's shelter on a large estate or farm or construction project (longterm).

Note: There are lots of ways to place your minigranny. Just look around your community or any area that appeals to you. Incidentally, we are working on an invisibility kit for minigrannies…with it you'll be able to make your microshelter actually disappear. Not even a French detective could find it!

"A cheap home will provide more than shelter…it will provide the time to enlighten and improve yourself.**"**

Lon Jackson

By putting your microhouse at the back of your property, it's possible to avoid all hassles as this "pool house" proves.

Minigranny Strategy

- Camouflage it by planting fast–growing vines or trees on or around it.

- Disguise it as a tool shed with a false front lobby full of garden tools and hay.

- Put it inside a garage or barn.

- Pretend it's a child's playhouse by draping a few dolls from the eves and putting a trike out front.

- Create a hobby shop in the interior. What's wrong if you happen to fall asleep on that old sofa in the corner each evening?

- Install it in that nearby hill with the entrance concealed by a large bush. Again, no tax collectors or Avon salespeople.

- Age it like they do movie sets. That way it will appear to have always been in your side yard.

Note: These are just a few tips. Naturally there are many more, but we don't want to give away all *your* secret ways of having a minigranny with no bureaucratic interference.

A Carport Enclosure

This type of project can be added under any existing roof—such as a patio over-hang or a breezeway. This example uses a carport roof structure to show you how to wall in a new storage space.

Millions of American houses have carports. Above is a way to create living space out of half of a carport. A few studs, some plywood sheets, a couple of sliding windows, and a door, and you have the basic needs for shelter. The person living in it can use the facilities of the house until such time as they can be added to the carport addition.

It's really not a big job to dig a trench to the house sewer line or to add extension water pipes and electricity. Once this is accomplished, the carport minigranny qualifies as a completely separate apartment, usable by a member of the family or a tenant. And keep in mind that this construction is totally legal in California under the Henry Mello act. Minigrannies and Granny houses can be separate or attached, whichever is most convenient for the homeowner.

So drive on down to the nearest lumber yard and pick up what you need. Either you or a carpenter can rough it out in a matter of a day or so. Have fun!

The Unitarian Minister

He had no home, and the church wasn't really suitable for permanent dwelling. So we built him a minihouse behind the church. It contains a comfortable bed and shelves for books and personal possessions. Plenty of room for clothes and a cupboard for snacks. He uses the church kitchen for his meals, but this is "Home Sweet Home" the rest of the time.

Of course, the small house could be completely self–contained—kitchen, dinette and even a small bath. It's been done before. They're called trailers and campers.

You can Build Your Own Minihome!

So far, the Holy Terra Church has built five of these minigrannies, or micro-houses or backyard bedrooms—no matter what you call them, they are still warm

Mini-Granny Assembly Sequence

1. Lay out pier blocks on an east-west line and plan a southern front exposure. Check county codes for setback distances from other structures and boundaries.*

2. Cut, drill and level up both 4 feet x 6 feet x 14 feet skids on the 6 pier blocks. Install Simpson "F-24" hangers in 20 places using #16 pound nails on 16 inch centers.

3. Install 20 2 X 4 floor joists between skids in hangers. Install 3 4 x 8 x 5/8 OSB panels as floor using '2" screw drive nails. Check to see that floor is square.

4. Fabricate front wall frame on floor and install 5 F24 hangers to top of wall frame. Erect and affix frame to floor in vertical position using #16 nails.

5. Fabricate rear wall frame on floor and install 5 F24 hangers to top of wall frame. Erect and affix frame to floor in vertical position using #16 nails.

6. Fabricate left and right wall frames on floor. Erect and affix to floor using #16 nails. Level and connect all four corners using #16 nails.

7. Cut and install the 5 2 x 4 rafters with 15˚ end cuts.

8. Affix the 3 4 x 8 x 1/2" sound board on top of rafters, white face down, using #4 nails.

9. Affix the 4 4 x 8 x 1/2" OSB panels atop sound board allowing 6" overhang on rear and sides with 10" overhang on front using 2" screw drive nails.

10. Cut and install 2 of 3 rear wall T-111 panels using 2" screw drive nails.

11. Cut and install side T-111 panels using 2" screw drive nails.

12. Cut and install front T-111 panels using 2" drive nails.

13. Pilot drill all cutouts from inside. Connect all pilot holes with pencil lines. Proceed to cut out all windows and door.

14. Install last rear wall T-111 panel.

15. Install all interior molding, calk and install windows.Install all interior molding. Affix exterior shutters.

16. Install door molding, fabricate and install door using #6 x 1 1/4 inch sheet-rock screws.

17. Affix roll roofing with 24" overlaps using 1/2" nails.

18. Affix and finish all exterior trim using #4 nails.

19. Apply exterior sealer to all outside wood.

20. Congratulations, you've finished.

*You don't need a building permit however, since the structure is under 120 square feet.

and dry and *low cost*! Here then are the complete plans with materials list and order of construction. Almost anyone with a saw and hammer can build one in a day or two.

Note: The interior is not planned because most everyone will have their own ideas. A loft bed clears the floor for a dinette, desk or other furniture. A Portapottie takes care of sanitation, and a small, trailer–type shower can be installed. These items along with a single–burner stove, a small refrigerator and a sink can accommodate one or two people indefinitely. What you end up with is the equivalent of an efficiency apartment, a small trailer or camper.

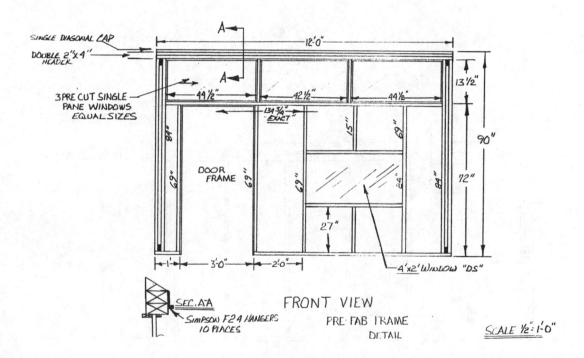

FRONT VIEW

PRE-FAB FRAME

DETAIL

SCALE ½" = 1'-0"

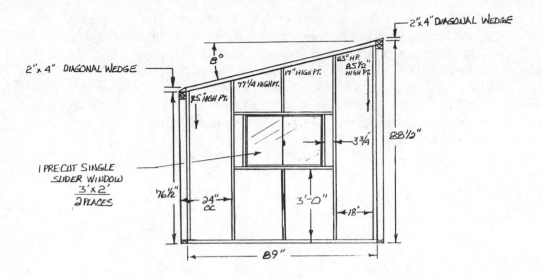

2" x 4" DIAGONAL WEDGE

8°

2" x 4" DIAGONAL WEDGE

23" H.P. 85½" HIGH PT.

17" HIGH PT.

77¼ HIGH PT.

85 HIGH PT.

88½"

I PRECUT SINGLE SLIDER WINDOW 3' x 2' 2 PLACES

3¾"

76½"

24" OC

3'-0"

18"

89"

LEFT SIDE SHOWN
RIGHT SIDE SAME
PRE-FAB FRAME
DETAIL

SCALE ½"=1'-0"

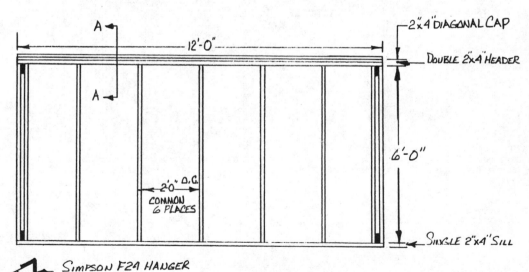

A

12'-0"

2"x4" DIAGONAL CAP

DOUBLE 2"x4" HEADER

A

6'-0"

2'0" O.C.
COMMON
6 PLACES

SINGLE 2"x4" SILL

SIMPSON F24 HANGER
5 PLACES

SEC A-A

BACK VIEW
PRE-FAB FRAME
DETAIL

SCALE ½"=1'-0"

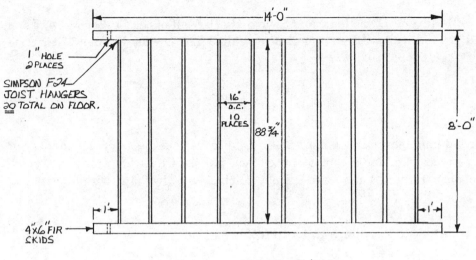

1" HOLE
2 PLACES

SIMPSON F24
JOIST HANGERS
20 TOTAL ON FLOOR.

14'-0"

16"
O.C.
10
PLACES

88¾"

8'-0"

1'

4"x6" FIR
SKIDS

1'

FLOOR PLAN

SCALE ½"= 1'-0"

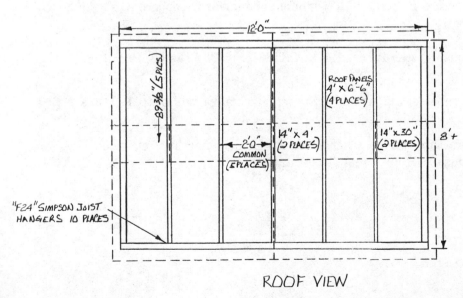

12'-0"

89⅜" (5 PLCS)

ROOF PANELS
4' X 6'-6"
(4 PLACES)

2'-0"
COMMON
(6 PLACES)

14"x 4'
(2 PLACES)

14"x 30"
(2 PLACES)

8'±

"F24" SIMPSON JOIST
HANGERS 10 PLACES

ROOF VIEW

SCALE ½"= 1'-0"

Information on Saving Money

Want to Build Your Own Home and Save Sixty Percent of the Cost or More? Then you should get in touch with an organization called The Owner Builder, 1516 Fifth Street, Berkeley, CA 94710.

Seminars

Owner–builder seminars are now being held in various parts of the country or hire an experienced builder or contractor to teach you. Alternatively, apprentice yourself to someone who builds and learn the old reliable way...by doing with an expert.

Some Sources and Suppliers to Contact:

- Pacific Frontier Homes, Inc., 17975 North Highway 1, (P.O. Box 1247), Fort Bragg, CA 95437

- Custom Cabinet Kits, Shea Corporation, P.O. Box 6536, Colorado Springs, CO 80934

- Wilderness Log Homes, 2051 Monument Boulevard, Concord, CA 94520

- Sierra Log Homes, Inc., P.O. Box 2083, Carson City, NV 89702

- Timberhouse Post & Beam, 696 Little Sleeping Child Road, Hamilton, MT 59840

- The Energy Independent Sun Cottage, Survival Consultants, P.O. Box 21, Rapidan, VA 22733

- Video Home Improvement Series for the Homeowner, Trulock Video Productions, 98 Main Street, Tiburon, CA 94920

Sun Valley, Idaho

I had stopped to check the water in my radiator. It was low, so I took a bucket to the little stream that tumbled down the adjacent hillside. Not wanting to pour the icy water into the hot engine, I sat down and enjoyed the view of the long valley that reached southward to the resort town of Sun Valley.

"Need any help?" A man in his early forties wearing jeans and a plaid western–style shirt had sauntered up. In the chat that followed, I learned that he had left the same company that I did and for the same reasons. Now he was living a relaxed and productive life in a large travel–trailer parked only a few–hundred yards from our meeting place. We agreed that once the high–overhead of a suburban tract house was eliminated, it only required a relatively small income to really enjoy life.

"It's easier to save a buck than it is to make one."

—Old American Saying

So that's the key: Low overhead. It's the secret of a successful business as well as a successful, stress–reduced lifestyle. The less you own and have to care for, the more time you have available for the truly worthwhile things of life. Have you had time to enjoy the fragrance of flowers lately? Or to sit on a green hillside and watch the clouds go by? Or just to curl up in a cozy corner with a book that you've always intended to read? If not, then you're spending too much time with the peripherals of life. As Thoreau said,

"I would rather sit on a pumpkin and have it all to myself than be crowded on a velvet cushion."

Extrapolating this to real life, I can say that I would rather saunter through the Sonoran desert near Tucson than live on Roxbury Drive in Beverly Hills. Or I'd rather row my dinghy along the shores of Denman Island in British Columbia than have a backyard swimming pool in Orange County.

Thus, the old saying that "the best things in life are free" is true beyond any doubt.

Communes and Coops

About ten years ago, while poking around in British Columbia, I chanced upon a most interesting commune. It seems that a group of college graduates agreed to focus their energies on a communal living arrangement rather than go to work in the Big City. They pooled their money and put a down payment on a 160–acre parcel of land near Vancouver Island. Then, by working cooperatively, they built log cabins, planted a large garden and developed a source of income by building vacation cabins for city folks.

Their commune is worthy of a calendar shot: a large swimming pond, a beach nearby, huge trees all around. Furthermore, there are lots of natural foods to be gathered for free: berries, fish, oysters and so forth. The air is fresh and the water pure, and their food is gourmet quality. They've managed to keep up the payments and each of the communal dwellers has his or her own snug cabin or lodge. To me, this is one of the best examples of what cooperation can do in the shelter field.

So that's our prologue to this discussion of cooperative living. Anyone can do it if they are willing to share a little and compromise as needed. Beyond that, it's just plain old work and gumption. Best of all, you'll find more and more people willing to live cooperatively, since it makes so much sense in every way.

Some Basics

Few people can afford one thousand dollars per month rent, but it it's split up five ways it becomes much easier. But economics aren't the only advantage. Here are a few more:

- By sharing, a better home can be enjoyed. Instead of a single small room or apartment, the group can have a garden, a hot tub, sun decks, even a pool.

- In living together, there is a sense of mutual protection. This is especially important for the elderly, who need someone around in case of emergencies.

- Living communally creates a better milieu for health. People can share meals, exercise, outings, child care and the usual ups and downs of life.

- When the hot water heater gives out or the roof leaks, you're not alone with the repairs or the entire bill. Often, in a group, someone can come forth with the skills to reduce maintenance costs sharply.

- Sharing a house can be a great learning experience, one in which possessiveness can be unlearned. After all, most of the world lives on a communal basis.

- One can think of oneself as a member of an impromptu, unrelated family with all that this implies. No one expects that a family will always agree in every detail, so one should rightfully and realistically expect to make adjustments and compromises as necessary.

The Big Secret

I found this out in several communal experiences. As long as everyone has a *private place* to which he or she can retreat, most problems of shared living can be resolved pronto.

Some Examples of Shared Living

In Santa Barbara, the city funds the costs of matching up partners as long as one of them is sixty years old or more. It's called Share–A–Home and could be duplicated anywhere. In San Francisco, there's a floating city near China Basin. Most of the residents are elderly and live aboard boats of varying age and condition. Today they have water and power, but several years ago they were almost run out of the area by bureaucrats. Fortunately, one of the group stood her ground and insisted that the city provide the means to continue the aquatic commune. And that's exactly what happened. An outstanding case of communal strength and solidarity. It's for certain that, if there had been only one or two boats there, they would have been tossed "down the river."

In Ridgewood, New Jersey, a church group formed SHARE, Inc. offering the elderly the opportunity to live together as a family. Everyone chips in to pay for all household costs, such as food and mortgage payments, and the only thing not shared is clothing and medical care. It's proving successful and points the way for any group, including churches, to do the same for the seniors of their area.

If you happen to find yourself homeless in Tucson, look up the group called Community House. They have launched a project that could be duplicated all over the United States. Taking the old, abandoned housing of downtown Tucson as a do–it–yourself project, they invite the homeless to fix up their own places to live. With donations from Tucson merchants and others, the street people are learning trades as well as enjoying homes in which they can live indefinitely. Many cities have derelict properties that could be rehabilitated, and who is better qualified to receive this kind of help/self–help than the homeless? If you want more information about the Tucson effort, write Community House, 347 West 22nd Street, Tucson, AZ 85701

Cooperative self–sufficiency is the keystone at Oz, a community on the north coast of California. Communal members have built both water and electrical systems that free Oz from any outside utility connections. They also have a large vegetable garden and orchard that provides organic food for themselves and the seminar guests who furnish cash income during the summer months. The latter are there to learn the techniques of building a community from scratch. Oz is representative of several communal projects; it not only functions successfully, it provides the know–how to others. For more information, write Oz, P.O.Box 147, Point Arena, CA 95468.

Speaking of cooperative educational projects, there's a school that provides both a general education and work experience in providing one's own food and shelter options. It's World College West and you can learn more about their programs by writing to P.O. Box 3060, San Rafael, CA 94902.

A Compendium of Assorted Ideas

Hay: Baled hay was used as though it were a giant brick in the prairie country of America. Bales were stacked, poles driven through for integrity, and the outside and inside plastered with mortar. With this material you don't need any insulation!

Scrap Wood: Trimmings from dimension lumber can make lightweight bricks. Imagine several thousand 2 x 4s cut to about the same length. Instead of mortar you simply nail them together, staggering the pieces as though they were common brick. Covered with wire mesh and plaster, the walls are sturdy and highly insulative.

Sod: Sod is the term for earth held together by grass. Many early pioneer houses were built of this material using giant sections, some as long as three feet. Laid like bricks with the grass–side down. The walls need no mortar. Often roofed with the same material, but wood and shingles are better.

Burlap Bags: Filled with sand and cement, narrow burlap bags can be stacked like bricks, held together with rebar and then sprayed with water to set. A finish coat of gunite will give you a fireproof house at low cost. Wood or tile can complete the project on the roof.

Telephone Poles: Often these are free or cheap from the phone or utility companies. They can be notched like a log cabin or placed vertically like a stockade. Another use is as foundation poles for houses built on unlevel ground. Creosote will keep them from rotting.

Metal: A round house was built from car tops—just one of the possibilities when you have a source of low–cost metal scrap. Think about those thousands of 55–gallon drums that often go to waste. One good use is as a floating platform for a houseboat.

Windows: As wood sash is replaced by aluminum nationwide, there are millions of old windows available cheap or free. I've seen houses built almost entirely from old windows, and they look great. Terrific for mild climates where drapes indoors would provide insulation and privacy. Fit them together like a giant jigsaw puzzle.

Rubble: There are millions of tons of broken concrete all over the landscape. This can be used for walls or fences. Let your imagination run with it. It's compatible with mortar and plaster, so there's no problem making it handsome again.

Trailers as Core Houses: A small trailer, especially one that is self–contained, makes a great starter for a bigger house. Eventually it can be completely surrounded so that no trace remains. Shingles are great for hiding modest origins.

Ferro–cement: It works for boats; it will work just as well or even better for houses. Make a simple framework of scrap wood, cover with layers of chicken wire, then plaster by hand or with a gunite rig. Add color to the last coat for beauty.

Note the stairway to the right of this highly imaginitive, sod–roofed home. Its counterparts appear in many areas of Southern California where cobblestones were piled and mortared together to make virtually indestructible houses. Stone houses are common worldwide, and the material is often free for the taking. Slipform construction is easy and quick, and requires no masonry knowledge to speak of.

Homes Under $25,000 and Land Under $10,000

Despite the fact that real–estate prices have escalated along with interest rates, there are still places where you can acquire a home or the land on which to build one quite reasonably. My own strategy would be to save the money in a region where salaries are quite high and then semi–retire to places where real estate is low priced. Another possibility is to have two places, both economical, so that one could take advantage of the best climate. How about a small ranch in Montana for summers and a mobile home in Arizona for the winter months? Each could be rented to those with hardy constitutions when you are away.

IN TRANQUIL VILLAGE

No. 143– 1/3 acre, $14,000. Take advantage of the low price on this small town home. 2 bedrooms, dining room, wood and coal heat; owner will repair or replace front porch. 1/3 acre. $14,000, owner financing. *Hico, W. Va.*

2 FAMILY MINI FARM

No. 225– 8 1/2 acres, $25,000. Village farm is a "hammer swinger's" special. Neglected home divided into duplex, total of 6 bedrooms, 2 baths, 2 kitchens, family room, dining room, enclosed porch. 2 story barn. 8 1/2 acres. Fronts state highway near large resort lake. $25,000. *Locke, N.Y.*

LAKE-AREA FARMETTE

No. 364– 10 acres, $24,200. Delightful farmette within 2 miles Kentucky Lake. Near state highway, 3 miles town. Well insulated home has 3 bedrooms, wood or electric heat, beautifully landscaped lawn. Utility building. 12x24 garage. 10 acres, large garden spot, fencing, family orchard, well. Make plans to see today– $24,200. *Waynesboro, Tenn.*

HUNT, FISH, SWIM, WATER SKI

No. 915– 5 acres, $3,000. Mostly wooded 5 acres adjoin 25,500 acres of government land with 1,005 acre lake. On old county road, mile to highway. $3,000, only $450 down, owner financing at 9 3/4% annual percentage rate. *Huntington, W. Va.*

COMFORTABLE & AFFORDABLE

No. 1596– $11,500. Live at outskirts of small town in central Florida farming area. Close to I-75 and Florida's Turnpike. 2 bedroom mobile home, 2 paddle fans, screened-in back porch, front porch, range and refrigerator included. Utility building. 75x146 lot. So much for so little at just $11,500. *Coleman, Fla.*

"HAMMER SWINGER'S" FARMETTE

No. 423– 10 acres, $22,500. Long view of surrounding farmland and prized privacy make this little place well worth repairing. Livable 2-story home with 3 bedrooms, bath, enclosed porch. 10 acres, scenic blend of pasture and woodland with stream, well, springs. On gravel road just 1/4 mile off highway, 3 miles town, 23 college town. Can't last at $22,500. *Appomattox, Va.*

VILLAGE FIX-UP SPECIAL

No. 618– 1/2 acre, $24,900. Needs paint, some carpeting, other finishing touches. 3 bedrooms, 1/2 acre, lots of trees. Less than 1/2 mile to state stocked trout stream, 3 miles to boat ramp access to Delaware River, 4 miles state game lands, 145 miles New York City, 150 Philadelphia. $24,900, owner financing at 10% annual percentage rate. *Beach Lake, Pa.*

$24,500 TAKES ALL!

No. 376– 26 acres, $24,500. Value packed small farm within 2 miles of county seat. 26 acres, 9 tillable, 12 improved pasture, 5 acres wooded, young orchard. 2 ponds, well, near-new fencing. Solid 3-bedroom and bath farmhouse needs some painting inside. 25x34-ft. barn, 20x24 workshop. $24,500. *Waynesboro, Tenn.*

FIX-UP FARMETTE

No. 306– 52 acres, $24,900. Remodel the 2-story 3 bedroom home and have 52 acres to roam– present owner has free gas. Half of land in native pasture, creek, well. Price reduced to $24,900, low down payment. *New Milton, W. Va.*

A PICTURE OF NEW ENGLAND

No. 146– 2 3/10 acres, $12,600. Delightful rural place features stone walls and split-rail fence enclosing scenic rolling meadow. Borders sparkling pond on 2 sides. An intermittent stream winds through. Attractive home only 3 years old and as yet unfinished, has huge 8x28 room serving as bedroom, 8x10 incomplete kitchen, big 8x18 family room with woodstove. Garden shed and root cellar complete the picture. Only 2 miles town. 2 3/10 acres. Finish the rest and enjoy the good New England life for only $12,600. *Shoreham, Vt.*

RIVERFRONT REC SITE

No. 2497– 11 acres, $4,900. Tract fronts navigable river and paved road. Power and phone on site. 11 acres, 4 tillable, balance wooded. The avid sportsman will enjoy this one at only $4,900, $1,900 down, owner financing. *Lyndonville, Vt.*

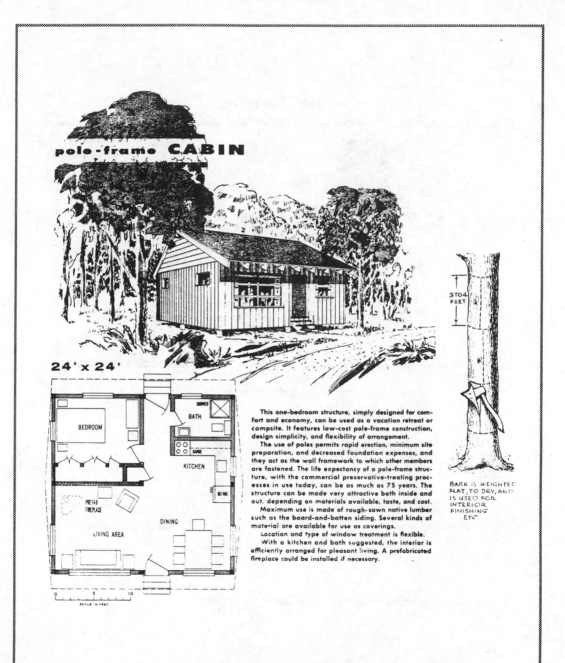

pole-frame CABIN

24' x 24'

BEDROOM

BATH

SHOWER

KITCHEN

RANGE

REFRIG

PREFAB FIREPLACE

DINING

LIVING AREA

0   5   10
SCALE IN FEET

3 TO 4 FEET

BARK IS WEIGHTED FLAT, TO DRY, AND IS USED FOR INTERIOR FINISHING ETC

This one-bedroom structure, simply designed for comfort and economy, can be used as a vacation retreat or campsite. It features low-cost pole-frame construction, design simplicity, and flexibility of arrangement.

The use of poles permits rapid erection, minimum site preparation, and decreased foundation expenses, and they act as the wall framework to which other members are fastened. The life expectancy of a pole-frame structure, with the commercial preservative-treating processes in use today, can be as much as 75 years. The structure can be made very attractive both inside and out, depending on materials available, taste, and cost.

Maximum use is made of rough-sawn native lumber such as the board-and-batten siding. Several kinds of material are available for use as coverings.

Location and type of window treatment is flexible.

With a kitchen and bath suggested, the interior is efficiently arranged for pleasant living. A prefabricated fireplace could be installed if necessary.

For low–cost plans, write the Superintendent of Documents, U.S. Government Printing Office, Washington, DC 20402. Ask for the price list of publications relating to the construction and maintenance of homes, farm buildings, and cabins.

The Hudson

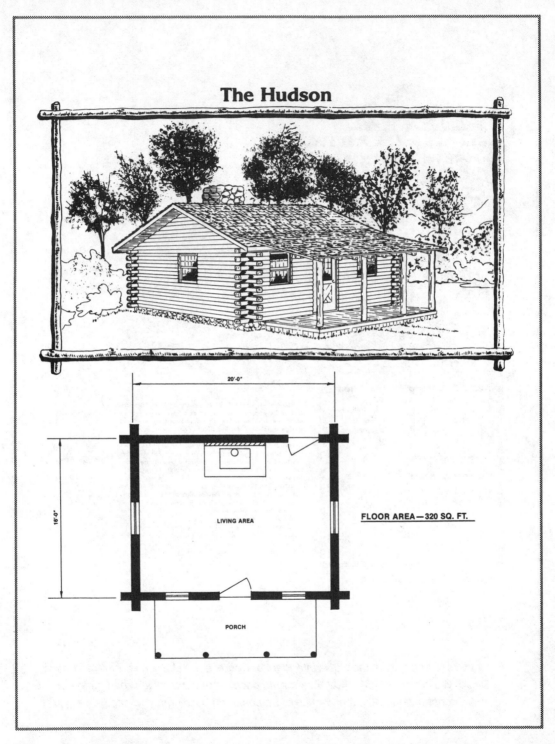

20'-0"

16'-0"

LIVING AREA

FLOOR AREA—320 SQ. FT.

PORCH

The Escanaba

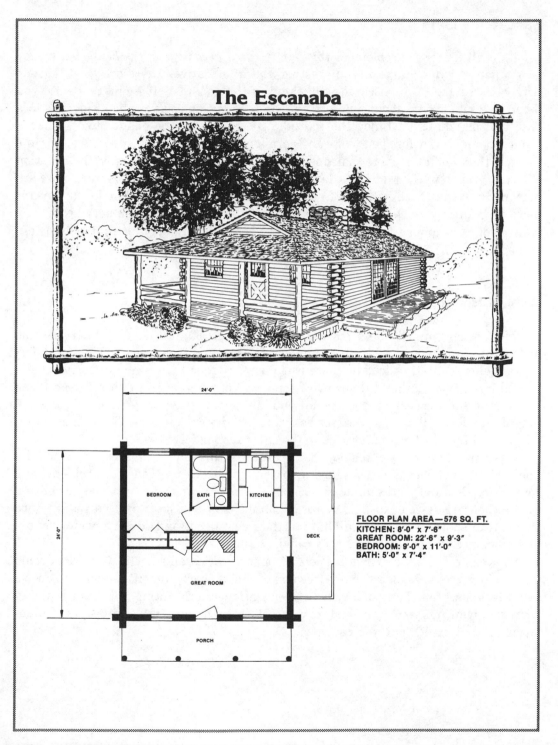

24'-0"

24'-0"

BEDROOM BATH KITCHEN

DECK

GREAT ROOM

PORCH

FLOOR PLAN AREA—576 SQ. FT.
KITCHEN: 8'-0" x 7'-6"
GREAT ROOM: 22'-6" x 9'-3"
BEDROOM: 9'-0" x 11'-0"
BATH: 5'-0" x 7'-4"

Back to the Land

I am all for it, but remember this, *many rural areas are unlivable* because they lack much of what makes life interesting and informative. There are good reasons why vast regions of America are still the way the Indians left them. So before you listen to a lot of hype about living off the land, go out and live in the boondocks in a tent, RV, or whatever. Enjoy the solitude, the fresh air, the chance to live like a human being, but before you make any permanent commitments, spend enough time to know that you'll last more than one winter. Take it from one who tried the isolation of a small ranch in the Mother Lode and found that cultural exchanges were more important than that backyard pine tree; that being close to a really fine library meant more than utter silence as snowflakes descended. It's all part of the paradox of "city mouse/country mouse," and you should try both before buying that wilderness spread.

Class K Housing

Mendocino County, California was once the scene of a pitched battle between the advocates of orthodox architecture and a large group of free spirits. The latter fervently believed that, as long as there was no harm done to anyone, property owners should be allowed to build their own homes without bureaucratic interference. The battle reached a crisis when the county building–inspection department threatened to bulldoze down "illegal" structures as defined in their code books. Cooler heads prevailed, and the matter was referred to the governor's office.

A compromise was worked out that prevails to this day. A landowner can build a house of his own design without having to comply with many of the requirements of a conventional home. For example, the home need not be wired for electricity or have a central heating system. Instead, kerosene lamps may be used along with a fireplace for heat. In short, people can build to suit their own needs and do not have to spend a lot of money and time on things they can do without.

This change in the law offers lots of opportunities and not just in Mendocino County. If it was possible to invoke freedom of choice there, then it's possible to do the same in your area. Thus, if restrictive legislation is preventing you from building what you want on your own land, take heart from the united stand people of Mendocino; if they could do it, you can, also.

Homes from Throwaways

Ours is a society of instant obsolescence—cars that last a few months beyond their last payment, appliances that just barely make it past the warranty, and so on. In this milieu of waste, it's possible even to build a home from the materials that are tossed on landfill dumps. Short of getting a job at one, it seems practical to make some arrangement with the people in charge to save anything that might be usable in building.

There are many instances where an entire house was built with nothing more than the new and used material tossed out on a local dump. Often contractors will discard perfectly good material that is left over from a building project simply because they have no place to store it until the next construction job Naturally, you would have to be creative to make use of all kinds of random materials, but, from my own experience in building, I found it fun. Much of what I used in building a small cabin in the Santa Monica mountains was recycled. By visiting other building sites after they were completed, I was able to load my truck with leftover sand, rock, damaged bricks, usable lengths of 2 x4s and lots of valuable plywood.

The way to take advantage of this free material is to keep a sharp eye out wherever you go. Having an empty lot or large garage to store the finds would be necessary. Alternatively, you could start your house and build it as the material was acquired. Also, don't forget that city, county and state agencies often have huge quantities of materials that they sell at auction, by closed bid, or simply give away. Check with your local civic departments and also with nearby railroads, electric companies and other utilities. I recall a friend building an entire house from old railroad ties that he got for the labor of transporting them.

Solving the Sewage Problem

The most difficult problem in obtaining low–cost shelter is eliminating human waste. Presently, most modern houses are equipped with flush toilets that use about *forty thousand* gallons of water per year. Further, there must be either a sewer system (more taxes) or a septic tank and drain field. Either of these add greatly to the cost of any dwelling.

Of the alternate systems proposed, from old–fashioned privies (unacceptable to most people) to the effective but bulky clivus miltrum, a new breakthrough design eliminates the problem of disposing of human waste—easily, effectively and inexpensively. It actually makes possible the use of otherwise unbuildable land. Thus, it extends greatly the possibility of everyone owning their own home...or inexpensively having a vacation home.

Here are two designs presented in the words of their creators.

HUMUS 80/M™

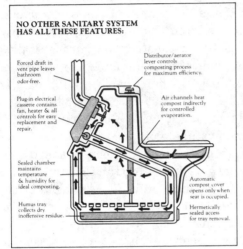

**NO OTHER SANITARY SYSTEM
HAS ALL THESE FEATURES:**

Forced draft in vent pipe leaves bathroom odor-free.

Plug-in electrical cassette contains fan, heater & all controls for easy replacement and repair.

Sealed chamber maintains temperature & humidity for ideal composting.

Humus tray collects dry inoffensive residue.

Distributor/aerator lever controls composting process for maximum efficiency.

Air channels heat compost indirectly for controlled evaporation.

Automatic compost cover opens only when seat is occupied.

Hermetically sealed access for tray removal.

The Humus 80/M is a completely self-contained system that requires only a standard electrical connection and the simple assembly of the supplied vent components for installation. Forced draft and thermostatically controlled heat, within sealed composting chambers, assure efficient operation without risk of odor or leakage. Human waste is reduced 90% by volume, and is removed as a dry inoffensive product—at intervals ranging from annually to monthly, depending on use—without contacting unprocessed material. The system is therefore completely compatible with contemporary U.S. standards of living. No plumbing, water or chemicals are required.

OPERATION: Inside the Humus 80/M, waste is decomposed and sanitized by a patented system of biodegradation. Recirculated warmed air evaporates urine and provides an optimum environment for the rapid composting of the solid human and paper fractions into a safe, dry humus. This humus devolves to removable collecting trays in an odor-&-liquid-tight compartment in the base of the unit. Daily agitation by an externally operated mechanism assures proper aeration for the biological process. A compost cover, which automatically retracts only when the toilet seat is weighted, conceals the composting chamber even with the toilet lid raised.

SPECIFICATIONS

TYPE: Electrically assisted aerobic biological decomposition (composting) waste treatment appliance. Self-contained, above-the-floor system requiring no plumbing or auxiliary holding tanks. Externally (rooftop) vented.

ELECTRICAL: Standard 110/120 VAC, single-phase, 60-cycle, grounded outlet for 3 wire plug.
Maximum power requirement: 225 Watts (200W heating element & 25W fan motor)
Average daily consumption: 2.0 kWh*

MEASUREMENTS:

Height: 73 cm (29″)	Depth: 83 cm (33″)
Width: 64 cm (25″)	Weight: 39 kg (87#)

Minimum floor space: 70×125 cm (27.6″×49.2″). If toilet is directly in front of bathroom doorway, to allow removal of the humus trays, length may be reduced.

CAPACITY*: Full-time residential—2 adults and 2 small children per unit. Part-time vacation—4 adults and 2 small children per unit. Toilet is designed to handle occasional overloads of short duration. A transparent external fluid-level indicator warns of overuse.

MATERIALS:
Shell: White, self-extinguishing polystyrene.
Process Components: Stainless Steel
Other metal components: Hot-dipped galvanized or electro-galvanized steel.
Fasteners: Bronze, electrogalvanized and stainless steel and plastics.
Vent Components: 55 mm (2.17″) diameter, PVC. 15′ lineal. Slip-fit sections. 1 m (40″) insulated and jacketed (4″ od) roof extension. 1 neoprene roof flashing.

WARRANTY: The Humus 80/M was developed and meticulously tested in cooperation with the Microbiological Institute of the Agricultural University of Norway. 1 year factory warranty on all parts. Write for "Warranty Certificate" for further information.

*Notes: Capacity may be increased and power requirements decreased by interaction with a SOLTRAN Solar Heating System. HUMUS 80/M is protected by patents in the U.S. and 29 other nations.

TROPIC

The **TROPIC** toilet has a beautiful appealing design, with a smooth and shiny surface on the entire enclosure. **15 years** of research and production has given us a superbly engineered toilet that meets all the needs of the cottage owner. Manufactured in the most durable materials available.

TROPIC is the ONLY biological toilet of its size which offers:

a) a **stainless steel HEATING ELEMENT** with sensitive thermostat located in a base under and *outside* the compost chamber. The **patented** position of the heating element is the same principle as an element under a pot of liquid on a stove. The purpose of the element is to evaporate liquid into the air and to supply heat to the compost.

b) **an adjustable fan speed control,** regulated from outside the unit. This ensures a comfortable noise level from air turbulence, if located close to a bedroom.

c) **shaftmixers** to provide aeration and excellent mixture of the compost. This simplifies maintenance by making the compost work more effectively at the bottom of the compost layer. A sturdy removable steel handle fits easily and directly into the shaftmixers behind the removable front door (no screws).

d) **an overflow security drain** to eliminate excess liquid, should the power fail or the toilet be over loaded by many extra guests.

TECHNICAL DATA:

Measurements: Width 57 cm (22½")
Height 70 cm (28")
Length 85 cm (34")
Seat Height 53 cm (21")

Weight: 21 Kilos (46 lbs.)

Ventilation: Electric fan through 38 mm (1½") plastic vent tube

Evaporation capacity: 4.5l/24 hrs.
(1½ US gallons)
However, with the overflow drain connected, the liquid capacity is practically unlimited.

Capacity: Family of 3 – 5. Dimensioned to handle temporary extra visitors.

Drain: 12.5 mm (½") if desired!

Enclosure: Made of extremely durable fire retardant fibreglass.

1. Vent Pipe 38 mm (1½")
2. Fan 30 Watt with speed control
3. Leveller
4. Bowl liner (removable)
5. Seat
6. Air channel
7. Inspection door
8. . Air tunnel
9. Clean out chamber
10. Grate
11. Heating pad 250 W
12. Connection box
13. Security drain
14. 3 prong plug
15. Main tank shell
16. Tank top
17. Insulation base
18. Shaft mixers
19. Crank (removable)

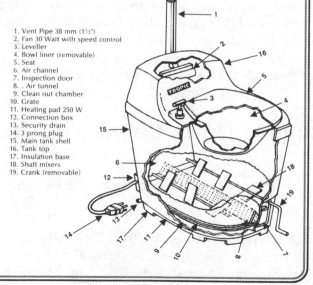

Tropical Island Living: That's the title of a newsletter that describes many diverse aspects of island living all over the world. Want to build a house in Hawaii, check out the charter business in the Virgin Islands, tour New Caledonia? Then write *Tropical Island Living,* P.O. Box 7263, Arlington, VA 22207 for availability of back issues of current prices. An outstanding service of this publication is its candor regarding health hazards and political instability in the tropics. I recall a friend who worked hard all of his life to retire to the Virgin Islands. Once there, he discovered that *his* race was the minority, and he couldn't adjust.

A recent tip from *TIL:* For data on health care while traveling, write the International Association for Medical Assistance to Travelers, 736 Center Street, Lewiston, NY 14092. They request a small donation.

Want to live on a deserted island and play Robinson Crusoe? Then here's the book for you:

Uninhabited And Deserted Islands, by Jon Fisher

The book is available from Loompanics, P.O. Box 1197, Port Townsend, WA 98368. It lists almost every island or grouping throughout the entire world. Typical item: Nihoa is located 150 miles northwest of Kauai. It has 12 fertile acres that were once cultivated. There are no inhabitants as of this writing. What are you waiting for?

Overseas Employment: Want to work overseas? Then perhaps this newsletter would be of value—*International Employment Hotline,* P.O. Box 6170, McLean, VA 22106. Ask for current prices. Many jobs are offered in tropical–island locations, such as the Bahamas and Java. From my own experience with relocation, I strongly recommend that you visit the area before you sign a contract.

City Mouse vs Country Mouse

"Come to me, my dear Bozzy, and let us be as happy as we can."
Samuel Johnson

In the film *Bonnie And Clyde,* Clyde tells Bonnie that if she joins up with him she'll never have a peaceful moment. Her response is "Promise?" Years of boredom and monotony in a small town have driven her to accept a life of desperate struggle just to escape.

Thoreau once explained that he "went to the woods because I wished to live deliberately, to front only the essential facts of life, and see if I could not learn what it had to teach, and not when I came to die, discover that I had not lived." My intent in introducing this discussion of where to live, with the opposing quotes above, is to show how complex this subject really is. Fortunately, I have had the wonderful opportunity to have experienced life in many settings from downtown, waterfront Oakland to a camper parked in remote Nevada deserts, from Baja California and Dubrovnik, Yugoslavia to the wilderness of British Columbia and the splendor of Tahoe.

Where is the best place to live? If I were permitted only one answer (and there are trillions) I would say:

"Wherever life is the most rewarding for you!"

And since change is the only certainty in life, then it follows that a person might change his location many times. For example, millions of young people are drawn to large cities to "make their fortune." then, after years of struggle, whether successful or not, they are often drawn back to peaceful, remote rural locations for retirement or just for relief from urban stresses. Wealthy people often maintain a number of residences—a cottage in Cannes, a cabin in the lake country of Wisconsin, a winter home in Montecito, California. Less affluent but nonetheless seeking changes and good climate are the "Snowbirds," the nomadic people who drive their motorhomes north in summer and south in winter.

For these and other good reasons, I've decided to simply prepare a comprehensive inventory of suggested places to live and encourage you to try as many as possible (beginning on page 168). In this way you'll be having the opportunity that I've had to "pick and choose," based on real life experiences rather than hearsay. Happy Hunting!

The Philosophy of Cooperative Living

One of my close friends is a man of such tremendous experience with life as to qualify him to expound on certain basic truths. In conversation one day, he pointed out that in any group of people of, say, over six or eight, eventually one of the group will become the "bad guy." This hypothesis was sharply delineated in a famous short story by Shirley Jackson called "The Lottery." In this story a person is chosen every year from the population of a village to be sacrificed.

When one is trying to cope with cooperative living, one needs all of the relevant data that can be obtained. So it is important going in to a communal housing effort to know that sooner or later one, or perhaps two, of the group will be singled out as the "sacrifices."

Now, what can be done about this situation? It is my belief that virtually all strained human relations result from a lack of honest, forthright, totally truthful communications. To prove this, think about a problem that you are having with another person. Wouldn't it be helpful if you would sit down with that person and "level" with that person?

That's the technique that I recommend for people who propose to live together in a house or on a ranch or boat or some other place where they will be constantly in contact with one another. By simply talking things out daily, the need for a "sacrifice" can be eliminated, or at least ameliorated.

One other technique that I have found effective in my own experience is to make certain that each person involved in a communal living experience has a place where he or she can enjoy *complete and total privacy*. Having served in the U.S. Navy during World War II, I know that the close confinement on board ship led to more fights among the crew than it did fights with the Japanese! So the answer is to generate a plan whereby each individual has a room or facility of his or her own, where he or she can be totally shut off from other members for as long as needed.

Another aspect that bears discussion is that of financing. If an arrangement is made whereby everyone pays an equal share and no one feels that they are taking on a greater burden, then you will eliminate many potential conflicts. Where a communal kitchen is used, it is important that any privately owned food be given a sanctuary so that it suddenly won't disappear after midnight and cause hassles the next day.

One of the best solutions to the food problem is for each commune member to contribute a certain amount toward a mutual food budget. Then when meals are prepared for all to consume, each participant can rest assured that they have made a fair and equitable donation.

There are many other aspects of communal living, but the ones cited are those that have been a part of the author's own experiences. And I am certain that if these basic problems are solved at the beginning, then it will be possible for a reasonable, happy communal lifestyle among nonrelated people to be achieved.

● Design Concept : Shared Living Community-Housing

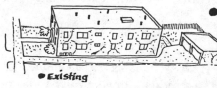

● Existing

● Scenario: A group of co-owner/ residents create exactly what they need & want by remodeling & adding improvements & by long term plans, self-help construction & the agreement & co-operation of each other.

AFTER REMODELING
BY THE CO-OWNERS!!

ARCHITECTURAL CONCEPTS for SHARED LIVING/CO-OWNERSHIP

Co-Own your own building & unit, or a large house, or cluster of houses, and, create as much shared community benefit as you want... affordability, social/family, living cost savings, ... and building re-design possibilities, such as,

Livelihood & Interests	Comforts & Esthetics	Energy & Utilities	Recreation & Relaxation	Social & Family
● home office(s)	● bay windows	● laundry & work room.	● play yard.	● child care & play room.
● meeting & studio space.	● skylights.	● tool maint-ainance shop.	● view/sun deck	● teen/game rm.
● craft shop.	● sleeping loft.	● auto repair	● patio courts & dining decks.	● group social & special activity rooms.
● computer room.	● balconies.	● bulk food, canning, stores.	● hot tub/sauna	
● add rental units.	● benches.	● solar w/h	● swim pool.	● Addit. sleeping & guest rooms.
● plant green house	● fountains & pools.	● insulation	● game courts.	
	● landscaping		● gardens.	
	● entrance gate & fences			

NEW DORMER   NEW LOFT   NEW LOFT   NEW SKYLIGHT

NEW SOLAR GREEN HOUSE   EXIST. BEDROOM   CLO   HALL   BATH   EXIST. LIVING ROOM or BED ROOM

An architect, Ken Norwood, has created the following scenario: A group of co—owner residents create exactly what they need and want by remodeling and adding improvements and by long—term plans, self—help construction, and the agreement and cooperation with each other. Here's what it looks like, before and after. For more information, write to Ken at: 1642 Arch Street, Berkeley, California 94709.

Elderhostels

There's no gain in spending valuable golden years in a sun city where the most exciting event is the daily arrival of the hearse. Instead, consider traveling at low cost the Elderhostel way.

Most Americans who travel to other lands do so as tourists—to see, to buy and collect, to travel. Elderhostelers will go beyond this. They will study intensively one or more aspects of the local culture, its history, its archaeology, its economy, its literature, its politics. The programs described will include an opportunity to learn about the people of another country by actually living with them—a one week homestay with a welcoming host family—coupled with two scheduled weeks of formal courses and many field trips related to the material being discussed and studied. This combined experience offers participants a unique perspective on the contemporary culture of the country visited, and is a practical way of contributing to international understanding at the personal level.

For more information contact: Elderhostel, 80 Boylston Street, Suite 400, Boston, MA 02116.

Some Additional Housing Options

Many schools and similar organizations are offering to pay you an income and let you live in your own house in exchange for the deed when you die. Makes sense, although it is merely an extension of an old English common law principle—the Life Estate. Wealthy landowners often granted "life estates" to their faithful servants. For a typical offering, write Claremont College, Bauer Center, Claremont, CA 91711.

Hancock County, Maine: Not too far from the congestion of Manhattan, this region contains pioneer country, beautiful and unspoiled. It includes the verdant mountainlands of the Acadia National Forest. With a small income, you could easily grow most of your food and thus live a lot for a little.

Coos County, New Hampshire: This region has been called one of the healthiest places to live in eastern America. Not far from the Canadian border, it would be possible to make use of the favorable exchange rates.

Culpeper, Virginia: It's hard to find relatively unpolluted land and water in densely populated regions, but this is, at last report, an island of refuge for city dwellers. Prepare to devote lots of time to growing things in the fertile soil with a long growing season.

The Ozarks: Once an isolated, hillbilly hangout, many people now make this picturesque region their home. Many lakes, dozens of major rivers and countless creeks make this a water lover's paradise. Land is still reasonable, even of the waterfronts.

Door County, Wisconsin: Sturgeon Bay on mighty Lake Michigan has a small population, or you can try the little villages of Valmy and Jacksonsport. With the continuing decline in some types of farming, it's possible to buy a farm for a modest down payment and convert it to other uses.

Thomas County, Nebraska: What impressed me about this area was the friendliness of the people. Even though it lacks the impressive mountain ranges of the west, the numerous woods and rivers make Nebraska and its low land prices appealing.

Montezuma County, Colorado: Combining mountain and desert, this region has low–cost land and many opportunities for an agrarian lifestyle. The climate is dry, the air worth breathing, and it's a great place to avoid urban confusion.

Flagstaff, Arizona: Coconino County is a land of contrasts with 12,000–foot peaks dipping down to desert sands. People have been migrating here from many parts of the United States and from the hotter parts of Arizona. Once you get there, you'll see why.

Jackson Hole, Wyoming: If you haven't seen the Grand Tetons, then at least visit this area for the astounding views. Lakes, fish–filled streams and thick green forests make this area a delight for any age.

Glacier County, Montana: A. B. Guthrie made this area famous in his book, *The Big Sky,* and much of it still looks the same as when the mountain men stalked game in the woods. Winters are severe, but I can guarantee you'll see scenery that will take your breath away.

Sawtooth Mountains, Idaho: Razor–sharp, silhouetted mountain peaks rise from the most fantastically active rivers you've ever seen. With many tourists coming to look, a service industry might provide the income you'd need to live here year round.

White Pine County, Nevada: Ruggedly beautiful mountains, a surprising amount of water, interesting caves and other attractions make this region appealing for short– or long–term living. Prices tend to be lower than most of the U.S., and all you need is a small income to live without depending on the local economy.

Big Sur, California: Famous worldwide, this spectacular seacoast region has few residents yet much potential. The famous Esalen Institute proves that, with the right "magnet," people will brave the winding roads that provide the only access to Big Sur. It's been a mecca for freethinkers for many decades.

The Mother Lode Country of California: From Mariposa to the northern mines, Highway 49 leads through a region steeped in history of the most intriguing variety. The Forty–niners built towns that are now near ghosts, but the scenery is still as lovely and appealing. Orchards and gardens are lush and provide the natives with sustenance that requires minimal cash income. You can do the same if you wish.

Cave Junction, Oregon: The beautiful Illinois River flows through this placid paradise of green forests and remarkably blue skies. Land costs are low because employment opportunities are quite scarce (as they are through much of rural Oregon). If you have a mail–order business, this would be a great base of operations.

Wenatchee, Washington: Land of the best apples you have ever eaten, the Wanatchee region is unbelievably lovely, especially in springtime when the trees are in bloom. Less rain because of the sheltering Cascades, many people declare this the ideal place to live.

San Juan Islands, Washington: Somewhat rainy in winter but spectacular the rest of the year, these islands number some 170 plus. A few have ferry service, but on most of the others you would have to depend on your own boat or be a Robinson Crusoe. Well worth a tour of review whether you decide to live there or not.

Classifieds Don't Lie

The best way I know to check out a place is to read the classifieds. In them is all you need to know: Help wanted, prices of houses, who's selling what at how much. So when you are interested in a place, just send for the local paper(s). The town's Chamber of Commerce is paid to present the most favorable view of any area, but the people who advertise simply cannot generate any swindles—they are too close to home.

Personal Observations

I grew up in a town of some eighteen thousand people about nine miles from Los Angeles. South Pasadena was a bedroom community for the big city, linked by an efficient electric railway system. To me, it seemed modern, up–to–date, well–developed but lacking in that quality that one reads into Tom Sawyer. There wasn't any true wilderness within a reasonable distance. In a word or two, it was simply too civilized to have much charm or appeal. I left it when I was still in my teens and have only been back once. It had not changed appreciably and was still a Lewisonian "Main Street" comfortable, older now, but devoid of charisma.

Los Angeles is, by my own definition, the anus of the universe. The air is unbreathable, the freeways are bumper–to–bumper most of the time, and the pace of life is frenetic and lethal. Elia Kazan, in *The Arrangement* described LA:

> "It was hot. The sun was shining. There was one place in the cover of smog brighter than the rest. My eyes smarted. I could smell the industrial waste. I could taste it. There was something malignant in the air."

If they made me a gift of the entire city with the stipulation that I had to live there, I would not accept it. I believe that LA was the city that Henry Miller had in mind when he coined the term, "The Air–conditioned Nightmare." Unfortunately, many cities throughout the world are "LAs." Not long ago I found myself fighting traffic in the southern outskirts of Paris, and it could have been the southern outskirts of LA, except the signs were in French and there wasn't a VW in sight.

For a number of years, I lived in a new tract house in a San Fernando Valley town called Canoga Park. Until the smog moved in during the early sixties (when I moved out), it was not an unpleasant place to live. Nearby were places to hike, several large parks, and friends who owned pools. My daughters seemed to enjoy the clean neighborhood and my wife, the life of suburbia. A certain stability is necessary for raising a family so, although the town was not my ideal, it served the purposes for which I lived there. As soon as polluted air began to waft over our rooftop, I made tracks for a more healthful environment.

Santa Barbara was my choice after I left the LA area, and, again, until it became overcrowded, it was like living in a picture postcard. Daughter Jill once remarked that everywhere you looked it appeared to resemble a tourist poster. And furthermore, she pointed out that "Where do you go when you leave Santa Barbara?" The answer to that was the Mother Lode country of California.

There are very few residents of West Point, a village in the lower foothills of the mighty Sierras. Whatever you do, it is a subject of discussion and concern, and unless you're a hermit, you are under constant surveillance. Then there are the monster lumber trucks spewing diesel smoke as they race to and fro with the corpses of magnificent trees. And always, the grating howl of chain saws, near and far. It was not long before I began to look for another home base.

Mark Twain called Tahoe the "fairest sight the world affords," and I will still agree, despite the encroachment of an overwhelming tourist industry near the north and south borders. Winters are severe, with lots of snow and ice, freezing motor blocks and the nuisance of chains. But in the intervals of spring and fall when tourists are minimal, Tahoe is most enchanting place to live. The lake is a giant jewel, now turquoise, later cobalt, at night a mirror for the galaxies. There are few places that would rate a return visit, but Tahoe, despite the periodic crowds, would be one of them.

Las Vegas would save space travelers some time. They could see everything larger than life in this unique, macro/microcosm of America. To paraphrase Dickens, it is the worst and the best of places all at once. If you like sunshine, you'll have it almost every day. If you hate rain, then enjoy Vegas—it has perhaps two to three inches a year. Restless: You can shop, see a show, watch the people panorama twenty–four hours a day, seven days a week, in more than thirty–five hotel casinos. Religious minded? Then this glittering city can provide you with *more churches per capita* than any other city in the country. But there are negative aspects—gambling and all the other vices—that almost cancel out the advantages. It was part of my education to live here for a spell, and I'm glad that I did. But I don't think I'll go back, ever.

Thermal Springs

Scattered all over the 11 Western States are more than 1700 hot springs. Some are located near old towns—others are in the wide–open spaces. There's a free directory that you can obtain from the National Oceanic and Atmospheric Administration, 325 Broadway, Boulder, CO 80303. Just ask for the Thermal Springs List for the U.S.

Ghost Towns

Scattered all over the West are towns that didn't make it. Most were mining towns built during a boom and then abandoned when the ore ran out. Many are completely vacated, but there are increasing numbers where all–year residents have taken up quarters that cost nothing.

To find a ghost town, check out one of the many books on the subject from your local library. Then take a trip to see if it meets your qualifications. I've often envisioned a colony of writers and artists occupying and restoring one of the many Nevada ghosts. After all, if you don't have to do the 9–to–5 bit, you're free to live anywhere you wish. Access to a post office for in–and–out mail is really all you need. Another source of ghost towns is large lumber companies. They've often built a complete company town and then abandoned it when the timber was cut. Check with some of the big ones in Oregon, Washington and northern California. There are more ghost towns in Alaska and British Columbia, some right on the coast where fishing is great. Abandoned canneries are another possibility.

Many years ago, lumber tycoons built towns directly within a forested area. The workers lived full–time in these towns. Today, most are abandoned but still in livable shape. Prowl around timber country and talk to some of the old–timers. You may luck out as I did. I found a complete village called Whitmore Meadows and paid a total rental of seventy–five dollars for the entire town. Several friends moved into the houses and fixed them up. We had a lot of fun and it was a great learning experience too.

The same would apply to mining towns or ghost towns. I recall visiting Ballarat near the Panamint range and finding pensioners living quite well in the old miners' shacks. And not far from there, I discovered more old people enjoying an Indian–style life in sandstone caves. It was not as rugged as you might think, since most caves maintain a comfortable temperature all year round.

The last time I checked, you could move into any house in Hardman, Oregon since the town was deserted many years ago. There were a few people there living like live ghosts. Although I've never been there myself, I understand that Bodie, California and Silver City, Idaho are quite lively ghosts with a modest number of residents who are proud of their contribution to maintaining a part of history by keeping the old houses intact.

Squatting

I know that many of my readers will take a somewhat dim view of the concept of squatting on land that you don't own, but hear me out. It's a legal method of acquiring land based on very old English common law that is still on the books today.

Colorado River Squatters

After World War II, many vets wanted a quiet, serene rural setting to get their heads together. A number of them parked old trailers alongside the Colorado River near what is now Parker, Arizona. When they needed more space, they added a screened porch. For income, they nailed together a pop–and–hot–dog stand to provide snacks for an increasing number of riverside visitors. As the years flowed along, these trailer homes became more substantial, and pop stands became full–blown restaurants. The owners of these enterprising businesses where really squatters in every sense of the term and thought that their tenure would go on indefinitely.

Enter the villains! Bureaucrats love to make their living from people who really have to work. So along came the license people, health department inspectors and tax collectors. They descended on the river squatters like a plague of horrible locusts. At first it was a nickle–and–dime operation which the entrepreneurs were willing to satisfy. But before long, government edicts demanding that they vacate were delivered. The squatters, being ex–combat soldiers and sailors, decided to fight for what they felt were their rights. They had settled the land, made it prosperous, had furnished useful services to their fellow citizens, and felt they had a strong proprietary interest in their riverside locations. I'll make a long story short by saying that after several bitter battles, the squatters won and now have full title to their land.

You can see why it's important to tell this story, because it lends credibility to my contention that squatting is an honorable and noble way to acquire a little elbow room on this planet.

A Good Place to Live, and an Income Too

Few Americans are aware that the 1871 mining law is still in effect. This law provides that any U.S. citizen can claim twenty acres of public land as a mining claim subject to a few simple stipulations. First of all, the land you claim must be open to mining. But don't worry, there are millions of acres, most of it in the west, that fall into this category. Second, you have to have a serious intent to actually create a mineral claim and work it. For example, if you have a gold placer mine in the high Sierras, you have to show that you're making a diligent effort to find gold and that according to the "prudent man" rule, there is a likelihood that gold is available. Third, you have to do the equivalent of $100 worth of work a year. As long as you abide by these major conditions, there is absolutely no reason why you cannot live on and work in your own mining claim...after all, there are tens of thousands of active mining claims in the U.S.

I recently visited a claim in the high Sierras where the owner asked me not to give its location. I went in to a hand–dug tunnel with this doughty miner, and with his flashlight he showed me what is called "jewelry–grade" or "specimen" gold. This means that chunks of almost pure 24–carat gold festooned the ivory–like quartz. He had worked this mine for many years and took out only what he needed to live. He was not a greedy person, and I know from friends that he shared his wealth with others less fortunate.

I'm telling you this story to prove that active and prosperous mining claims do exist and that, if you're one of the lucky ones, you too may find one. Incidentally, I encountered a similar situation on the banks of a Mother Lode river. Here a young couple had taken over an abandoned mining claim and were making enough money to pay the bills with just a few hours work per day.

This brings up an important point—if you don't want to go out prospecting, just go to the recorder's office in the county of your choice and ask to look through the list of mining claims that have been abandoned. The recent boom in the price of gold and silver has made this type of claim scarce, but keep in mind that claims are constantly being abandoned as the owners lose interest, move away, die or otherwise let them go.

Even fewer people know about what is called the five–acre mill site. This is discussed in the same 1871 mining law. In an area where mining is or may be conducted, it is legal to claim five acres of public land to erect a facility for milling any kind of ore. You see, most ore has to be reduced in size before the minerals can be extracted. So crushers and stampers become an integral part of routine mining operations. If you build a mill site and hang up a sign, you will be fulfilling the majority of requirements for claiming the five acres on which it is built.

While traveling through southern Nevada, I discovered a mill site that had just been claimed. The claimants had selected a favorable location adjacent to an abundant flow of hot mineral water. They had already built a loading platform and brought in electricity. I am sure their next step was to drill into the source of the mineral water so that they too would have a bountiful supply. Once a mill site such as we have described has been established, it's only natural that you would want to build an administration building, including living accommodations. If you happen to like tomatoes, chilis and beans, you could certainly plant a garden out back. And since you would be guarding your property against vandals, you would simply have to stay there all year round. By the way, after you've improved your mill site, you can apply for a "patent" on the land, which is simply legalese for full title. Once this has transpired, the mill site is yours forever, and you can sell it, rent it, give it to your heirs or do anything that's normally done with real estate.

The River Island People

A lot of land comes and goes in America. For example, floods can create islands in the middle of a river and they can also destroy them. In the interim, these unclaimed parcels of land make great spots to squat. Once, while driving through Idaho, we chanced to rest by the banks of the mighty Salmon River. We noticed a quaint dwelling on a heavily forested island. Upon further inquiry, we learned that a group of young people had settled on the island, built themselves a rustic house, planted a huge garden, and were enjoying a poineering lifestyle without payments or taxes. I have found similar islands in the vast California Delta between San Francisco and Stockton. Here, islands, from as little as a city lot to some that number acres, are homes to people who have no other. Sometimes their home floats, and they merely use the island for moorage and for garden space.

In travels throughout the largely unpopulated west and Canada, we have found any number of places where living on an island or otherwise unclaimed, unregistered land is not only possible but feasible. So I suggest that you simply travel to an area where you would like to live and start checking around.

Gate Five

Gate Fivers live aboard all manner of floating stock from restored yachts to virtual derelicts in their community near Sausalito, California. But it's a community where there's more life per square yard than in most other places. Dogs, cats, kids and far–out architecture plus a strong arts and crafts orientation make this floating city a vision of some past or future age—an age when life was totally unstructured and free. Incidentally, I found another small, but similar floating community in the mouth of the Umpqua River near Reedsport, Oregon. Here I found full–size houses built aboard old barges and floats of cedar and redwood logs. Most residents were quite old, enjoying what may be the last of a water–borne village.

Other Places

In the eastern United States there are far more places to tie up your floating home, and this takes some of the pressure off water lovers. For example, the Inland Waterway which reaches from New York to Florida has thousands of protected bays, inlets and canals where small boats may tie up without anyone's feathers being ruffled. It's also possible to find this relaxed watery real estate along major rivers such as the Mississippi and Missouri. Even in crowded California there's many good spots along the Sacramento and San Joaquin, particularly where they form the 1500–square–mile Delta region between San Francisco and Stockton.

Creative people often combine boats with shore living in a pleasant mixture that offers the best of each. Up the Napa River north of Vallejo in California there is a meandering community of mostly retired people who have built small places on stilts. No one seems to mind since the land is marshy and unusable otherwise. The clannish group lives half–ashore, half–afloat, finding much of their provender in the river. Fish, clams, crayfish and other fresh– and salt–water foods are theirs for the taking. With no rent to pay, they can afford to buy gas for their small vessels and thus enjoy boating at its lowest cost.

I recall meeting a man who had been reduced to a pittance after a disaster in business and another in marriage. He told me that he lived for almost a year on an uncharted island in the Delta using his rowboat to fish and dig clams. His only expenditures were for oil, salt and kerosene for his lamp. He built a shelter of driftwood and found his recreation in a battered guitar and the stars.

Finding Old Boats

For many years I lived aboard an old Coast Guard cutter converted to a houseboat. In the process I learned how easy it is to obtain old boats. Many marinas have a back lot where boats that have been put on blocks are stored. Often the owners lose interest, and the boats decay. You can buy these for storage charges and often get them for free—the marina managers just want them out of the way. I once bought three old boats for $50 and one was a restorable, 30–foot fishing boat.

Also check out the backwaters of harbors. Boats that have been leaking a lot are often towed to a sand bar and parked. If abandoned, you can check the numbers and ask the owner if you can take possession. Check with insurance companies in your area. Often boats are sunk or burned and can be obtained for few dollars or even salvaged for free.

Free Boats Can Be Found in Many Maritime Locales

It's lots of fun to wander around in the back-waters of a harbor or in a scenic area like the California Delta. At left is a plywood cruiser complete with engine. I checked the wood, and it was still good. Very little would have to be done to turn this derelict into a livable home…most of the work is cosmetic rather than repair. One quick fix for a boat of this type would be to put a camper on it. That way you'd have a livable home pronto.

I fell in love with this old railroad–company house barge. In the early part of the twentieth century, railroads provided much of the housing for their working people. And this was typical of the low-cost, self-propelled floating home that they built by the hundreds.

Now there are only a few left, and I could have bought this one complete with engine and living quarters for just five hundred dollars! I already had too much boat, so it slipped by. But I think of it often and fondly.

Here's a metal lifeboat just about covered with sand. It would take a bit of diligent digging to get it afloat, but, personally, I think it would be worth it. Those old steel lifeboats have been converted into some of the most comfortable floating homes I've ever seen. Because of their great sta-bility, you can build both up and out. And if you keep them painted, there's no limit to their life-span. And surely the price is right!

Fixing Up Old Boats

There's a method that has been used successfully by many fishermen that's cheap and effective. Haul the leaky old hull out of the water and clean it by scraping or sandblasting. Then staple on several layers of chicken wire, about half–inch mesh. Then plaster the boat with a thick layer of very sticky, almost–dry cement. If you have a friend with a gunite rig (blown cement), you can use that method. But either one works. Keep the setting cement damp until it cures—several days. When you re-launch it, you shouldn't have any more leaks. This can save boats that would otherwise be lost to the chainsaw gang.

Once the hull is dry, you can make it livable for a peanut budget. For example, many rug dealers will give you rugs that they remove from homes. Cut out the worn spots and use the balance to give yourself a wall–to–wall carpeted cabin. Since boats are usually quite small, you don't need much furniture; often plenty of big pillows and back rests will make a snug living area. Cooking facilities can be as simple as a one–burner stove run by gas or kerosene, and lights can be 12–volts recharged by a small generator or, if you have some bucks, the new solar cells.

The best way to see how to live aboard cheaply is to visit people who are already doing it. You'll learn all the shortcuts as to furnishings, utilities and food.

There's a very large subculture in America that lives afloat, and they've generated a large inventory of valuable information on low–cost shelter. To me, waterborne living is one the best ways to enjoy life with little money. I recall one summer when friends and I were living on the old Flying Goose and we discovered we were spending less that twenty–five cents per day per person for *everything*! That was food, utilities, entertainment...the works. So I know that it can be done!

Freedom Afloat

The cost of land in buildable areas has sky–rocketed. Even the smallest, meanest little old lot can cost 30, 40 or 50,000 dollars. At even moderate interest rates, the payments on the lot plus a house goes beyond most people's ability to pay. So what's the answer? Simple, forget the land...try water.

The earth is about three–fifths water with millions of acres of quiet, usable, protected inland waterways. So why pay a fortune for a scrap of polluted land in some crowded area when you can roam waterways free aboard a floating home?

Barnacle Bill

I met Bill when I was living aboard my own Coast Guard cutter converted to a house–boat. His cozy home was a Navy launch from Pearl Harbor days that he had found rotting on a mud flat. He patched the leaks, hosed it out and then proceeded to restore it to livability. Priority was a comfortable and spacious bunk that served as a couch in the daytime. Next was a compact galley with an oil–burning stove that could be converted to wood if the oil ran low. Bill loved the outdoors so most of the hull was open deck with an awning for shade.

He retired from a job as a therapist in a mental institution on a small pension. As he said, he could have struggled along paying high rent somewhere but preferred the life directed "by wind and tide." (Often, to save fuel, he would just let go the mooring lines and let the elements move him about; wherever night fell, he would cast his anchor and enjoy the unexpected scenery.)

I spent some time with Bill in the Delta region and we often discussed how easy it was to live a free life aboard a small boat.

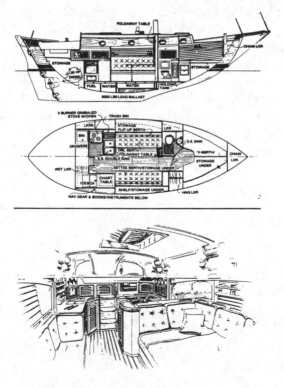

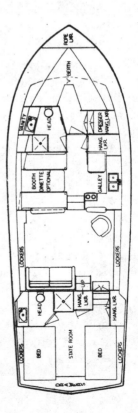

Open Your Mind

It's true...once you discard the linear thinking that keeps most people land bound, another water world opens up. Here are some examples from real life.

Many older Americans have special problems. No longer able to work, they must depend on small pensions. Housing is a particularly acute and critical area, since older people cannot get around as handily as the young. Often they have no means of private transportation. Finally, boredom is an ever–present menace, since living in an urban area offers limited free entertainment and recreation.

Solving most of the above problems are the people I met at a small backwater harbor near San Francisco, They managed to acquire old yachts too far gone for sea— WWII landing craft remodeled to contain living quarters, and trailers on pontoons and ancient barges. This motley armada was once clustered together in a Hong Kong hodgepodge until a bond issue created a modest marina. Now they have utilities, slips with walkways and parking. Along the shore many have planted small gardens, and a flock of ducks has come to stay.

It wasn't easy to bring this about; at one point the city authorities threatened to clear them out. But a resolute woman brandishing a shotgun persuaded them that there were alternatives, and thus the new China Basin livaboard marina was born.

Not too far away is the houseboat community called Gate Five near Sausalito. Here the residents are mostly young people who have opted for the free life afloat. Again it hasn't been all water lilies. They have often had to fight to keep their boats in place. At the present time there's a Mexican standoff with each side learning to compromise.

Interlude

Now that we have reviewed a few real–life examples of privacy afloat, let's take a look at some further possibilities. With millions of boats afloat on this planet on millions of square miles of interesting waterways, it's obvious that your opportunities are virtually limitless.

Note
If you don't know a great deal about boats, then I suggest you send for International Marine's free catalog. Their books are up–to–date and written for amateur sailors as well as pros—marine education at low cost. Everything you'll need to know, from buying your first boat to long–distance navigation. Write to Box BH, Camden, Maine 04843.

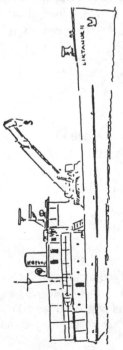

Comfort, economy and privacy through mobility are the strong characteristics of modern houseboats. With plentiful water, generators, holding tanks and such, they can provide every amenity that one is accustomed to in a home or apartment. Because they can be moored almost anywhere, the high cost of using land is eliminated. I know of many people who keep on the move and thus eliminate docking charges. Even if those are necessary, they are often much less than the rental of a studio apartment in some smoggy city.

Privacy is easy with a houseboat, since one can just touch the starter button and move on when noise, confusion or unwanted visitors appear.

Houseboats are usually restricted to quiet waters; inland bays, estuaries and rivers are perfect for these flat–bottomed craft. Fortunately, there are millions of square miles of waterways in these categories. The Inland Waterway on the east coast of the United States is one good example, while the St. Lawrence seaway between the U.S. and Canada is another. Personally, I recommend both the Georgia Strait area between British Columbia and Vancouver Island and the fabulous Sea of Cortez east of the Baja peninsula, Mexico. I've cruised both and want to go again soon.

In summary, a modest investment can assure far more privacy afloat than one can find ashore when that investment is in a floating home. Once you try life on the water, dry land will seem dull and unexciting. As one friend said, "living on the water is like being in a movie 24 hours a day." I agree one hundred percent.

Your Own Tramp Freighter

If there is one pervasive dream that every corporate executive has it's to chuck it all, buy a small steamer, and set sail for the far horizon. Can this dream become a reality? Can a couple or small group experience the romantic life of a sea gypsy? Can the ultimate in privacy be achieved? Can you be in Rangiroa while that certified letter languishes in Raiatea?

Most people are astounded when they learn that a small, ocean going vessel can be purchased for less than the meanest, most miserable shack in drab Inglewood.

But here's proof—the three vessels shown on the next page are typical of what was offered in a recent issue of *Boats and Harbors*. The least expensive is twenty–six thousand dollars, and remember, that's the *asking* price. They might even take a trade of one of your white elephants.

My personal fantasy is to buy that 185–footer for seventy–five thousand and turn it into a floating publishing company. I'd sail it north in summer, say to the Victoria, British Columbia area, and south in winter—the Sea of Cortez around Mulege or Loreto. To help pay for fuel, I'd invite friends to join me on a joint–venture basis.

103' FREIGHTER

Twin 6-110's. 2 2-71 G.M. Diesel 20 KW generators. 7' Draft. 200-250 Ton capacity. 3000 Gals. tankage. Recently rebuilt. Sound.

reduction to **$26,000.00**

185' Ex Navy P.C.E.R. Vessel 33' beam - 732 Gross tons. Twin GMC 278A V-12 engines - 3 Ea. 100KW AC generators - 3 Ea. 20 KW DC generators - Drydocked and painted with all new zinc's 6-84. **$75,000.00.**

Re-Sale Price Reduced — 176' L.O.A Freighter 1943 Steel U.S.A. registered. 34 Net tons. 2 Hatches, 2 refrigerated holds. 1 - GM 371 40 KW - 2 3-268 100KW-D.C. 2-GM 6-278 Falk Westinghouse. All engines running cor dition. **$35,000.00.**

In any large library, you'll find all the information you'll need about documentation and marine law. Did you know, for example, that once a ship is documented, it cannot be boarded except for good reasons and lots of complex paperwork. You can treat everyone else like the pirates they are.

Now here's an idea: Collect your friends, form a shipping company, and buy *all three* vessels. Send one to the South Pacific, the other to the Caribbean and the third to the Mediterranean. Now you'd have a choice of where you would enjoy maximum privacy!

Cruising

In the quest for privacy and peace, many people have given up on *civilization* and sailed their way to a better way of life. Paradoxically, it can be far less costly in terms of money and stress. Save up your money and create the goal of a seaworthy craft as shown. Today, with electronic aids, it's far easier to navigate the seven seas. Also, new safety devices take away most of the hazards.

The Vava'u Islands

The poetic description of Vava'u is best given by Robin Graham, author of *Dove*, when he says. "This must be one of the loveliest spots on all the earth." It is easy to understand why Chief Kaho said to me "You will be happy here until the end of the world. How different they are, these islands, different as flowers from flowers, trees from trees. People are too..."

The Tongans are Polynesians with an easy and natural charm inherent in a people who live close to the land and sea. The Tongans are proficient navigators and from trees. People are too..."

The Tongans are Polynesians with an easy and natural charm inherent in a people who live close to the land and sea. The Tongans are proficient navigators and fishermen, with Tonga being one of the few remaining places where whales are hunted using hand harpoons. The women are skilled in tapa making and basket work, with Tongan handcrafts considered among the best and most sought–after in the South Pacific.

Tongans are noted for their gentle and proud manner, but of all the many unique Tongan characteristics it is perhaps the Tongan friendliness which is best remembered by visitors. Certainly Captain Cook thought so in 1773 when he named Tonga "the friendly islands."

The waters of Vava'u are noted for their variety of game fish—barracuda, tuna, marlin, and sailfish—to name a few. The coral reefs are virtually untouched in beauty and variety. They are equal to any in the world, with drop offs, caves, extensive reefs, and lagoons to be explored. Vava'u offers a wide selection of shells common to the Indo–Pacific region.

The best way to describe the Vava'u islands it to compare them with other bareboat areas in the Caribbean. Vava'u would best be described as a cross between the Virgin Islands and the Bahamas. It has the deep water and relatively high mountains you find in the Virgins, and most of the islands are within close proximity to each other. As in the Bahamas, Vava'u has numerous outlying atolls rimmed with white sand beaches and protective reefs, many with good anchorages.

The cruising area is approximately 30 square miles within which lie over 50 islands. Countless hours can be spent exploring many of the *uninhabited islands* with their abundance of good anchorages and white sandy beaches. The diving and snorkeling opportunities are excellent. The waters are beautiful shades of turquoise and dark blue, and the trade winds blow constantly, making every day a sailing day.

Liveaboard/Income Combinations

Several years ago while living on my own 75–footer, a friend suggested that we take a group on tour. An ad in a San Francisco paper yielded a capacity load. We asked for a twenty–five dollar donation to cover meals and fuel, and that worked out just fine. Everyone had a great time during the three–day, two–night cruise of the San Pablo Bay and Napa River areas.

I've often wanted to try this way of creating an income while living on a boat again, and probably will eventually. In the meantime, I'm always on the lookout for boats similar to those shown.

The *Miss Tahoe* would function like the U.S. Mint during the summer months, while the vessel known as *Romance* could be used in many parts of the world all year

U.S.C.G. LICENSED 100 PASSENGER TOUR BOAT — 1981 Volvo Diesel - Full cocktail & snackbar, PA, VHF radio, and stereo. Modern interior. New carpet and seating. Fully equipped and ready to be shipped anywhere in the Americas. EXCELLENT BUY. **$110,000.00.**

1963 CHRIS CRAFT
44' Roamer (Cruiser)

Steel hull, fresh water. Excellent condition. Sleeps 8. Reconditioned gas engines. 28-Mile radar, autopilot, trim tabs. Beautiful mahogany interior. Many extras. 2 Mansfield heads and shower. Microwave, aft wet bar, etc. Moored in Chicago. **$45,000.** Video tape on yacht available

133' x 30.5 x 12.6, 755GRT 15 Dble Staterooms w/private facilities. Crew qtrs for 12 One-sitting Dining rm. Lge Saloon. Cocktail Lounge. Sun Deck w/BBQ. 500Hp Dsl. 30 gph.

long. Consider doing a joint venture with a vessel like the *Romance*; you supply the energy and know–how, the owner simply supplies the boat.

You could operate solo on something the size of the *Roamer*. Live on board and charter it out whenever the need for some income arose.

Boat Acquisition Ideas

Introduction: Want to go to sea but don't have much money? Then use your creative abilities to acquire the vessel you desire. Several years ago, a friend wanted a large sailboat but could not afford to pay the full cost. So he sent his name to various insurance companies that provided coverage for yachts and asked to be notified if a large sailboat was "totalled." This means that the company pays off the loss because it is considered total and then resells the salvage. Shortly thereafter, the opportunity to bid on a 45–foot ketch occurred. It seems that the crane operator dropped this new boat and it broke in half—just like a big bottle since it was of fiberglass construction. My friend bid the most—$15,000—and became proud owner of a luxury yacht in two big pieces. A creative man, he simply fitted the two halves together, strengthened the joint with reinforced aluminum ribs and lots of glass and ended up with a perfectly usable vessel. It was done so expertly, he was able to re–insure it! Total cost for the two hundred thousand dollar ketch was under twenty–five thousand dollars!

The same man also acquired a 75–foot coast guard cutter conversion for very little, made some repairs and sold it to me for $10,500. I had a lot of fun with it until dry rot and a careless marina owner compelled it to be salvaged out. Even then it provided a source of materials for a handicapped person and a tax writeoff for me.

Rebuildable Boats: Send your name to casualty insurance carriers and ask to be informed of salvage bidding.

Lease/Charter: Make a deal with a charter or leasing company to operate the vessel on a joint–venture basis. This can be done with all kinds of boats from pleasure yachts to fish and workboats.

Repair Specials: Do as my friend did—find a boat for a low price and fix it yourself.

Big Boats at Liberty: There are big boats all over the globe, and many could be acquired on some equitable basis—joint venture, coop chartering, operation as a school for sailors, cargo vessels from one small port to another and so on. Often boats sit at their moorings simply because the owners don't know quite what to do with them or have been unable to sell them. Go find the boat of your dreams and make an offer of any kind. You might be surprised what develops.

Foundation Acquisitions: Form your own nonprofit group and seek donations on a tax–deduction basis. This has been a very popular way for a boat owner to let his boat serve a useful and humanitarian purpose while he also gains a needed tax credit. Remember that many older boats are very hard to sell because they don't qualify for insurance coverage. Some companies make a hard and fast rule not to insure a boat over sixteen years old.

Workboats vs Yachts: Most people want a pleasure boat, but you can have just as much fun on the water and an income if you invest in a reasonably priced workboat. Big enough for a family, you'd never have to pay rent again!

No–Money Special: If you have experience or gain some via schooling, this can be for you: Living aboard and getting paid for it. Makes a fine ship–shore balance so you never tire of either.

In summary, get out those boat ads and put your brain in gear. It can be done if you are persistent and creative.

Sailing

You can find many ads that offer boating in exchange for your services and skills, and vice versa. For example, let's say that you want a cruise to Cabo San Lucas. Just check the list of *Men Needing Crew In Mexico* and their specifications. If you fit, you may have the opportunity for the experience of a lifetime! And who says that you have to stop at just one cruise—it could become your way of life. And the more you sail, the more experience you can offer to a prospective cruiser!

This is typical of the often overlooked possibilities in this world. The more you read, especially in rather specialized publications, the more chances there are that you can find exactly what you want at a price you can afford.

If you want more information, I suggest you write to *Latitude 38*, Box 1678, Sausalito, CA 94966.

Health is Your Responsibility

❝Health is wealth.❞ —Anonymous

❝What can a sick man say but that he is sick.❞ —Samuel Johnson

Introduction

Who is the best doctor you know? It's yourself. All you have to do is apply common sense to your daily life, and you won't need those pills.

Let's take a look at a group of people who are world–famous for health and vigor as well as longevity. They are the Hunzas, who live in the shadow of the towering Himalayas. They breath pure air, drink mineral–rich glacier water and enjoy a diet consisting mainly of grains, fruits and vegetables. Meat is a rarity. Their real love is apricots—fresh or dried—including the vitamin–rich apricot–seed kernel.

Investigators have found that the Hunzas not only live eight or nine decades or more, they enjoy robust health during each and every one of those years. After all, the quality of life is more important than the quantity, but if you can have both, why not?

Obviously, what we are advocating in this entire book is to learn to live a healthy life as well as one that is frugal. And it's really no accident that the two are not only compatible but symbiotic and synergistic.

As may be seen from the brief description of the Hunza lifestyle, health is not really difficult or complicated to achieve. Most of it consists of *letting go* of things and situations we really don't need. Who needs a giant house with a thirty–year mortgage (millstone)? Who needs one of those throwaway cars that must be replaced just as the last payment is made? And who needs to live amidst confusion and congestion when *there is so much of the world that is both beautiful and quiet*?

So what we'll be considering is alternatives to the corporate imperatives. But in addition to that basic principle, here are some basic requirements for good health.

Diet

You are what you eat, no question. Every cell in your entire body depends on your bloodstream, and it better contain the things the body really needs. That means

189

eliminating weird chemicals and ingesting only what nature really intended you to have.

Alan Hopkins Nittler, M.D., created one of the most compact and efficient guides to good diet I've ever seen. Follow it closely, and I guarantee that you will feel better in days. And if you stick to it religiously, there's no question that you'll be as healthy as diet can make you.

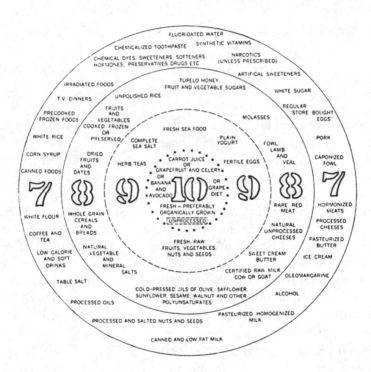

Your Attitude

You could eat nothing but yogurt, wheat germ and sunflower seeds and still get an ulcer. What you are thinking is equally or perhaps even more important than what you are eating. Negative thoughts and a harried lifestyle will put you in the hospital faster than a speeding bullet. Conversely, if you live a tranquil life with copable stress, you'll outlive your doctor. And remember that stress isn't "out there" somewhere, it's *inside of you*. It is your reaction to any situation or circumstance that makes the difference. As Marcus Aurelius said, "Nothing is either good or bad. It's thinking that makes it so."

Exercise

Try carrying a good arm around in a sling for a few days. Soon it will have less strength than a wet noodle. "Use it or lose it" is the watchword where your body's muscular–skeletal system is concerned. Every bookstore in the country is awash with books on how to exercise, but your really don't need them. Just take a good walk every day, do some lifting to keep those arms limber and strong, practice deep breathing, and stretch like a cat. It can be as simple as that, since that's what I do, and I feel like 23 instead of 63!

Occupation

Zen has it best: *"To do is to be and to be is to do."* Thus, whatever you find yourself doing for a living or otherwise determines largely what kind of person you are. Compare, for instance, the harassed salesman who's on commission only. Every day is like frontline combat as he seeks to zero in on a hapless client. No wonder Arthur Miller chose that profession as one that invited tragedy. Sure, we all sell something to make a living: goods or services. However, we don't have to try to live under *constant* pressure to outperform ourselves.

While it is true that the stress of life is present in doing everything (including doing nothing, by the way), one can be selective and try for an occupation that is not damaging to one's health.

The solid principle behind this book is, again, "It's much easier to *save* a dollar than it is to *earn* one." So every time you make a saving, you're relieving yourself of the pressure to go out and hustle.

Recreation

Ever notice how many American recreational activities are competitive? Football, baseball, tennis and even sedentary golf depend on having a better score. In Israel, they play a game of keeping a small ball in the air and the object is to make your fellow players look good. How much more humanistic that is than constantly trying to beat the other guy.

My own recreational preferences are motorcycling in scenic regions, flying (when I can afford it), touring the world in a camper or trailer, or preferably both. Not only do I stay close to nature in this way, I constantly learn about this fascinating planet.

What I have sought to combine is work and play, an occupation that incorporates recreation, and in many instances I've been successful. For example, for a number of years I've been able to tour thermal springs and write about them in a series of books. Could you do the same? Of course!

Vitamins, Minerals, Supplements and Herbs

There's a lot of debate on whether we really need the above items. Some physicians and lay people swear by them; others at them. My own view is to give them a try, and, if they make you feel and perform better, take them. Be sure you know the source of each item and whether they are *fresh*. Stale, lifeless, devitalized, rancid *anything* can be harmful.

Philosophy and Religion

We've left this for last because it's an appropriate subject to summarize an over-all health concept. In examining the writings of Swedenborg, we find these classic principles:

(1) that God is impersonal and unitarian, the life–giving force which exists in the universe and which is shared by every creature that inhabits it; God, in fact, is the substance of the cosmos;

(2) that no one is redeemed by the vicarious atonement of a Godman, but that every human being may create in himself, by ethical conduct, which he is free to embrace or reject, a character which will fit him for blessed immortality;

(3) that the Bible is throughout the word of God, but that it possesses a spiritual sense which cannot rightly be understood except through an inspired interpretation which reveals its true significance, often quite at variance with its literal meaning;

(4) that whatever we become on earth we continue to be after death—in short, we will take it with us;

(5) that if we practice the best ethical code of our own society, there need be no fear of punishment hereafter;

(6) that productive activity, both intellectual and material, is the highest ideal of the ethical man;

(7) that the neighbor is all mankind and that we best express our love for him in performing useful and reciprocal services;

(8) that the highest charity consists in dealing honestly with our fellow men and in doing our work well at all times; and that the comforts of life may be enjoyed and wealth obtained by methods completely just and virtuous;

(9) that the pursuit, possession, and temporal enjoyment of material comforts and even luxuries are highly laudable, so long as these are obtained through honest service to our fellows or the creation of social wealth, and so long as the money so gained is not the sole or the principal objective;

(10) that the Second Coming consists simply in the proclamation of reconstituted Christianity; and that the New Jerusalem, of which we read in Revelation, is that reconstituted church;

(11) that the Last Judgement and the Parousia are purely spiritual events, consummated without the cognizance of the people on earth;

(12) that there is a universal, vitalizing, and beneficent influx or emanation from God—the central sun of the universe—which, if we allow it to flow into ourselves, fills us with vigor, health, and moral virtue;

(13) that the failure or refusal to accept this divine influx is simply a failure on the part of our understanding or a misuse of our free will; thus, sin is really only a form of error or ignorance;

(14) that sickness and disease, whether mental or physical, are caused by lustful thoughts, evil desires, or corrosive hatred, which destroy a person's peace of mind and, *transferred to the bodily functions* bring on every form of malady and illness;

(15) that sickness may be cured and eliminated from the body by permitting the divine influx to permeate our beings entirely;

(16) that both heaven and hell exist within us as subjective states, which are simply transferred to the next life at the transition called death;

(17) that the punishments which ultimately overtake the wicked are self–inflicted; and

(18) all this being true, that a scientific religion is demonstrably possible which has, as its objective, the well–being, health, happiness, success, and prosperity of its communicants in this life and an immortality of joyous activity and pleasure for eternity.

Can our minds really make the difference between sickness and health, disease and total wellness? There's increasing proof that the universe is more a great thought than a great machine. On this foundation one can build a strong case for alliance with the concept that we are really manifestations of spirit. If that is true, then health does begin in your mind as does sickness. It's up to you to choose what it will be. If you are enjoying your life, then it's apparent you would choose to continue it. But if you are under constant harassment, perhaps illness is a socially acceptable way of bowing out.

In closing, I recall a surgeon once telling me that very seldom do happy people get cancer; so it's apparent that how you live your life determines its quality.

"If you have good health, you are young at any age." —Old Proverb

The Best Ways to Create Your Own Fountain of Youth Nutritionally

Here are several ways to stay young if you are already young, and to achieve greater youthfulness if you are older.

Vitamin C

There is only one vitamin that the body can't synthesize: Vitamin C. Thus, you need to keep yourself supplied with this vital metabolic building block. Here are just a few reasons:

1. Vitamin C has a stimulating effect on all glandular activity, helping to produce the hormones that keep one youthful.

2. Vitamin C protects you from being poisoned both internally and externally.

3. It keeps collagen, the cellular cement, healthy. Thus, your skin won't lose its smooth, tight appearance.

4. It can help prevent atherosclerosis, the leading cause of heart attacks.

5. It is important to the functioning of sex glands in both men and women.

Thus, if you want to look and feel younger almost immediately, up your intake of C, both from natural sources like rose hips or oranges or from taking ascorbic acid stirred up in fruit juice.

Open Sesame

Widely used in the Middle East and considered a staple food rather than something you toss on a baking bun, sesame seeds:

- Have more calcium than milk.

- Contain more protein than meat.

- Are loaded with unsaturated fatty acids, vitamins B and E.

- Offer the key element of lecithin.

- Taste great in many ways: as a garnish, an oil, in a sauce called tahini and even as a healthy candy.

Try this on your sugar–freaks. It's called halvah and is sold in many health–food stores, but you can make your own. Grind a cup of sesame seeds and mix with two teaspoons of honey until it forms a stiff dough. Smooth out in small pan about 1/4–inch thick and cut into bars after chilling.

Kefir

Kefir, a cultured milk, has been consumed for centuries in countries where the longevity records are indicative of long–term health. Somewhat similar to yogurt but thinner in consistency, it can be made in your own kitchen by using what are known as "kefir grains" which last indefinitely. If your local health–food store doesn't stock them, try RAJ, P.O. Box 167, Blue Point, NY, 11715.

One of the main benefits of kefir is that it has a high nutritive value due to the abundance of yeast cells. More information may be obtained by reading Beatrice Trum Hunter's book, *Fact Book on Yogurt, Kefir and Other Milk Products*, available in your library or from Keats Publishing Co,. 212 Elm Street, New Canaan, CT 06840

Multi–grain Cereal

Grind one–fourth cup each of the following grains in your blender: whole wheat, whole rye, whole oats, whole barley, whole millet. Add a tablespoon each of bran and raisins. Shake well, and you have the makings of several fine breakfasts, chock full of health and vigor. Be sure and store in sealed jar until used. To cook, simply add twice the quantity of water and simmer for thirty minutes until tender but not mushy. Eat immediately with skim milk, add chopped fruit or nuts. The contribution of each grain will make for a bountiful nutritional feast for your entire body.

Bircher–Benner Apple Muesli

People with ailments spend thousands of dollars to travel to the famous Bircher–Benner Clinic in Switzerland where the emphasis is on fresh raw foods. You can stay at home and make one of their most popular and rejuvenating dishes. Soak two tablespoons of regular rolled oats (not instant) in twice the quantity of water overnight. In the morning, shred two apples and add to the oats along with two tablespoons of chopped almonds and skim milk and honey to taste. Stir vigorously and eat immediately.

A breakfast like this each morning will soon have you bounding out of bed. It's the antithesis of the junk breakfasts purveyed by supermarkets. A sprinkle of wheat germ and bran makes this an even better energizer.

Sprouts, the Living Food

If your goal is to remain slender and youthful and have boundless energy, then sprouts must be in your diet. We've discussed these at length in another part of this book, but it's worth a reminder here in the health section. An interesting aspect of sprouts is that they yield more protein than meat on a weight–for–weight basis.

Nutritional Yeast

Often called "brewers" yeast, this is one of the best sources of B–vitamins and trace minerals. Inexpensive in terms of food value, it should be in your daily diet to keep your nervous system in top condition. Just add a tablespoon or two to fruit juice or raw milk and stir.

Sunflower Seeds

Do you know what parrots eat? Sunflower seeds and water. And on this diet alone, they live longer than any other bird on this planet—often to 100 years or more. Just be sure they're fresh, as any oil seed can become rancid, especially if they're broken.

Pumpkin Seeds

One of the best–tasting seeds I know, this one can assure the integrity of your glandular system long beyond the point where non–seed eaters have given up the active life.

Sauerkraut

It's interesting that in countries where people live to be a hundred years old or more they consume a lot of fermented foods. One of the best and cheapest is sauerkraut, which you can make yourself. You'll need a ceramic or glass container and cabbage, plus a few optional items. In its simplest form, sauerkraut consists of thinly sliced cabbage that has been placed in a non–metallic container and allowed to ferment for three or four weeks. If you'd like added flavor, sprinkle a few hot pepper slices between layers or add a sprinkle of freshly ground cumin seed. Strips of raw vegetables can be used because they will be preserved by the sauerkraut juice that is formed in the process. Here's the step–by–step instructions:

1. Place sliced cabbage in the container, compressing tightly.

2. When full, cover with clean cloth and weight with a stone.

3. Let ferment for several weeks, periodically removing resultant foam and adding clean cloth.

4. When fermented, store in refrigerator in glass jars.

It's better for you to eat raw but it can be cooked in many ways. Keeps almost indefinitely and thus makes a great winter vegetable.

Rye Bread

Why do Russian peasants live so long? Part of it may be due to that wonderful coarse, tasty Russian rye that we sometimes find in the market. But you can make it yourself and thus enjoy good health and save money simultaneously. Here's how:

Mix eight cups of freshly ground rye flour with three cups warm water and a half cup of sourdough. You can make this yourself by simply leaving a saucer of flour and water in a warm place. Natural yeasts will create leavening as if by magic. Alternatively, you can buy sourdough starter in many specialty food stores. It lasts indefinitely if you keep feeding and using it.

Let the mixture of flour, water and sourdough stand overnight. If too wet, add more flour and mix well. Place in baking pans and allow to rise until double in bulk. An unlit oven is a good place for rising dough. Bake for about one hour in a 350° F oven. Remove and cool on wire rack. This bread will not only be tasty, but will provide a workout for your teeth also. It's delicious when spread with sweet butter or cream cheese and fantastic caraway–seeded Monterey Jack cheese.

What to Leave Out

It's as important to avoid some foods as it is to eat others:

- Anything white…sugar, flour, margarine and so forth.
- Coffee, tea, salt.
- Anything highly refined and adulterated.
- Any foods that are canned, preserved or irradiated.
- Foods that have been sprayed, coated or otherwise treated.

Staying far away from your local supermarket can be the wisest move you can possibly make.

> **"**O health, health. It is the blessing of the rich, the riches of the poor. Who can buy thee at too dear a price since there is no enjoying this world without thee?**"**
>
> —Ben Jonson, *Volpone*

Rice Polish

Few people have tried this "waste" product. To make rice more appealing and whiter, all the valuable outer layers are removed—exactly the part of rice that contains most of its valuable food value. It's sold to gas stations to soak up oil, but fortunately some of it reaches health–food stores. A bland product, it will add high–quality nutrition to your cereals and baked goods. Inexpensive and long–lasting, it should be on your shelf at all times.

Wheat Germ

The germ of wheat is the part that contains the oil, vitamin E and other nutritives. Just be sure when you buy it that it's fresh; wheat germ deteriorates quickly, so it must be refrigerated or it will turn rancid and bitter. In the better health–food stores, you'll find it in their refrigerator, so keep it in yours. If you consume a lot of whole–grain wheat, you're getting the germ at its best and freshest, so you won't need to buy additional supplies of the germ alone—another telling point for the strategy of eating *whole* foods rather than components. In that way you get all the nutrients just as nature intended.

Garlic

The Greeks and Romans were convinced that garlic was the cure for many diseases, and that conviction has survived to this day. Fresh garlic can be used in salads, pasta sauces, vegetable dishes and even baked whole in the oven to make a delicious buttery spread. Surprisingly, it loses very little of its nutritional value by being cooked, only the sharp flavor and the characteristic odor. Among the many benefits of garlic are the following:

- It has been found effective in preventing and treating cancer.

- It lowers blood pressure, probably through dilating arteries.

- It can help cure various respiratory infections and prevent colds.

- Generous amounts in your diet can prevent or relieve arthritis.

- Fresh garlic daily can act as a liver and blood cleanser.

What could be better than to have such a delicious bulb add so much flavor to your foods and at the same time be so healthy? Lately the price has fallen due to larger amounts being grown, so stock up!

Lecithin

A natural substance derived mainly from soybeans. Its major use is as an emulsifier, but it has also been found to reduce cholesterol in the human body, as well as arterial plaques. It may be purchased as an oil or in granular form. Either way, it's easy to use by just adding it to blended drinks, baked goods or as a preventive for foods sticking while cooking. Stores better if refrigerated.

Honey

A far superior sweetener than white sugar, since it contains vitamins and minerals, honey is a complete food for bees. It's sweeter than sugar so you use less in recipes. (You'll note throughout this book that honey is the preferred sweetening agent.) Among honey's features are:

- It contains a high percentage of fructose (40%), a preferred sweetening agent;

- It is a natural product, unlike refined white sugar;

- The two main sugars, glucose and fructose, are predigested; thus honey can be a quick energy source;

- Older people with digestive problems can better assimilate honey.

One caution. Be careful where you buy your honey. It's possible to get honey that has been diluted with ordinary sugar. So be sure of your sources.

Kelp

This usually appears in the form of a dried powder and is made from seaweed. Kelp is unique in that it contains almost every mineral known. Keep it in a shaker to add to foods such as salads, baked potatoes and soups or stews. It adds flavor and nutrition and takes the place of salt and pepper.

Sea Salt

You'll notice that in recipes throughout this book salt is never mentioned. This is because it's not needed and is harmful in large quantities. If you feel you must use some salt in your diet, at least make it sea salt, which contains some trace minerals and is usually free from the additives in regular salt.

Dry Milk Powder

Inexpensive because you eliminate the high cost of transporting plain water, milk powder can be used in cooking, to make yogurt or to mix drinks. Add a bit of pure vanilla and a smidgin of honey to improve flavor. Blending makes a frothy drink to which can be added nutritional yeast, lecithin, and other health–promoting supplements.

Bran

In David Reuben's book, *The Save Your Life Diet*, he proves beyond doubt that it is lack of adequate fiber in the American diet that causes much disease and death. A simple fix is to add a couple of tablespoons of bran to your cereal, baked goods, soups or stews. It is low in cost, keeps almost indefinitely and actually tastes quite good, so there's no reason not to ensure your longevity and health with this easy–to–obtain real food. If you eat lots of whole grains you probably won't need bran, but why not make sure you have quality fiber anyway?

Carob

Most of us have grown up liking the taste of chocolate, which really is not too good for us. It's always mixed with lots of sugar and contains oxalic acid, which can throw off your chemical balance. A delicious substitute which, to me, tastes better than chocolate, is the powdered dark–brown bean from the St. John's tree, carob. Known as manna in biblical times, it is a nutritious food without the disadvantages of chocolate. Use it in cooking, drinks, and any way that you would use cocoa or chocolate. You'll save money and have a better diet.

Formulas for Good Health

The Rinse Formula

Atherosclerosis or hardening of the arteries has become one of the greatest threats to longevity. Plaques of calcium and other minerals gather on the artery walls, eventually closing them off. Short of getting a surgical "roto–rooter" job, what can be done? One method that has won support among holistic healers is the nonsurgical Rinse method. Developed by Dr. Jacobus Rinse, he used it to clear up his own arteries.

You can make it in your own home from ingredients from your local health food store. This recipe makes two cups, and it's advisable to keep it in your refrigerator. Mix 1/2–cup each of bran, rolled oats and wheat germ with 3/8–cup of lecithin and 1/8–cup of sunflower seeds, plus one tablespoon each of nutritional yeast and bone meal. Serve with fruit, nuts and skim milk that has been blended with a teaspoon of safflower or other polyunsaturated oil.

If you know of anyone with angina pain, this could be their salvation, since that anguish usually accompanies diminished arterial flow. It's certainly worth a try since the cost is low and the side effects are zero.

Ana Aslan's Age–Reversing Strategy

Dr. Aslan of Hungary has worked for many years in the area of aging and has developed a remedy for what is, inevitably, a problem for all of us who reach our senior years. The problem is a gradual reduction of our physical and mental capacities, depression and stresses that only the older generation can know.

The good doctor discovered that a mixture of procaine hydrochloride (you know it as Novocaine, a dental anesthetic), several other chemicals and vitamin/mineral complexes administered in tablet form not only arrested aging, but provided the stimulus for the efficient metabolic processes.

You may have read of this remedy under the names *GH–3* or *KH–3*, since several books have discussed it at great length. If you have further interest, check your local library for copies.

The formula, for those who like to do it themselves:

To make yourself: (per tablet)	mg.
Procaine hydrochloride	46.
Dimethylaminoethanol bitartrate (DMAE)	20.
Calcium hydrogenphosphate	100.
Calcium pentothenate	5.
Mono–magnesium DL–aspartate	30.
Iron (II) sulphate	10.
Nicotinic acid amide	15.
Folic acid	.10
Vitamin A	1000.
Vitamin B1	.75
Vitamin B2	.8
Vitamin B5	1.
Vitamin B12	.003
Vitamin C	30.
Vitamin E	15.

The ingredients can be obtained from any complete chemical supplier, particularly those devoted to research. A source I have used is Sigma Chemical, P.O. Box 14508, St. Louis, MO 63178.

I have tried it with good results. Taken (one per day), it would not be harmful, and it is certainly worth a try since the benefits can be so great.

The Fresh Air Cure

Got the blahs? Life becoming a drag? Always fatigued?

Here's a suggestion from an M.D. who has studied the problem. Move to an area where there is abundant fresh air—central Nevada, northern British Columbia (avoid paper mill towns), Newfoundland. Alternatively, buy cylinders of purified air from a hospital supply company and fill you house with something besides an atmospheric garbage dump.

If fresh air doesn't revive you, then you can try some of the other fixes that follow.

Desiccated Liver

There is a dye, once widely used, called "butter yellow." It can produce liver cancer in rats in five months. In an experiment, one group of rats was fed butter yellow and rice, the other group the same diet plus 10 percent desiccated liver. The first group all died of cancer while the group protected by the liver survived. Since 70 percent of all cancer is caused by chemical pollutants in our environment, it makes sense to give yourself all the protection you can get.

Be sure that the desiccated liver you get is not from American beef liver. That's full of harmful chemicals. Get your dried liver from out of the country where they don't inject hormones and other junk into their cattle.

Herbal Healing

Long before there was an ethical drug business, people employed natural herbs to ease their pains and restore their health. Fortunately, there has been a renaissance of interest in herbal remedies with the publication of such books as:

Back to Eden by Jethro Kloss
Stalking the Healthful Herbs by Euell Gibbons
Earth Medicine by Michael Weiner

You'll probably find these and others in your local library or bookshop. Here's a sampling of what you'll learn:

Sore throat: A tea made from slippery elm or white pine needles is helpful.

Sedative: Ordinary hops used in making beer can be used as a tea for a calming effect. Wild lettuce is used for the same purpose.

Rheumatism: Appalachian folk practitioners have used a wine made from pokeweed berries to alleviate this ailment.

Laxative: Boil cascara sagrada bark and drink for a natural way to regularity.

Kidney Ailments: Indians made a tea from bearberry or milkweed to stimulate the kidneys.

Insomnia: Forget the drugstore remedies and try a teaspoonful of powdered lady's slipper root in a glass of warm water. As a medical botanist once said, "It produces beneficial effects in all nervous diseases and hysterical afflictions by allaying pain, quieting the nerves and promoting restful sleep."

Goldenseal: This perennial herb is used as a tonic, stimulant and astringent. I've heard it makes a great blood cleanser.

Chaparral: This desert bush has been used by Indians for centuries to prevent or cure cancer. The tea is rather bitter, but a taste for it can be acquired as I've discovered.

American Hemp and Dogbane: Both have been used for heart and circulatory problems.

Hair: Have you noticed how most Indians have a fine head of hair? Perhaps it's because they use such natural herbs as Apache plume, scouring rush and columbine as shampoos and hair conditioners.

Ear ache: The Kickapoo Indians of Wisconsin used crushed and steeped mescal beans for this problem. The strained, warm liquid was poured into the ailing ear.

Hawthorn Berries: Great for regulating the heart and eliminating palpitations.

There are many herbs for many ailments, these are just starters. Before you take any synthetic drug, why not try the natural way of herbs? They are available in many health–food stores or by mail. Check your local telephone directory.

> "In the history of science and medicine, there is no instance known of any chronic or metabolic disease that has ever been cured or prevented except by factors, water or oil soluble, normal to the diet and/or to the animal economy."
>
> —Dr Ernest Krebs, Jr.

Laetrile

The word is a buzz word. It has been plastered on post–office walls, reviled against in the media, and targeted for the most vehement put–down campaigns by the medical establishment. And yet, the strangest event has occurred recently. The AMA, which fought its use with all its great power, now admits it to their pharmacopia under other names.

Laetrile is the extracted form of amygdalin usually derived from apricot kernels. It is also known as B–17, a vitamin. It has been used successfully in the treatment of many kinds of cancer. And it was this success that brought down the wrath of the medical hierarchy which claims that only surgery, radiation and chemotherapy are effective in the treatment of cancer. They were especially wrathful since the "cut, burn and poison" methods haven't proven themselves. More than a thousand Americans are dying every twenty–four hours from cancer despite all that orthodox medicine can do with their billions of dollars worth of equipment.

Few people are aware of these facts:

1. If you go the "cut/burn/poison" route, you have only a 7.5 percent chance to survive five years.

2. People with cancer who undergo *no* treatment by conventional means live up to four times longer than those who are treated.

Dr. Alan Nittler once told me that prevention of cancer was one thousand times easier than its cure, and that it's possible to avoid cancer by eating foods rich in natural laetrile or B17.

Here's a list:

- Kernels or seeds of fruit, particularly apricot. While bitter, they can be ground up in a health drink.

- Beans of all kinds including lentils (sprouted), lima, mung (sprouted), chickpea, scarlet runner.

- Nuts—bitter almond, macadamia, cashew.

- Berries, including all wild species, blackberry, chokeberry, cranberry, elderberry, raspberry, strawberry.

- Seeds—chia, flax and sesame.

- Grasses—acacia, alfalfa, (sprouted) aquatic, Johnson, milkweed, Sudan, tunus, velvet, wheat grass, white and red clover.

- Grains, including oat groats, barley, brown rice, buckwheat groats, chia, flax, millet, vetch, wheat berries.

- Miscellaneous, including bamboo shoots, fuchsia plants, sorghum, wild hydrangea, yew tree (needles and fresh leaves).

Naturally, you would want to consume the right amount. If you ate three apples, seeds and all, you would probably have the right amount of B–17. About one apricot kernel for each ten pounds of body weight per day would be sufficient.

It took many years for the British Navy to learn that scurvy could be prevented with ease by ingesting a small amount of Vitamin C each day. How long will it take for Americans to learn that B–17 in their daily diet can eliminate the cancer epidemic? Not long if many people check with these sources of information:

Freedom From Cancer, by M. L. Culbert, '76 Press, P.O. Box 2686, Seal Beach, CA 90740.

The Committee For Freedom of Choice in Cancer Therapy, Inc., 146 Main Street, Suite 408, Los Altos, CA 94022.

The Two Best Health Guarantees I Know

1. *Create an interesting life for yourself.* Eliminate boredom. Do what *you* want to do, not what other people tell you that you should do. Remember, to be is to do, and vice versa. All the organic food in the world won't help if you're trapped in some boring office job or routine factory slot. Nor will diet help if you are constantly under emotional stresses or financial pressure. There are ways to leave them behind, as we discuss in our lifestyle alternatives section.

   This is the most important aspect of health, as I have learned by actual living experiences. Everything else is subordinate to what you are doing inside your head on a day–to–day basis. If you are frustrated, uncreative, bored and thwarted in self–fulfillment, then don't expect to be healthy no matter what else you do. It is worth all the effort you give to achieving freedom and the opportunity to let yourself *grow*! Remember, like plants, we're either growing or going.

2. *Your body is constantly being rebuilt from the foods you eat, the water you drink, and the air your breathe.* Through cell replacement, you get a new heart every two months, so be sure that it is built from quality ingredients. Just like assuring yourself of good food for the mind in what you do, make sure that the food for the body is equally nourishing and satisfying. Whole grains, fresh vegetables and fruits, raw milk and homemade items are well within almost anyone's reach. As we've shown elsewhere, they are not only cheaper, but better, and you

can nearly always grow your own fresh foods even in an urban environment. The easy way out is a packaged goodie from the local convenience store, but your body knows the difference and will soon tell you about it in the form of severe complaints. So take the time and trouble to put the best food you can possibly get into your body.

Julie

Julie was dying of cancer. A quiet, thoughtful woman, she had been successful as a real–estate entrepreneur and lived in a posh apartment on Wilshire Boulevard in Los Angeles. A mutual friend suggested that I might be able to help her in some way; a nutritional cure perhaps. So I visited her and suggested that she and her husband drive up the coast with me—a change of scene and some fresh air would supplement any other healing modes.

We took my camper because it had lots of room, a place to rest and freshen up, and was ruggedly built for the terrain I had in mind. I drove the couple to one of my favorite spots; a large swimming hole on the Santa Ynez River a few miles outside Santa Barbara. Willows, cottonwoods, and sycamore grow in thick stands along the river, but here and there are sandy beaches decorated with granite and sandstone cobblestones. As a backdrop to the pool, a lush growth of cattails merges into a picture–pretty hillside reaching up to a blue sky.

I couldn't get Julie or her husband to swim with me, so I dove in anyway. The water was absolutely perfect, perhaps 72° F. They watched while I cavorted. After a good swim, I dried off and began preparing a simple lunch from the camper fridge. A vegetable salad with some tuna, olives and chopped red onions, accompanied by slices of hearty Russian rye bread. We sat around the picnic table enjoyng the food, the warm breezes, the sight of dragonflies skimming the still water. Occasionally a swallow would dip his beak in swift flight and scoop up a tiny drink.

Julie took it all in without saying anything, but I knew what she was thinking. It was on her face as plainly as though it were written there. She was stunned by the realization that *there had never been any good reason to work so hard*—hard enough to end up with a serious disease. All she needed was to acquire a small camper, and the world would be hers to enjoy. The money for gas and food could be earned in any number of nonstressful ways. Finally she said, "Do you...live like this a lot? I mean just traveling around, swimming, going where you want and so forth?

"Isn't that what life's all about?" I went on to explain that I had learned to *minimize "things"* so as to *maximize free time*. "Satchidananda says it best," I said. "Give up the drop and gain the whole ocean."

I drove them back down the coast as the sun slowly set into the Pacific, and some months later I learned that Julie had died quietly. Although it had been too late for her to change, perhaps it won't be for others who read this true story.

Epilogue

In Kazan's book, *The Arrangement*, he says:

"This society is insane. All of it—the customs, the work, the hours devoted to work, the way people spoke to each other without looking, the homes they lived in, the streets they walked, the air, the noise, the filth, the bread—all the basics."

Happy to report, this situation is changing: People are buying boats, building small hideaways in the forests of America, traveling as a way of life. I see this transformation as a true "greening of America."

Will you be part of this greening? It is entirely up to you!

"Life is not a spectacle or feast; it is a predicament." —Santayana

Getting a Handle On Life

If you read a book of quotations, you'll find that life is defined in myriad ways: Life is (among other things):

A bowl of cherries	Anonymous
A sojourn in a strange land	Aurelius
A walking shadow	Shakespeare
Like an autumn leaf	Wilde
Just one damned thing after another	O'Malley
Vain	Montenaeken
Short	Montenaeken
Can be bitter	Masefield
An adventure in experience	Peattie
Is real, earnest	Longfellow
Just the stuff to try the soul's strength on	Browning
All a cheat	Dryden
A jest and all things show it	Gay
Worth living? Depends on the liver	Anonymous
Made up of sobs and sniffles	O. Henry
A hassle	John F. Kennedy

There are thousands of other definitions—and millions more if you were to ask people for their interpretation. But one thing is sure: No two people agree on just what life *really* is. However, there is some agreement on how one can put a handle on it. Of all the books I've read on this subject, two stand out:

Psychocybernetics, by Maxwell Maltz, M.D.

How to Live 365 Days a Year, by John Schindler, M.D.

These writers are in close agreement as to what can be done to not only cope with life but to make the most of it. For example, Maltz points out that everything we learn in life is by trial and error—walking, riding a bicycle, playing tennis, making love or money. Naturally, we make lots of mistakes until finally we learn how to make a "hit" or succeed. To continue to be successful, we have to remember what we did that gave us that achievement. How ridiculous, both men agree, to constantly recall our *errors* and *mistakes*. And yet, this is what many people do. They mope around criticizing themselves for what they did or didn't do. "I failed yesterday, therefore, it follows that I'll fail again today," is the way Maltz puts it. And Schindler has this to say: "The present and future depend on learning new habits and new ways of looking at old problems. There simply isn't any future in digging continually into the past."

The secret key to being successful is to

Ignore Past Failures and Forge Ahead

Maltz points out that:

Hypnosis furnishes convincing proof. When a shy, timid wallflower is told in hypnosis and believes or "thinks" that he is a bold, self–confident orator, his reaction patterns are changed instantly! He currently acts as he currently believes. His attention is given over completely to the positive desired goal and no thought or consideration whatsoever is given to past failures.

Marilyn Ferguson, in her wonderful book, *The Aquarian Conspiracy* says,

The past is not our potential.

Just think, while you are reading these words you can, if you really want to, *completely change your way of life.* If you're a smoker, you can toss those cancer sticks out the window and never smoke again (I did when I was 39—then a three–pack–a–day smoker—and have never smoked since). You can get up and quit your health–destroying job and forge a new life in another, more desirable region (I did when I was 41 and left a "safe" job for the adventurous life of a freelance writer). You can stop eating all those junk foods and completely restore your health. I regained my health and now feel 23 at 63! I mention my own experiences, not in boast, but to prove that Schindler and Maltz are absolutely right!

Once, while living at Tahoe, Jack Benny was giving one of his few live performances, and, in an interview, he said "Fuck the past." I got a kick out of this candid, ribald remark that, no doubt, was heartfelt. I really can't think of a more succinct and decisive way to express that imperative.

The Way to Wellness

The Green Light!

Try this simple test.

1. Rate yourself on a scale of one to ten where one is terrible and ten is terrific with respect to the way you feel about your life and your accomplishments.

2. Have there been times in your life when you were closer to ten?

3. What are the barriers and obstacles now holding you back? Make a list of at least ten.

4. Make a list of ways in which you could overcome the barriers and obstacles.

5. What would you be like and what could you accomplish if you had unlimited time, financial resources, and the physical and mental attributes necessary to your tasks? Write this in the form of a short essay.

6. What would be the payoffs that you would gain from this ideal state of affairs? List all you can think of.

7. Now rate yourself in terms of where you would be in six months and one year if all your fantasies come true through the hard work that it will take. Use the same scale as No. 1.

Summary: It's strange that by taking this self–evaluation, self–direction test you will find new strength and resolve simply because you wrote it all down! I did it myself, and it gave me the necessary impetus to get down to business and finish this book.

You Say You're Too Old To Start Something New?

Person	Accomplishment	At Age
Michelangelo	Best paintings	80+
Goethe	Wrote *Faust*	80+
Edison	Still inventing	Past 90
Shaw	Writing plays	Past 90
Grandma Moses	Started painting	At 79

Now what other excuses do you have to offer?

> ❝In the midst of spiritual bankruptcy came a new way of life. I asked myself, 'What are thou afraid of? What is the sum total of the worst that lies before thee? Death? Well, Death and say the pangs of Tophet too and all that the Devil and man may, will or can do against thee. Hast thou not a heart; canst thou not suffer whatso it be and as a child of freedom, trample Tophet under thy feet while it consumes thee. Let it come then, and I will meet and defy it!❞
>
> —Carlyle

The Big Three

Alan H. Nittler, Joseph Walters, and Henry Bieler had much in common. All three were MD's, tops in their field and dedicated to bringing in the coming era of health through good nutrition. Dr. Bieler was the pioneer of the three. Although surrounded by physicians who did little but prescribe drugs, he prescribed lightly cooked string beans and zucchini, allowing the body to heal itself with appropriate foods. His book, *Food is Your Best Medicine*, is a classic, and you should read it. There's a current printing in the bookstores, and, if not, try the library.

A doctor to many of the Hollywood stars, Joseph Walters eschewed vitamins in favor of pure foods containing the necessary elements of good health. He started a food company so that his parents could have the best that money can buy.

Until he was several years into his practice, Alan H. Nittler believed what he learned in medical school. But then the remarkable recovery of his dog through metabolic nutrition motivated him to study that field. His book, *A New Breed of Doctor,* was a best seller and contains a summary of the knowledge of all three healers. Again, find a copy and read it; by following its basic principles, regain and maintain good health.

Food is Your Best Medicine

Dr. Bieler was a student of the pioneers of the movement to find the real cause of disease. In this book, he quotes Sir James McKenzie, an English M.D.:

1. Diseases are the result of long–developing processes which begin early in life and finally lead to saturation of the body with toxins.

2. Improper eating, living and thinking habits are the prime cause of this degeneration.

3. The same type of toxin when localized in a joint causes arthritis; when localized in the liver, hepatitis; in the kidneys, nephritis; in the skin, dermatitis; in the pancreas, diabetes; in the brain, insanity.

And from Thomas Sydenham, called the English Hippocrates:

66Disease is nothing else but an attempt on the part of the body to rid itself of morbific matter.99

The Dutch clinician, Hermann Boerhaave, followed Sydenham's lead with:

66Disease is cured with the help of nature by neutralization and excretion of morbific matter.99

And just prior to Pasteur's day, Rudolf Virchow in his pioneer work on cellular pathology said:

66If I could live my life over again, I would devote it to proving that germs seek their natural habitat—diseased tissue—rather than being the cause of the diseased tissue; e.g., mosquitoes seek stagnant water but do not cause the pool to become stagnant.99

Dr. Bieler summarized his own conclusions thus:

"I have reached three conclusions:

1. The primary cause of disease is toxemia caused by improper foods which results in cellular impairment and breakdown.

2. The use of drugs to treat patients is harmful. Drugs often cause serious side effects and sometimes cause new diseases.

3. Disease can be cured by the use of correct foods."

He proved his conclusions in fifty years of successful practice during which time many people, who could afford any type of medical care, came to Bieler and left with gratitude.

Don't fail to find and read this book several times. Check your bookstore of library for it.

Health and Longevity Tips

In the USSR

The Russians have seven times the number of centenarians per million population than Americans and are known for endurance and good health. What do they eat: Their basic staples are the famous "black" or whole–grain bread and lots of cabbage, onions and potatoes. Millet or buckwheat cereal is a breakfast favorite, and meat is consumed once a week or less.

Shangri La?

The Hunzas of the Himalayas are free of cancer, heart disease, diabetes and most other degenerative diseases common in the West. Their diet? Grains (wheat, millet, barley and buckwheat), fruits (especially apricots), lots of vegetables, and very little meat. Certainly no refined foods.

Seventh Day Adventists

This religious group has a health program that specifies no smoking, no eating of meat, and no drinking of alcohol, coffee, tea or cola drinks. They also avoid sugar and refined starches. The result? A lung–cancer rate of practically zero, forty percent less coronary disease, and a mortality rate two times lower than that of the general American population.

Fasting

This therapy is practiced by our animal friends. I'm sure you've noticed that whenever a dog or cat is sick or injured, it takes no food at all.

And fasting is so simple and cheap. Here's why it works:

- Inferior tissue is consumed first, and that includes tumors and fat.

- The cleansing capacity of the eliminative organs is increased.

- Your digestive tract gets a much–needed rest.

- There is a regenerative and normalizing effect on all parts of the system.

Try this test. If you have any kind of chronic ailment, such as a skin problem, try a three–or four–day fast (water or liquids only) and see if the problem isn't alleviated, if not completely cured. After all, the body can react quickly if it's given the opportunity.

Spend Your Money on Health

My philosophy of life has been to spend whatever funds I have on having fun, learning, and simply enjoying each day as it comes. I call this my "investment in health," and, to date, it has paid off handsomely. I have the most precious possession in the world—good health. I play tennis, hillclimb with my motorcycle and even change a split–rim tire! So instead of saving up for pills and potions, doctors and disease, invest in *joy*!

The Two Most Common Complaints

If you read the publications sent to doctors, you'll see ads that picture a doctor and his patient with the latter saying something like:

"It's just that I feel anxious and depressed." The ad goes on to prescribe one of the new drugs that will *suppress* these symptoms, not really *cure* them.

Interestingly, the side effects of these drugs often produce exactly what the drug is supposed to prevent! For example, Valium, which is supposed to relieve anxiety, often causes it. Furthermore, dependency on a drug often fosters a sense of weakness and defeat for the patient. To not be able to function in life without popping a pill has to be one of the most negative conditions there is.

So what hope is there? Plenty, according to two doctors, David Sheinkin and Michael Schacter, who have authored the book *Food, Mind and Mood*. In a series of actual case histories, they prove beyond any doubt that what you eat can influence your mood.

Mr. B was a chemist in his mid–forties and complained of having felt depressed for seventeen years. This state of mind was initiated by an acute attack of anxiety at a company staff meeting. The doctors diagnosed him as a hypoglycemic (low blood sugar) and prescribed a two–fold approach: elimination of certain foods including milk and the introduction of minerals into his diet. Within a matter of days, Mr. B's depression lifted and never returned.

It might be possible to argue that Mr. B had faith in Sheinkin and Schacter and that diet had nothing to do with it; however, in a test it was found that by drinking milk, the depression returned.

If you have a health problem, there's a simple approach that costs nothing: Fast for a day or two and then introduce foods one at a time. If a reaction occurs when you eat a certain food, you may have the culprit identified. Another method is called kinesiologic testing, which you can do in your home for free. It involves testing muscle strength with and without certain foods held in the mouth. The two MDs admit that the exact mechanism of this type of test is not totally understood, but it does delineate food–allergy problems accurately. I strongly recommend this avant–garde book. If not in your library, try the publisher or a used–book store. It could be that your pill–popping days will be over!

Two Cents a Day to Keep the Doctor Away

The Key to Survival We All Throw Away

Dr. David Reuben is the author of a number of best–sellers including *Everything You Wanted to Know About Sex*, and *The Save Your Life Recipe Book*. (His *Everything You Wanted to Know About Nutrition* didn't make the bestseller list because it offended the major food interests.)

The book that you should read as soon as possible is *The Save Your Life Recipe Book*. To prevent such diseases as:

Cancer of the colon and rectum

Heart disease

Diverticular disease of the colon

Appendicitis

Phlebitis and resulting blood clots to the lungs

Obesity

all you need do is add two to three tablespoons of ordinary bran to your daily diet. It's that simple. Adding this roughage may eliminate constipation and its related problems. This amount of bran would cost around two cents and would be no problem to add to such things as drinks, baked goods or cereals. Try it and see if you don't fell better just knowing that the protection of roughage is part of your daily routine.

With more than 100,000,000 Americans suffering from being overweight, Reuben's *High–Roughage Reducing Diet*, which is in the book, is most appropriate. The basics involve:

- Reduction of the amount of low–roughage foods or those heavily refined.

- A diet high in such high–roughage foods as whole–grain cereals, high–fiber fruits and vegetables and nuts and seeds.

- Eliminating anything synthetic or imitation.

- The bran as specified above on a daily basis.

Reuben points out that one can eat all one wishes of the specified foods because they are really nonfattening. So, at last, a diet that eliminates the hunger pangs! And proof is offered by pointing out that obesity is seldom a problem in cultures where the diet is "high–roughage."

In summary: a simple change can ensure your health for your entire life, and this one is so easy and cheap it would be foolish *not* to try it.

> Cancer has been called a disease of civilization. The more primitive a society and the simpler its diet, the less the incidence of cancer.

The Cancer Answer

In her book of that title, Maureen Salaman says:

The principal mechanism of the body's defense against a foreign substance is its reserve of white blood cells, continually circulating throughout the body; they have the ability to destroy invading viruses or even errant deviating cells if they are recognized. The first malignant cancer cell should be destroyed at this point. However, science now recognizes that the cancer cell wraps itself in a protein coating having the same electrical charge as the white cells. The two identical charges repel each other. The cancer cell, in this clever protective disguise, could remain unattacked and free to proliferate, were it not for another marvelous mechanism: the enzymes that continuously circulate in our bloodstreams and have the ability to dissolve the protein coat from the malignant cell. Once robbed of this protective coating, the cells are recognized and overwhelmed by the white cells. This, then, is the body's intrinsic method of ridding itself of malignancies.

You can read about enzymes in Chapter 7 of this same remarkable book. You'll also learn:

- A simple rule–of–thumb to maintain a cancer–free body (eat as close to the diet of our primitive forefathers as is possible in a modern world).

- About foods containing cancer–blocking agents (alfalfa sprouts, sweet potatoes, blackberries, garbanzo beans, buckwheat and the kernels of most fruits, especially apricot, to mention a few).

- About a gourmet guide to cancer prevention, including what to put in your child's lunch box.

- What are the alternatives to orthodox treatment (the usual cut, burn and poison methods which have often shortened rather than extended life).

- Where to find physicians who practice nutritional cancer prevention and therapy and where to get more information on your own.

In summary, the prediction is that one out of four Americans will die of cancer. I firmly believe that if the information in this book became widely disseminated, that would change to one out of a hundred or more.

Note: The cost of the book is *far less* than the first visit to your doctor to check cancer symptoms.

> **"**What you need is a little madness. You must cut the rope to be free.**"**
>
> —Zorba the Greek

More Tips on Health—This Time on Lifestyle

In March of 1985, my wife and I flew to Paris where we rented a new car for a leisurely tour of France and nearby countries.

We drove from one scenic village to another, stopping at quaint hotels and enjoying the gourmet meals for which the country is famous. At first I missed my work; I had almost never stopped either writing or researching since I left corporate life some twenty years ago.

Gradually, a day at a time, a new way of life took over. I began to really see things, notice details, enjoy the moment. Here was a fisherman intent on his nets. Was he aware of the crystal clarity of the Mediterranean? Then that chef near Bedoin—what was it like to prepare food every day of one's life? Research again—yes, it was, but of a new variety. I found I had the time for an in–depth examination rather than the quick once–over.

Then serendipity! At a small outdoor market, I found an English–language edition of Elia Kazan's book, *The Arrangement*. I began reading it in the same way that I was observing the flora and fauna of the region: slowly and carefully. I found parallels between Kazan's central character, Eddie Anderson, and my own life in the corporate rat race. I found two cogent statements:

> "I went on to think of everyone as living in a disguise. I began to think of all appearances including that of things—clothes, cars, food, public buildings—as false fronts. Our entire civilization as poses and attitudes...

> "I'd lost the knack. I'd killed the gift. I didn't know what I wanted anymore. I felt only that I must do this and should do that and I was expected to do such and such and it was my duty to perform this–a–way and my obligation to see this thing through and it was demanded of me to fulfil—always. The worst of it was a whole other set of imperatives that I had allowed myself to become subject to. These were the Expedients. Again, not what I wanted but what was useful at a certain time in any situation. Expedient. The word was written on the tomb of our generation. They did what was expedient, especially me."

Civilization as sham, people living it as though it were real life. That's what his observations delineated.

Now, perhaps this would not be so tragic, except that for millions of people it means that their lives are as imitation as nondairy creamer. And beyond that, it's lethal, often long before one's expected three score and ten.

Take ordinary business for example. It's really a continuous battle that goes on twenty–four hours a day, seven days a week, fifty–two weeks a year. The soldiers are the businessmen who wield their commercial acumen like crusaders swords, but with one important exception. The crusaders rested between battles while a "good" businessman never lets up. If he did, he'd be slain by his unresting adversaries.

Take cities as another example. They are really the trenches of modern business wars. How else would they end up being described in these terms:

> **❝**Money had made it necessary for me to be in certain places at certain times—places I loathed. What possible excuse was there for any man to live in New York City or Los Angeles? They were not fit habitations for men.**❞**

One morning in Provence, I went for a walk. On either side of the road were vineyards. I "bon jour"ed a man who was puttering about, and he smiled back. I could not help but compare this obviously healthy man with my late brother–in–law, who spent the last few years of his life commuting from Santa Ana to Beverly Hills—two hours each way on bumper–to–bumper freeways. Lung cancer finally carried him off, and I think he felt relieved.

I could give many more examples. After all, I am 63, and I've seen a lot of people come and go on the stage of life. But here's my point: *Good health*, which is the foundation of a happy life, *is really a way of life* rather than any set routine of what you eat or how you exercise or where you go on your vacations. Your day–to–day lifestyle is the key, and it must be one that is based on the natural state of the human body—not the shams and scams that have been substituted for profit motives. What are the parameters, the ingredients of a real life? Here are mine:

Environment—it must have at least reasonably pure air and water and freedom from major toxins, noise, overcrowding, and so on.

Activities—what you do is really what you are and are becoming, so make some intelligent choices from the myriad that exist.

Nutrition—you are and are becoming exactly what you eat and how you make use of it internally. The best, natural and organic foods won't do you any good if there's heavy stress from any source.

Exercise—just sitting around will stagnate your system. Running water purifies itself while stagnant water becomes poisonous.

Self–reliance—it's a lot easier to achieve than you think, especially when you learn to outwit the hucksters and do what is intelligent rather than expedient.

Philosophy, religion, family friends—all the peripheral that are so important to your mental well–being.

Put all of these together and see if your life doesn't take on a new vigor and enthusiasm of its own.

The Compendium

Here are odd facts and unique tidbits that I've gathered from many sources. I like to browse through a catalog, and that's what this is: a catalog of unusual information. It can be added to periodically, and that's exactly what I intend to do. I hope you enjoy—it was a pleasure compiling it!

Overcoming the Information Explosion

Millions of words are pumped into the media daily. Many of them concern a vital issue: Your health. How to keep up with this flood of data? Not to worry. Just subscribe to *Alternative Medicine Digest*. I strongly recommend you have this information for the arduous, stress–filled days ahead. And if you cannot afford the price yourself, join with others until you can. Write: *Alternative Medicine Digest*, 11 Bloomfield Street, London EC2M 7AY, England. The author of the digest reads and condenses more than two hundred alternatives and holistic medical journals every month. You get the benefit in a few minutes reading.

Living Abroad

If you are planning to take your retirement income to a foreign country, I suggest that you learn all you can about it before leaving. Then go on a trial basis. Don't burn all your American bridges until you become reasonably certain that the new environment will be all you want it to be.

Thousands of Americans are living happily in such countries as Mexico, Canada, Costa Rica, the Caribbean area, Europe, Australia and New Zealand, and in South America and the South Pacific. At any given moment, hundreds of yachts from the west coast are enjoying cruises in such faraway dreamlands as Samoa and Micronesia.

During a recent trip to Yugoslavia, I fell in love with the country. I found the people simple and uncomplicated, the food abundant, tasty and often ridiculously inexpensive. The scenery was absolutely fantastic—waterfalls more spectacular than Niagara and a coastal region that rivaled or surpassed the Santa Barbara coast. I calculated that I could easily live there on just my own social security check of about three hundred dollars. A small apartment would be around one hundred and fifty dollars, and if I did my own cooking, which I usually do anyway, food costs could be around one dollar a day. If I lived in a camper or trailer, these costs would be even lower.

More recently I toured part of British Columbia and discovered small towns where you could park you RV for one hundred dollars a month. This, coupled with the purchase of fresh vegetables and fruits which are abundant in many parts of Canada, would allow one to live quite wonderfully on a social security check.

In summary, go traveling. See for yourself. Try different places, including the many different regions of the United States; in the vast state of Nevada, there are remote valleys so beautiful they make Shangri–La look like a garbage dump (Meadow Valley and Pahranagat for example).

And always remember that nothing is forever. Even if you enjoy La Paz or Dubrovnik now, you can always boogie on to Lilloet or Nogales.

❝Ever let the fancy roam, pleasure never is at home.**❞** —John Keats

The Straight Skinny About Health

You may obtain it by writing to *The National Health Federation*, P.O. Box 688, Monrovia, CA 91016. They publish a magazine and also many books on the latest in health care by alternative means. Well worth any investment you care to make for magazines or books.

Rather than risk redundancy with the wealth of health books that exist, why not send for the catalog offered by Aurora Book Companions, P.O. Box 5852, Denver, CO 80217.

❝Give your life your best shot and maintain your sense of humor. Drugs are not always necessary. Belief in recovery always is.**❞**
—Norman Cousins

DMSO

DMSO or dimethyl sulfoxide is a most unusual solvent derived from wood. Simply applied to the skin it has proven effective in the treatment of a vast spectrum of ailments including arthritis, bursitis, tendonitis, back pains, muscle strains and various acute inflammatory or traumatic conditions. Many physicians have reported almost miraculous cures.

From a user: "I attribute all my success to DMSO for not having to go through the amputation of my right leg. I was told by several doctors that I would not be able to stand the pain otherwise. With all this in mind I was brought in a wheelchair to see Dr. Jacob. Thank God for the day. From that day on, I began using less and less pills until there was nothing but DMSO. I walked, did my own shopping, my own housework." —E.M.F.

Although DMSO has not been officially approved for more than a few conditions, it is available in many health–food and similar stores, and the cost is quite reasonable. Since it has no side effects except a garlic odor if used correctly, it is worth a try if you have an ailment that DMSO can help; if used *improperly*, DMSO has unpleasant side effects.

Check your library for books on DMSO. One of the best is *The Persecuted Drug, The Story of DMSO* by Pat McGrady, Sr. Another is *DMSO, The Pain Killer*, by Barry Tarshis.

The leading expert on the subject of DMSO is Dr. Stanley Jacob at the Oregon Medical Sciences Center, Portland, Oregon. He's been working with the compound since 1963 and has records of thousands of successful applications.

Adventure at a Modest Cost

Many people want to explore remote regions of the planet but do not have sufficient funds. Here, for your review, is a story by a woman who is living on a 32–foot sailboat in the Sea of Cortez, the body of water between the Baja peninsula and the west coast of Mexico.

Is it safe to travel and live in Mexico? Yes, according to a survey made recently by *Motorhome* magazine. From my own personal experiences there, I believe that a person can be as safe as they are in the U.S. by taking reasonable precautions. Travel in groups, don't park in isolated places, stay in company with other Americans. There are fewer crimes in Mexico City than in L.A.

Cruising in Mexico on Dollars a Day

After getting our foot caught in the Sea of Cortez, we are now well into our second year here, cruising on a very limited budget. I have a few provisioning tips to share with people planning to cruise into the Sea of Cortez who are also concerned with stretching their pesos.

First, a little insight to our mode of cruising. We are non–meat eaters. We eat seafood and sometimes chicken. We provide ninety–nine percent of our main dish entrees direct from the sea by snorkeling and fishing. As we sail all summer rather than "hurricane–hole out," my categories will reflect areas on the Baja side of the Sea of Cortez, all of which are north of Puerto Escondido. We like little–known anchorages and remote areas best of all. Thus we stock up so that we only need to reprovision, re–beer and re–water every three weeks.

Most often the village stores are so few and small that I find it best to make a quick buzz through them without buying anything. This gives me an overall picture so I don't end up buying tomatoes that run through my fingers in one store, while the one down the street has good ones. If the town has a *Conasupo*—a government run grocery chain—you'll probably find the best overall prices. *Conasupo*, however, has the worst record for availability.

The following items are readily available most places at prices usually much lower than in the United States.

Canned and packaged beans such as garbanzo, green, refried, and black. Corn, mangos, mushrooms, peas, peas and carrots, peppers, pineapple, tomato sauce, peanut butter, corn starch, baking soda, baking powder, cake mixes, white flour, gelatine, honey, vegetable oil, pancake mix, vegetable shortening. Sugar, powdered and white. Syrup: maple, chocolate, and karo. Yeast, soy sauce, A–1 sauce, bouillon, catsup, jam and jelly, mayonnaise, mustard, salad dressing, tomato salsa, vinegar, coffee, cocoa mix, Tang, tea, rice, pasta, instant Ramen, cereals (Kellogg's), Jello, milk (canned Nestle's), soups (Campbells), juices, tuna, clams, sardines, Vienna sausage, deviled ham, whole chicken, most basic McCormick spices.

If a company has a factory in Mexico, the prices are much lower because import duty doesn't have to be paid. Some of the well–known brands at lower prices are: McCormick, Kraft, Campbell, Kellogg, Nestle and Del Monte. Paper goods are available at prices comparable to the U.S. west coast. Some are U.S. brands like Alcoa and Kleenex.

Toilet paper and paper towels are very inexpensive. You can also find: wax paper, aluminum foil, plastic wrap, napkins, tissues, coffee filters, beauty products, shampoos (many U.S. brands), hair colorings, hair permanents, very basic make–up items, sun oils, hand/body lotions, toothpaste (Crest/Colgate).

Good paper plates are hard to find and expensive, however.

Under the heading of "rare finds" are those items that are hard to locate and/or terribly expensive if you do:

Cocktail olives, cocktail onions, pitted olives, canned peaches, canned pears, fruit cocktail, pickle relish, pickles canned spinach, canned asparagus, water chestnuts, bamboo shoots, canned nuts.

Help for Your Heart

Nearly a million Americans will die of heart attacks in the coming year. It is the leading cause of death, so it's obviously worthwhile to learn about some of the ways you can avoid this killer.

Stress is certainly a major factor, and it can be avoided, as we've related in the health section of this book. Exercising regularly is helpful also. But one of the major defenses against heart ailments is to ensure that you have nutritional support. Here are some factors to consider:

- Salt, or sodium chloride, is one of the most dangerous cardio–toxic agents. Avoid it at all cost. One of the best reasons for eliminating prepared, processed foods is that you eliminate all the salt that is mixed with them.

- Potassium obtained from natural sources is one of the best elements to ingest to counteract the effects of salt. Raw fruits and vegetables will usually provide an adequate amount of potassium.

- Keep your lecithin level up by taking liquid or granular lecithin or by eating lots of soybean products. It emulsifies fats and cholesterol.

- Calcium and magnesium are two elements that can lower your chance of a heart attack.

- Deficiency in B–vitamins can impair the function of the heart and cause hardening of the arteries. The best sources of all B–complex vitamins are nutritional or brewers yeast, desiccated liver, wheat germ and unrefined grains, seeds and nuts.

Alzheimer's Disease

This invariably fatal malady *may* be the result of eating food cooked in aluminum pots and pans. Until the facts are in, I suggest you try cast iron, ceramic or stainless steel. Better yet, eat most of your food raw.

Holistic Health

There are lots of references to this subject in the book titled, *The Whole Again Resource Guide,* by T. Ryan and R. Jappinen. In fact there are lots of directions in every field in this comprehensive annual.

Your Heart is the Most Important Organ in Your Body

Here's how you can protect your heart and your life! Read it and act. Carnitine is available at most health and vitamin stores. I take it myself and have no apparent heart problems.

Carnitine

Carnitine, sometimes referred to as Vitamin B_t, is a "mover and a doer." It is the great mobilizer of fatty acids throughout your body. We manufacture the amino acid carnitine in the liver. Although kidney and brain tissue also produce some carnitine, the liver synthesizes most of what we need from lysine with the help of methionine and a few attendant nutrients before sending it out to the other tissues of the body. There it fulfills an important role in each cell.

Carnitine carries fatty acids into the mitochondria of each cell. Carnitine waits in the membrane of the mitochrondria, anticipating the approach of fatty acid–carrying Coenzyme A. Coenzyme A races up to the molecule of carnitine, and hands the fatty acid baton to it. Carnitine then sprints across the inner membrane of the mitochrondria, eventually to hand the baton (fatty acid) to another molecule of Coenzyme A that has been waiting inside the tiny but powerful mitochondria.

The mitochondria are the power centers of each cell. It is there in the sixteen or so mitochondria that glucose and fatty acids are oxidized in order to generate the energy that powers us; that moves our skeletal muscles, that makes our stomachs knead food, and that keeps our hearts drumming out the music of life.

The heart derives so much of its energy from the burning of long–chain fatty acids (48% to 70% of its total energy output), and its energy needs are so constant, that it is to be expected that carnitine will be concentrated in heart tissue. Indeed, large amounts of the amino acid are found there. Your body is very wise. It knows through a myriad of as yet undiscovered communication channels that the heart must keep working or all is lost. It sends carnitine there to assure that the efficient operation of that vital organ will continue.

If dietary intake of carnitine or of its lysine and methionine precursors is insufficient to meet bodily needs, health status is compromised and continuance of life itself may be at risk. Diseases of the gastrointestinal tract such as Crohn's disease, diverticulosis, ulcerative colitis and celiac disease can prevent the uptake of adequate lysine, methionine and preformed carnitine from foods. Malabsorption syndromes brought about by allergic responses to foods or by dietary habits which provide grossly out of balance quantities of essential nutrients can also block the intake of the amounts of lysine, methionine and carnitine needed to sustain health. Systemic carnitine deficiency could result.

Carnitine can be manufactured in your body through the activity on lysine and methionine of Vitamin C, Vitamin B, niacin, five enzymes, and reduced iron.

In the absence of adequate carnitine, serum triglycerides skyrocket. Lacking efficient transportation to the cell mitochondria due to a deficiency of carnitine, fatty acids remain attached to circulating glycerol molecules in the form of triglycerides. Since elevated triglycerides are considered a potent risk factor in the development of coronary heart and artery disease, low carnitine levels which give rise to elevated triglyceride levels can also be identified as a risk factor of cardiovascular disease.

Carnitine supplementation has been shown of value in treating many of the cases of carnitine deficiency. Oral supplementation with one to three grams of DL–Carnitine or L–Carnitine per day have restored patients to functional lifestyles more times than not. Straight carnitine supplementation may not be in the ultimate answer, however. Many patients do not respond adequately to carnitine supplementation. These patients tend to be those with a defect in the transport mechanism carrying carnitine into the tissue or, sadly, those unfortunate infants whose carnitine deficiency begins shortly after birth.

Two Useful Publications on Health

The People's Medical Journal, P.O. Box 81, Kentfield, CA 94914 and *Freedom in Health Care*, 3A, Gate 5 Road, Sausalito, CA 94965. Send along a small donation to cover their mailing expenses.

To Do Is To Be and Vice Versa

This basic Zen principle is often lost in the maze of bandaid solutions to our cultural problems. Write to National Holistic Institute, 5299 College Avenue, Oakland, CA 94618 for information on how to be doing the work you love rather than the work you hate. In my own case I don't have enough hours in the day to do all the things I'd like. But every bit of what I do is *fun*—no tedium, no watching the clock, except to note how fast time goes by when you are doing what you love!

The American Death Ceremony

The death ceremony started as a crude ritual, back in the days of witchcraft. In recent years it has been developed into a science. It usually takes from 10 to 15 years, however modern scientific advancements are shortening this period of time.

It starts with one simple aspirin for a simple headache. When the one aspirin will no longer cover up the headache, take two. After a few months, when two aspirin will no longer cover up the headache, you take one of the stronger compounds. By this time it becomes necessary to take something for the ulcers that have been caused by the aspirin. Now that you are taking two medicines, you have a good start. After a few months these medications will disrupt your liver function. If a good infection develops, you can take some penicillin. Of course the penicillin will damage your red blood corpuscles and spleen so that you develop anemia. Another medication is then taken to cover up the anemia. By this time all of these medications will put such a strain on your kidneys they should break down. It is now time to take some antibiotics. When these destroy your natural resistance to disease, you can expect a general flair–up of all of your symptoms. The next step is to cover up all of these symptoms with sulfa drugs. When the kidneys finally plug up you can have them drained. Some poisons will build up in your system but you can keep going quite a while this way.

By now the medications will be so confused they won't know what they are supposed to be doing, but it doesn't really matter. If you have followed every step as directed you can now make an appointment with your undertaker.

This game is played by practically all Americans, except for the few ignorant souls who follow nature.

Another important organization to contact: Cancer Control Society, 2043 North Berendo, Los Angeles, CA 90027.

Wonder Herbs

- *Alfalfa*—It's extremely nutritious and primarily used for arthritis, bursitis, rheumatism, and hay fever.

- *Dandelion*—It is also very nutritious and good as a blood purifier, to balance blood pressure and a diuretic.

- *Cascara sagrada*—Probably the number one herb sold in the United States. It's very good for constipation.

- *Cayenne pepper*—It's good for circulation (cold hands and feed), stomach problems, blood pressure and hemorrhoids.

- *Chickweed*—It helps to emulsify fat and is a diuretic.

- *Gota Kola*—It's brain food and good for memory depression, senility and mental fatigue.

Rural Living Information Sources

Two of the best I know are:

VITA (Volunteers in Technical Assistance), 80 South Early Street, Alexandria, VA 22304.

Cooperative Extension Service, University of Alaska, Fairbanks, AK 99701.

If you are interested in becoming a self–reliant person, urban or suburban, you'll find a wealth of information in every booklet, and the cost is often negligible.

Videotapes

More costly than books but more likely to help you learn how to do anything you want are videotapes from the Video Schoolhouse, 805 Airport Road, Monterey, CA 93940.

The Depression Garden: When I was growing up in the 30s, there was no TV, so people provided much of their own amusement. One variety always intrigued me: The strange and lovely salt crystal garden that one colud grow with bluing. Here is the formula. Try it and see for yourself that there was something better than television.

RECIPE FOR GROWING A "SALT CRYSTAL GARDEN "

In a glass or plastic bowl, put some pieces of coal, coke, porous brick, tile, cement or sponge. Over these pour two tablespoons of water, two of table salt (iodized or plain) and two of Mrs. Stewart's Bluing. The next morning add two more tablespoons of salt. On the third morning pour in the bottom of the bowl (not directly on the base material) two tablespoons each of salt, water, and Mrs. Stewart's Bluing, and then add a few drops of mercurochrome, vegetable coloring or ink to each piece. By this time a beautiful flower-like growth should have appeared. If all conditions are not ideal, it may be necessary to add 2 tablespoons of household ammonia to aid the growth. A free circulation of air is necessary, and these formations will develop better where the air is dry.

To keep it growing, just add more M.S.B., salt and water from time to time. It will "bloom" indefinitely into beautiful rosebuds, coral and crystal. Try it! Mrs. Stewart's Bluing is just as indispensable for these flowers as it is for good washing. Don't experiment with anything else for either purpose. The M.S.B. Salt Crystal Garden is ideal for Elementary School Rooms, Nursery Schools, Cub Packs, Bluebirds, and has won many a blue ribbon at Science Fairs. More of these recipes are available by writing to the address below. You can also receive FREE, Mrs. Stewart's new "Home Washing Guide", complete with stain removal chart, by writing to: **Mrs. Stewart's Bluing, 100 No. 7th St., Minneapolis, MN 55403.**

 **USE IT FOR INK**

NOW AVAILABLE!!

Complete Easy-to-Use Kit for growing a "Salt Crystal Garden"
Write For Information

Free Space for Your RV

A friend of mine took a job as a camp host in an ocean–front park and believes that the freebies he gets would cost him six hundred dollars a month. He has parking for his trailer, free electricity and water, trash pickup and a phone.

He also has all the free firewood he wants.

Thus, he needs only to earn money for food, and that is done by attending flea markets with items he has picked up from various locations for free. Now there's an alternative lifestyle!

It's all clearly presented in this excerpt from a brochure. Perhaps your state has a similar program.

Do you like to camp? Enjoy helping people? Have talents that you'd like to share with others? Then there's a place for you in the California State Park System's *Campground Host* program.

As a friendly, helpful on–site representative of the Department of Parks and Recreation, Campground Hosts help park visitors in a variety of ways.

- Welcoming campers and helping to enrich their camping experience

- Acquainting visitors with activities and facilities of the park and area

- Doing minor maintenance jobs

As a Campground Host you'll get free campsite, plus an identifying cap.

Alaska

The name still evokes excitement and thoughts of adventurous experiences amidst tall peaks and vast green forests. And to be sure, this can be a reality if you plan for it. But it's best to get some information in advance, particularly concerning employment. And that's why we have included this list of Alaskan employers. It would be a lot better to arrive there with a job than without; there is still much unemployment in our largest state.

Alaska Division of Agriculture, P.O. Box 1088, Palmer, AK 99645

U.S. Department of Agriculture, P.O. Box 1628, Juneau, AK 99802

Alaska Division of Economic Enterprises, Pouch EE, Juneau, AK 99811

Alaska Division of Fisheries, 210 Ferry Way, Juneau, AK 99801

Fairbanks School District, P.O. Box 1250, Fairbanks, AK 99707

Office of Public Affairs, 7th Floor, Gruening Building, Fairbanks, AK 99701

Alaska Department of Health, Pouch 11, Juneau, AK 99811

Alaska Department of Fish and Game, Subport Building, Juneau, AK 99801

Northwest Alaskan Pipeline Co., 1001 Noble Street, Fairbanks, AK 99701

Alaska Oil and Gas Conservation Commission, 3001 Porcupine Drive, Anchorage, AK 99504

Alaska State Job Service, P.O. Box 3–7000, Juneau, AK 99811

Alaska Division of Occupational Service, Pouch D, Juneau, AK 99811

Alaska State Job Services, P.O. Box 1010, Fairbanks, AK 99707

Alaska Division of Lands, 323 East 4th Avenue, Anchorage, AK 99501

U.S. Bureau of Land Management, P.O. Box 1150, Fairbanks, AK 99707

Alaska Railroad, Pouch 7–2111, Anchorage, AK 99510

Alaska Department of Transportation, Pouch 2, Juneau, AK 99811

Alaska Division of Marine Highways, Pouch R, Juneau, AK 99811

Alaska Division of Parks, 619 Warehouse Avenue, Anchorage, AK 99501

National Park Service, 540 West 5th Avenue, Anchorage, AK 99501

Alaska Division of Geological Surveys, 5001 Porcupine Drive, Anchorage, AK 99504

U.S. Department of Mines, P.O. Box 550, Juneau, AK 99802

Alaska Oil and Gas Commission, 3001 Porcupine Drive, Anchorage, AK 99504

Alaska Pipeline Company, 1835 South Bragaw Street, Anchorage, AK 99504

Alaska Executive Search, 510 L Street, Suite 609, Anchorage, AK 99501.
    Call: 726–5707

Kelly Girl Services, 101 Benson, Anchorage, AK 99503. Call: 276–1425

Snow's Recruiters, 880 N Street, Anchorage, AK 99501. Call: 276–8087

North Employment Agency, 519 West 4th Avenue, Anchorage, AK 99501.
    Call: 277–8682

Professional Services, 814 West 2nd Avenue, Anchorage, AK 99501. Call: 279–7679

Anchorage Daily News, Pouch 6616, 200 Potter Drive, Anchorage, AK 99502.
    Call: 274–2561

The Times, 239 I Avenue, Anchorage, AK 99501. Call: 279–0012

Municipal Utilities System, 654 5th Avenue, Fairbanks, AK 99701

Fairbanks Memorial Hospital, 1650 Cowles Street, Fairbanks, AK 99701

Fairbanks Daily Miner, P.O. Box 710, Fairbanks, AK 99701

All Alaska Weekly, 419 2nd Avenue, Fairbanks, AK 99701

City Hall, 410 Cushman Street, Fairbanks, AK 99701

Bill Seavey at P.O. Box 864, Bend, OR 97709 has a three page, single–spaced leaflet on Alaska for three dollars. Well worth the investment, since it tells it like it is with no holes barred. He also has other newsletters on additional "greener pastures."

Privacy (How to Get it and Enjoy it)

If you need it for serenity and happiness, buy the book of the same name. It's just one of many from Eden Press, P.O. Box 8410, Fountain Valley, CA 92708. And there's more of a similar nature from Harian Publications, 1 Vernon Ave, Floral Park, NY 11001. One of their long–lasting titles is *Where to Retire on a Small Income*—another is *Retirement Paradises of the World*.

More than Two–Thirds of the World's Population Live in Port Cities

That piece of information should trigger some interesting ideas. It certainly evokes a picture of people relating to maritime activities.

Here's a sample of what we have in mind...an opportunity to participate now!

Ship Ahoy!

The ship shown on the facing page is the M/V *Anastasis*—a 12,000 ton, long–distance ocean vessel with a mission to serve the nations with a three–fold purpose: Mercy Ministry, Missions Training, and Evangelism. Designed 30 years ago, the passenger/cargo ship sailed on her first mercy mission in 1982, newly christened as the M/V *Anastasis*—Greek for "resurrection." In her first year the *Anastasis* delivered, free of charge, more than 1,300 metric tons of relief goods at an estimated value of 1.3 million dollars.

More than two–thirds of the earth's population live in port cities. The *Anastasis* is equipped to help meet their needs with a two–handed approach—spiritual and practical.

The ship can hold 3,000 tons of emergency food, medical supplies, clothing and construction materials for disaster relief and development. In a crisis, the *Anastasis* can carry almost 700 passengers to and from a disaster area. An 18–bed medical/dental unit brings help to many who would never receive it any other way.

People from over 20 countries make up the over 200 staff and crew. Each one is trained to serve on board, as well as to be actively involved in sharing the gospel at each port. Several hundred students are also mobilized into mission service each year through the Discipleship Training School (DTS) and the School of Missions (SOM) that are held right on board.

How You Can Help

If you'd like to get involved with the *Anastasis* as either a short–term volunteer or a long–term crew member, write to: Mercy Ships International, c/o YWAM, San Pedro, CA 90733, and mark the envelope "Attn: Personnel." For information on schools that are run on board the Anastasis write to the same address, "Attn: Registrar."

Did you Know

- That two–thirds of the world's population lives in port cities?

- And that the earth is three–fifths water?

- That's why it makes sense to emphasize the opportunities inherent in water or waterfront living.

- Boats that are often more livable and practical than houses can be obtained for far less than the average house.

- I believe that by the year 2000 a large segment of the American population will be living aboard boats.

- Furthermore, there will be new methods of building and restoring boats that will increase the number available and lower the costs.

There are many opportunities like this, and, if you don't find them locally, make your own. You'll find abandoned boats in almost every seaside city. In Alaska, they can be found in places where rough seas have damaged them.

Let There Be Light!

Want to live in a remote area but concerned that you won't have such amenities as good lighting? Then perish the thought. Aladdin to the rescue. There are some lovely kerosene lamps put out by this company that produce as much light with lamp oil as a hundred watt bulb. So kiss the power company goodbye, forever, and enjoy the romantic lighting of the last century with twentieth–century candlepower.

For a catalog and information write Aladdin, Box 100255, Nashville, TN 37210.

Aladdin® Incandescent Mantles and Burner Assembly
…Produce a brilliant white light, fully adjustable in intensity. Light output equivalent to 10 wick lamps. Burns approximately 12 hours on one quart of lamp oil.

Optional Electric Converter
For versatile operation, most *Aladdin* lamps may be ordered with an optional electric converter.

MITSUBISHI DIESEL GENERATOR

MODEL NM 155E · RADIATOR TYPE WITH ELECTRIC STARTER

FEATURES

1. More durability through special roller bearing, Bosch type injection pump, and alloy steel usage.   2. Low fuel consumption from unique pre-combustion chambers and Bosch type injection pumps.   3. Vibration-free from extra balancing system.   4. Easy maintenance through forced-feed lubrication and condenser cooling systems.   5. Easy starting with double injection system. (NM 130, 155 & 180)   6. Cam operation with a silent fuel injection pump using a specially designed nozzle.   7. Unsparing use of high quality materials brings you the assurance of durability no other brand dares to offer.

ENGINE SPECIFICATIONS

TYPE . . . . 1 cylinder, 4-cycle, water cooled, horizontal

BORE × STROKE . . . . mm 96 × 110 in 3.78 × 4.33

TOTAL DISPLACEMENT . . . . cc 796 cu in 48.6

COMPRESSION RATIO 20:1

ONE HOUR RATING . BHP/rpm 15.5/2400

ENGINE TORQUE . . . . kg.m/rpm 4.8/1900
(AT 1 HR RATING) . . . . lb ft/rpm 34.7/1900

COOLING SYSTEM . . Condensor/Radiator

REDUCING VIBRATION SYSTEM . . . . By counter weight on the crankshaft and extra double balancer shafts

GOVERNOR SYSTEM . . . . . . All speed mechanical governor (centrifugal weight type)

DRY WEIGHT . . . . kg/lbs 166/366

STARTING SYSTEM: . . . . 12v Electric

LUBRICATING SYSTEM . . . . . Forced feed circulation by trochoid-pump with relief valve and oil pressure signal

DIRECTION OF REVOLUTION . . . . Counter clockwise

AIR CLEANER . . . . Oil Bath Tye

FUEL SYSTEM . . . Special Bosch type fuel injection pump & nozzle with fuel filter

FUEL TANK
CAPACITY . . . . liter/US gal 13.5/3.6

Construction and Function

Longitudinal Sectioned View of Engine

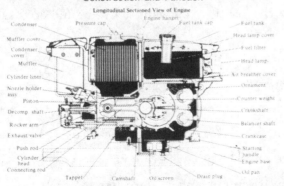

With one of these on your farm or ranch, you would be almost self–sufficient. Or course, you would neeed diesel fuel. But it's possible to grow corn and other grains and distill your own fuel! In South America, alcohol is commonly substituted for gas and diesel.

Tips and Pointers

- Send for a sample copy of *Nutrition Action Newsletter*, 1501 16th Street N.W., Washington, DC, 20036. A guide to better food for you and your family.

- Definitions: Success is making the most of what you have been given. Failure is making the least of it.

- If you are interested in communal, cooperative living, send for these directories:

   1. *Directory of Intentional Communities*, RR 7, P.O. Box 388A, York, PA 17402;

   2. *Guide to Cooperative Alternatives*, P.O. Box 426, Louisa, VA 23093

  Send a postcard first to determine availability and price. Both offer such important information as lists of intentional communities, how to start one, organizations that are involved in this field, plus references and index and bibliography.

- Among the many myths of America is the one that holds that we should work hard so we'll live well in our retirement years. My friend E. J. Cossman has pointed out that the average American dies with an estate of less than three hundred dollars. What is the answer to this enigma? Mine has been to live well each day and let that be my life.

- Barter is rapidly becoming a way to live without money. There are many good books on the subject.

- During my lifetime I have observed the United States government lie in the areas of food, defense, inflation, oil, health and many other essential subjects. For further data, consult *The Politics of Lying* by Wise.

- Want a job as a caretaker? Pick the location you want to live in and do these things:

   1. Check the ads in the local paper(s) daily;

   2. Place an ad offering your services;

   3. Print up posters and tack them up all over town;

   4. Go to likely places and ask in person (lumber yards, rock crushers, mines);

   5. Write to various resorts and other facilities offering your services;

   6. Travel around in your RV until you see a place you'd like to caretake.

- Gold is Still Where You Find it: I personally saw some being found along the Fraser River in British Columbia—nuggets the size of large pumpkin seeds. This, of course, is just one location among tens of thousands. With the price of gold quite high, it makes more sense than ever to combine outdoor living with making a living. For further information, write to the Department of Mines in the state of your choice and also check your faithful local library. There is a good publication on mining, *The California Mining Journal*, 9032 Soquel Drive, Aptos, CA 95076. Inquire about a sample copy. It lists many opportunities including mining claims from one thousand dollars or so up.

• Walk into the Elenbass Company in Sumas, Washington with just twenty–five dollars, and you'll stagger out with a 300–pound load of freshly harvested, whole–grain wheat. It's ready to grind into hot cereal, flour for bread, muffins, pancakes, biscuits and other delicious food. Three hundred pounds of whole–grain makes up into nearly half a ton of high quality food, almost the entire food needs of the average person—all for just twenty–five dollars!

Wheat as a commodity is selling for less than it did in 1932. That's what's bankrupting all the grain farmers—everything else went up except the price of what they grow.

You can find whole–grain wheat all over the country. Check your local feed–and–grain store or call a health–food wholesaler. Be sure and buy it as close to home as possible since the weight of grain would greatly diminish savings if it were shipped a long distance. A good method of storage are #10 cans topped by plastic lids available from restaurants. Drop a lighted match in just as you seal to burn off oxygen and kill weevils and such.

Unusual Books

Want to read some books that you are not likely to find in your neighborhood bookstore? Then send for the *Loompanics Catalog*, P.O. Box 1197, Port Townsend, WA 98368.

Water

It is the one essential for living anywhere. With a simple rig you can drill your own well. Enough have been sold to prove that the concept is valid. For more information and a comprehensive brochure, write: DeepRock, 2200 Anderson Road, Opelika, AL 36802.

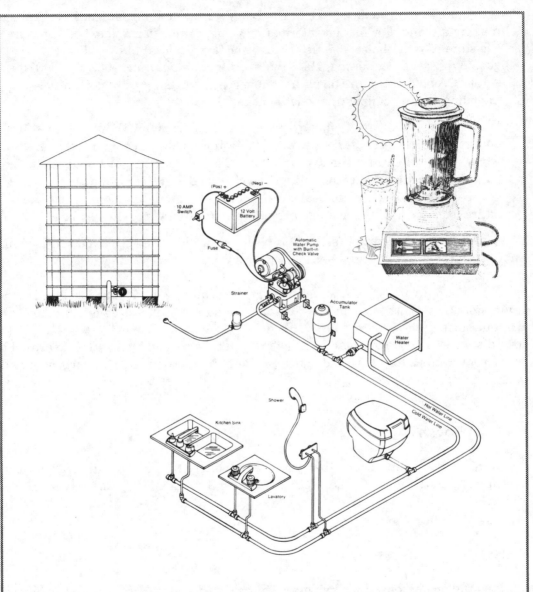

The Automatic Multi-fixture (Diaphragm) Water Pump System

The automatic multi-fixture pump system (shown above) delivers water the instant a faucet is opened, just like home. Pump starts automatically when a faucet is opened or a toilet is flushed. When all water outlets are closed, pressure in the discharge side of the pump rises to shut the pump off automatically.

Pump draws water from a non-pressurized water tank. Standard household fixtures are used throughout. The heart of the system is the automatic water system pump.

Power

It's becoming more feasible than ever to obtain power from the wind and/or the sun. And it doesn't have to be 110 AC. The low–voltage systems are gaining ground and appliances are appearing to meet the demand.

Solar Electric Generation

Sunlight is a kind of energy that is permanent, free, and universally available. The sun is really a nuclear power plant that generates radiant energy at an enormously high kilowatt (Kw) rate estimated to be a staggering 110–trillion Kw/hours. Even though less than one–billionth of this energy is intercepted by earth, every eleven square feet of the earth's surface facing the sun is estimated to receive about one Kw or 1000 watts per hour.

A photovoltaic device or silicon solar cell converts light into DC (direct current) electricity. It does not use heat from the sun as does thermal solar hot water. In fact the higher the ambient temperature, the less efficient a solar electric cell becomes. The common commercially available solar cells is a small wafer or ribbon of semiconductor material, usually silicon. One side is positive (+) and the other side is negative (–). That there is no additional material between the two sides is the key to generating electricity. When light strikes the positive side of the solar cell, the negative electrons are activated too and produce a tiny unit of electrical current.

When a group of solar cells are connected or the semiconductor ribbon material is applied to a predetermined surface area, a solar module is created. Quantitative electrical output is determined by the number of cells or ribbon material connected together within the module and then further determined by the number of modules connected together. More than one module connected together is called a solar array.

A properly planned photovoltaic system consists of the simple components described in the introduction. They are: (A) A system based on the number of Kw you will use each day, with back–up or secondary generator (wind, hydro etc.). (B) The choice of a roof, ground, pole or passibe tracker mounting. (C) A charge controller system. (D) Metering Panel. (E) Battery Storage. (F) Inverter (if desired).

Usually a battery storage system is necessary to act as a buffer between the solar array and your home on nights and sunless days. Although a solar array will generate some electricity on cloudy days (sometimes up to sixty percent of the rated output on a bright cloudy day) and even under a full moon, it varies greatly on both a daily and seasonal basis. A battery system smooths out some of the variation.

There are exceptions to the need for a battery storage system for solar electric power generation. Some appliances and equipment run directly from the power produced from one or more solar modules. These are called sunsynchronous devices.

The World Health Organization has determined that the average person on this planet lives on food worth about twenty–five cents.

Minimums

Bookstores are awash with them; you see them advertised in the business section of newspapers, and they often make the bestseller list. What are they? Books on how to invest, preserve, enhance your assets, that's what. There's a new batch every year saying essentially the same thing:

- Diversify; don't put all your assets into gold or silver or real estate.

- Hedge; no one knows what the future will bring.

- Be cautious about any investment; remember what happened to so–and–so during the you–know–what.

- Look out for (here follows a long list of don'ts).

After reviewing a number of these inventories of financial fears, I'd like to create one of my own. It's based on Gibran's precept:

> **"**There are those who have little and give it all. These are the believers in life and the bounty of life and their coffer is never empty.**"**

Go back with me a century or so in time and a distance in space to visit the plains Indians of what is now Montana. Living communally in tribal segments, the Sioux probably had more real fun and enjoyment out of this country than anyone since. North in summer, south in winter, their tipis had no mortgages. Food was every-where—buffalo, deer, bear, elk, moose, not to mention millions of rabbits and other small game. There were wild onions, nuts, seeds, grains, beans, peas, fruits and ber-ries for the trouble of gathering them. Most could be dried or otherwise preserved for use in winter.

Food and shelter, the basics, were there for the taking, and they never gave one thought to T–bills or tax–free bonds.

If you're feeling adventurous, you can find native populations in many parts of the world who still live in the manner of the Sioux. Northern Canada has a popula-tion of Indians who live just as their ancestors did with only a few exceptions, such as rifles instead of bows and arrows for game. Along the shores of the Sea of Cortez, one often finds the *vagabundas* or Mexican wanderers/vagabonds who live the life of itinerant fishermen. Their small boats allow them to fish for their supper, and the overturned boat acts as a house at night.

I'm not suggesting that you become a *vagabunda*, but just that you consider the following:

* It really doesn't require much to live a happy life;

* Both shelter and food can be simple and, in so being, better for you;

* Most of what we own is really superfluous to our real needs. We may *want* a TV set but we don't really *need* one to live;

* A life of simplicity can be one of the most rewarding.

None of this is new. Just listen to some of the great philosophers on this subject:

> **"**Remember this—that very little is needed to make a happy life.**"**
> —Aurelius

> **"**You are king by your fireside as much as any monarch in his throne.**"**
> —Montaigne

> **"**Man is born free and everywhere he is in chains.**"**
> —Rousseau

> **"**Most of the luxuries and many of the so–called comforts of life are not only not indispensable but positive hindrances to the elevation of mankind.**"**
> —Thoreau

> **"**That man is richest whose pleasures are cheapest.**"**
> —Thoreau

> **"**It is preoccupation with possession more than anything else that prevents men from living freely and nobly.**"**
> —Bertrand Russell.

Here then are some examples of life lived with minimums. Decide for yourself whether they would have appeal for you.

The Minimums

What is needed to provide for basic human needs? Well, one of the best ways to find the answer is to study plans for small boats; a small boat is a universe unto itself. Once afloat in the vast seas and oceans, it must provide for its owner's basic needs.

Take a look at the two small boats presented on the facing page. Both are designed by a naval architect of rare perception. He has combined classic charm with a real knowledge of what it takes to be comfortable. Even in the little 17–footer, one finds everything that is needed on a day–to–day basis: comfortable beds, a small but efficient kitchen, and a micro–toilet. Although a shower is not indicated, one could be installed to provide the cleanliness we all need.

This would be a perfect live–aboard for one or two persons who wanted maximum utility in the smallest possible space. Imagine cruising in a boat this small on the Sea of Cortez or the great reaches of Georgia Strait in British Columbia. With a draft of only twenty inches, it could go virtually anywhere. And with a small diesel, fuel economy would be of the highest order.

Here is a somewhat larger vessel that would provide a lot of comfort for two and could accommodate more—perhaps a small family.

Unlike many yachts which waste room, this design takes advantage of almost every cubic inch. Note the rear cabin with its wraparound seats. A luxurious place to stretch out with a good book, with a compatible companion and listen to the rain beat overhead! Easy to heat and clean, the cabin areas would make snug quarters for almost any kind of maritime adventure.

Having owned a few boats, I can really appreciate how beautifully this one is arranged. I especially like the privacy of the forward cabin with its large double berth. Deck space isn't shorted, either, with a comfortable place to sit on either side to enjoy the sea and sky.

The hull material is ferrocement, which is one of my favorites; long–lasting, impervious to rot and bugs, it can be handled by amateurs as long as there is some expert advice available during the critical phases (plastering, launching, etc.).

I see this small boat as a cozy home for adventurous people in any part of the world. Why stay at home and die of the mullygrubs when you can explore the seven seas and never have a dull moment!

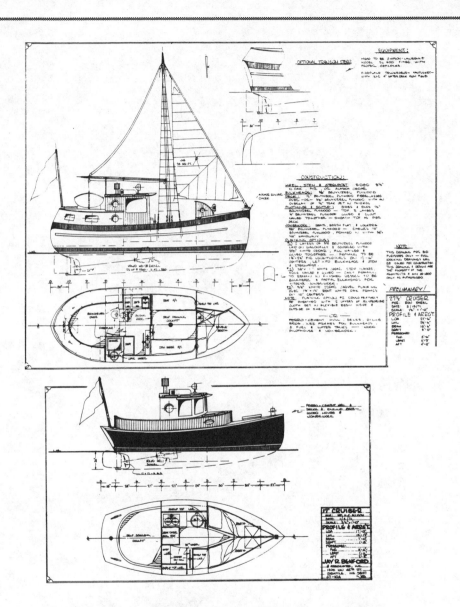

This delightful mini-cruiser evolved from our popular 17' catboat. Intended for use as a snug cruiser for two, she would also make a grand fisherman -- able to take some nasty weather much better than the typical open runabout. Headroom in the pilothouse is a full 6'3". Stock plans, including corrected offsets, are available.

For more information on these boat designs, write to:
Jay Benford, 1405 NW 45th Street, Seattle, WA 98107.

Alternative Scenarios

Introduction

If the old 8–to–5 has got you down, if living in a Sun City is evocative of the total blahs, then you should consider alternatives.

Resort Management

Robinson's Bar

In the Sawtooth Mountains of central Idaho lies an enchanting resort called Robinson's Bar, or it was when we were last there. We remember it as the ultimate location for dream fulfillment. A young couple living in Boise wanted to take their two children and get back to more natural surroundings, so they checked the ads and ran a few of their own. In time they were offered managership of the Robinson's Bar resort on the Salmon River, about two hours northeast of Sun Valley. This lovely place has everything: a rushing river out front, a crashing creek alongside and, best of all, a wonderful hot, hot spring that fills two pools, one quite warm and the other "just right." The lodge and outbuildings are built of logs, and all are as picturesque as a movie set. The backdrop to this resort is a range of jagged peaks often draped with snow of the purest white.

The couple's children attend a nearby rural school, but most of their education comes from helping their parents operate the resort. Imagine growing up in the heart of Idaho's tourist country!

Income is, of course, derived from guests, and they come winter and summer just as they do to Sun Valley about one and a half hour's drive south.

It is one of the most ideal settings for an alternative lifestyle and best of all, there are hundreds, perhaps thousands of similar resorts that will need management from time to time.

Want to follow this lead? Then go to your library and research directories of vacation facilities. For example, there is a directory of nothing but dude ranches, while my own book, *Great Hot Springs of the West*, lists most of the best hot springs resorts in the eleven Western states. Once you have a location, then get busy with the letters or phone calls. From then on, it's a matter of a lot of persistence and a little bit of luck.

On the Waterfront

Free Floating in the Sea of Cortez

Waterborne opportunities are everywhere. While the first thing that most people think of is fishing, there are many other possibilities. Here's one from real life:

Jack was a former Air America pilot who loved and lived the adventurous life. When he retired, he bought a large, old schooner in Maine. It had once been used for fishing, but Jack had other ideas. With his wife, Ann, he worked for a solid year cleaning, repairing and polishing. When they finished, the 85–footer gleamed! They headed south toward Florida using the calm waters of the Inland Waterway for most of the journey.

Their first income was earned by taking a boatload of scuba divers out to the Bimini banks for underwater tours. Their boat was so handsome and picturesque that they didn't need any ads to charter it to parties of tourists anxious for a day's sail. It became obvious to Jack and Ann that they had something close to a human magnet!

After a year in Florida waters, they headed for the Panama Canal with a cigar box full of travelers checks. While they didn't need the money, they couldn't resist taking parties of cruise–ship guests on short exploratory sails around the Canal Zone. The same fun–filled "work" occupied them as they made their leisurely way up the west coast of Mexico. From the fishing port of Topolobampo, they crossed the usually tranquil Sea of Cortez to La Paz. Once they dropped the hook in this city of pearls, they knew that they had found their personal heaven. Neither too large or too small, La Paz was the perfect place for two, sea–loving Americans. They could enjoy both the interaction with citizens of their own country and also the culture of Mexico in a laid–back and easy–going way.

They made contact on many levels and finally ended with a berth alongside a peaceful old pier. By handing out cards with a picture of their boat at the resort hotels, they had all the tourist charters they could handle. Just imagine a lifestyle where you meet people having fun and show them how to have even more fun! That's exactly what Jack and Ann found themselves doing on an all–year basis. They would stock up with plenty of tortillas and beans and then add the lobsters and scallops as they slowly wended their way along the Baja coast. Campfires on the remote beaches, daily swims in the crystal–clear water, and good conversation with their guests were just a small part of their daily enjoyments.

A remote and unreachable objective? Hardly. There are small ports worldwide where a well–equipped boat could easily earn a comfortable living in a dozen different ways. And old fixer–upper boats are available in almost any harbor. All this takes is gumption and some elbow grease to start (the team of Jack and Ann added a few

Mexican crewmen to do the really hard work).

One often wonders what people are doing when they drive endlessly to and fro on crowded urban freeways when the world is a storehouse of aquatic opportunities. I recall noting how few tourist resources there were in Dubrovnik, Yugoslavia. A large sailing vessel moored at the old walled city would need a crew armed with belaying pins to ward off eager tourists!

So what are you waiting for; check out lists of boats currently available on both American coasts!

Claim *Your* Mine Now My Darling Clementine

A stone's throw from one of the best hot springs in the United States is a rather odd collection of buildings and trailers. A sign out front announces that this is an ore–reduction plant: a mill site, in federal parlance. What is so special about this desert installation? Just that the land on which it is located was obtained for a filing fee of just $10. That's all. No down, no payments, no interest, no long–term mortgage. In fact, after a five–year period, my friends will own it outright. Of course, it will then be subject to taxes, but, considering Nevada in general, they are sure to be reasonable (no state income tax in Nevada and other taxes are equally moderate).

Examine how you can obtain free land in this day and age of outrageous real–estate costs if you and your family want to be landed gentry on a twenty–five acre parcel. The key is a simple booklet that you can obtain free.

The mining act of 1880 is still in effect in the United States. It allows any U.S. citizen to claim land that has mineral values or is intended for use as a mill site. We won't go into all the details here but suffice to say that you should send for this information. Then you can pursue your goal with intelligence and authoritative guidance. It is entitled "Staking a Mining Claim on Federal Lands," and is available from Superintendent of Documents, U.S. Government Printing Office, Washington, D.C. 20402.

My own fantasy is to locate a lovely little canyon somewhere in Nevada or Idaho, one with a spring or all–year flow of pure water. Then I would build the most picturesque mill structure ever seen in the west, using the same lumber the early settlers used. Of necessity, I would have to live there to provide mill services.

To live there would require that I have food. Thus, a garden of some size would be necessary. And to eat up the leftovers, there would be a hen house and perhaps a few rabbits. To get into town in rough weather when the creeks are high, a horse and stable would be mandatory. And, as the mill site prospered, it would be strategic to put in a small landing strip for my mill–site plane, a Cessna 150 commuter. Then there would be...but I'm sure you get the picture. All legitimate, all according to the book and everything approved by the local BLM and forestry and mining people. And all for a ten dollar investment in the land!

A tip that I think is worth a lot—check out Meadow Valley Wash, northeast of Las Vegas: Water, lovely willows and sycamores and old 1880's ranches scattered here and there. I've driven it from one end to the other and even flown over at 250 feet—wonderful and remote and mystical—a place like no other in the world. See it soon.

Fifty—one Acres Near Chilliwack for $500

That was an offering in the September 11, 1985, *Sun*, published in Vancouver, British Columbia.

As the warning note at the bottom said, the properties are for mining purposes, and not for residential purposes. But this does not mean that you cannot live on your mining claim, only that the *primary use* must be mining. Obviously, if you are running a mine, it's logical that you would put up a cabin to sleep and eat in while carrying on your work. I'm sure you get the picture.

Incidentally, the same philosophy applies to U.S. mining claims. Many rather poor claims are still being worked by their owners who live nearby and enjoy the fresh air and vegetables so readily available in most outlying regions.

Chilliwack? It's a delightful area in southern British Columbia not far from the impressive Fraser River. Some other locations are remote but that may be just what you refugees from the rat race desire.

So get a map of British Columbia and spot your home in the wilds; then phone or write the people in charge One Resources Canada, 448 Seymour Street, Vancouver, BC V6B 3H4, British Columbia.

Mail Order: An Income in Your Home

Many people say, "If I could make a living somewhere else, I would certainly leave this smoggy, overcrowded city." But you *can* make a living almost anywhere that has a post office, and here is proof.

The classic way to start a mail—order business is at your kitchen table with no more than twenty dollars in capital. That's exactly what Barry Reid did about fifteen years ago in southern California.

Barry's first book, one that is still bringing in a substantial income, was *The Paper Trip*. It's about now a person can rejuvenate his or her life by simply changing one's name. Reid observed that many people who, perhaps, had made one mistake with the law, were saddled with a lifetime of prejudice due to their past record. With a new name it was possible to create a brand new life, free of the impediments of the past.

The book sold well from the beginning. Soon, Barry added other books, and the business began to prosper. He is careful to point out that it was not easy to make a success out of mail order. It took several years before the business was truly in the black. But Barry is one persistent entrepreneur, and he never gave up his vision or his long hours of writing, editing, promotion and order filling.

His big break came when he appeared on *60 Minutes*, the TV show, and his business doubled almost overnight. But even with this breakthrough, he had many obstacles to overcome in the ensuing years. One of his books displeased the establishment to the point where they made him the patsy for an obviously framed—up legal case. Even though he ended up in a Federal prison for a year, he kept up his business and research. When he emerged, he was ready for a new and streamlined mail—order book enterprise, one that is racing along as these words are written.

What are the secrets to Barry's success? Hard work, persistence, creative efforts and lots of guts. While it is possible to "luck out" in the mail—order business, that happens very seldom. Citing the Pet Rocks and other runaway successes does not in the least negate the fact that mail—order is simply a business that is conducted by mail and requires the same diligent effort as any other business.

For Barry's catalog: Eden Press, P.O. Box 8410, Fountain Valley, CA 92708.

If you want to take advantage of the privilege to live anywhere you choose, be prepared to study and educate yourself. Then also be ready to work long hours and accept many defeats. From this preparation comes the ability to last out the early periods of testing and re—testing.

The important tasks are to:

1. Study the field in depth, reading all the books available on the subject.

2. Then forget the rules and be so creative that you'll gain success from innovation.

This theory is based on real—life successes. I once did ghost writing for Joe Karbo, who originated the famous "Lazy Man's Way to Riches" ads. He told me that it was only when he bought full—page ads in major dailies that his book began to sell in appreciable numbers. It took a lot of guts to gamble thousands of dollars on a one-time ad, but he did and succeeded. Robert Ringer followed in his footsteps and was also successful in book sales through massive advertising.

And there are many other approaches! See your local library/librarian, for books on the mail—order and direct—mail business.

Food For All: Sharecropping

This word often evokes a picture of a poor black or white walking behind a primitive plow on some Alabama farmstead. And at one time this may have been true. However, the current joint effort of those who own land with those who work it has become highly sophisticated. Also, it can be conducted on almost any level.

Let's give a small–scale, real–life case. Just north of where I currently live on the California central coast is a parcel of rich farmland owned by an electronics executive. Since he has no interest in farming, he has leased it to a young and enterprising young farmer who grows organic vegetables. Everyone benefits: the owner gets a regular lease income, and the farmer has a place to grow his crops without tying up a lot of money in land ownership. The people who buy those snappy carrots and fresh lettuce are grateful that there is an alternative to the usually pesticide–laced produce in the supermarket bins.

The Delta

Several years ago, I was given the use of fifteen acres of land on an island in the bountiful California Delta region. We found that the ground was so rich that one almost had to jump back out of the way after dropping a seed in a hole. Only a small part of the acreage had to be used to supply all that we could eat and barter.

While I was engaged in this bit of sharecropping (the owner just wanted the land used and a few improvements guarded), I discovered many other parcels, large and small, that could have been sharecropped. One parcel was overwhelming—the lessors of an entire 110–acre island were willing to let anyone farm it for free. They had a duck club on the property and part of the arrangement with the state was that the land be used for agricultural purposes. They didn't have the time themselves and, thus, were ready to strike almost any deal with anyone. Although I didn't have the time myself, I finally found a young farmer who proceeded with a sharecropping arrangement.

Finding the Land

If you have flown over America, you know that much of it is unpopulated. Even in the east, there are large segments of land that are unused. And out west, most of it is virtually untouched. There are many fertile valleys in Nevada, for example that require only the barest effort to be productive. Seeding could be done casually in many places, and the rewards would be great. Water, often thought of as scarce, is abundant in many regions. I recall seeing a giant fan of watercress growing from a small thermal spring in central Nevada near Auburn. In the Amargosa area, I was once offered as much land as I needed for melon culture. The owner of this ranch was experimenting with grapevines but wanted to make some use of his unused property.

Summary: land is everywhere; it's just a matter of finding the right parcel for you.

Getting Started

Several years ago, I wrote a book, entitled *First Time Farmer's Guide*, which took the reader by the hand and led him through a step–by–step orientation into becoming a successful small–scale farmer. This book is available in many libraries and can provide all the data you need to make a start. Or contact the county farm agent in your area for advice on what to grow and how. Don't feel limited by this advice; many times it is the innovative crop that can be most successful. For example, not far from where I live a young family has created a marvelous gourmet herb farm, growing chives, shallots, garlic and other items for the many fine restaurants that purvey elegant dinners in this affluent region. This coming spring, I intend to experiment with the culture of therapeutic herbs on an acre that was donated to my church.

Actually, there is such an abundance of both information and needs that no one should be constrained in the ambition of becoming an independent grower.

What You Can Earn

While many farmers are having hard times, I know many others who are doing better than ever. Most of these are providing exactly what the market needs: fresh, organic, natural, unsprayed produce; out–of–season berries, especially strawberries; herbs like gotu kola and comfrey for the many new holistic therapists and nutritionists, and so on. For these items, you will be paid well because they are often in short supply. They are the antithesis of such crops as wheat and corn, which now bring prices so low as to make paupers of farmers who specialize in them. But there is no lack of demand for the best by the increasing number of people who know that the best investment they can make is in their health.

Summary: You can help yourself and others, find a rural place to live (many farms already have dwellings and others will allow trailers to be parked), have a happy, outdoor lifestyle and, best of all, fulfill this old Chinese saying:

When the sun rises I go to work.
When the sun goes down, I take my rest.
I dig the well from which I drink,
I farm the soil that yields my food;
I share creation.
Kings can do no more.

Let's Get it Together: Communes, a Sharing Lifestyle for Anyone

66I'm living on a commune in Massachusetts, sharing my life, my resources, my property, my energy, my thoughts with a group of people. It's an organic farm. We can live comfortably. Twelve adults and two children on ten thousand dollars a year. We have gardens, cows, pigs. We sell hay, milk and maple syrup.99

—Studs Terkel
The American Dream, Lost and Found

Brotherhood of the Sun

In the early 70s, a spiritually motivated seeker of truth, Norm Paulsen, began to gather friends about him in an effort to provide a better–quality food supply for the Santa Barbara community. At first they only had the wherewithal to gather wild herbs, dry them and sell them. This led to finding some land on which to grow organic vegetables which, in turn, led to the opening of a produce store.

Ten years later, the Brotherhood operates four stores, sells wholesale up and down the California coast, and is into many other related ventures. All was done with communal effort, since all of the brothers and sisters renounced material possessions for the common good. In turn, they receive food, shelter and incidentals without charge. Today, the Brotherhood has a giant ranch, hundreds of square miles in size, in northeast Nevada; they are developing it as a self–sufficient community.

Norm has proven beyond doubt that communes work, and work well, if the members are dedicated and hard–working. It's that simple!

Denman Island, British Columbia

My favorite example of a commune is one that was started in the early 70's on an island north of Vancouver, British Columbia. This was a simple arrangement whereby each participant contributed part of the cost and then received (by lot) a choice of acreage on the 160–acre spread. The last time I visited, it was doing extremely well. One important accomplishment was to integrate their activities with those of the "natives." Often this can be the most formidable problem, since people who have lived in an area for a long time do not welcome "outsiders."

Orr Hot Spring

I can't think of a better place to form a communal activity than around a geothermal artesian well. This is what the people who now operate Orr Hot Spring Resort in northern California have done. They bought the facility by pooling their funds, and each participant has a 1/18th interest. Some of the owners live there; others visit when they can. A part–owner can sell his share as long as the new owner is compatible to the structure of the hot springs effort. This has lots of possibilities for those who have limited funds and high ambitions.

Stelle

This communal town is most interesting; I suggest that you write for a copy of their brochure. Write to: The Stelle Group, P.O. Box 75, Quinlan, TX 75474

Informal Communes

While traveling about the country, I've noticed that groups of people often gravitate to a specific area and then function as an informal communal group. I noticed this in the north coast counties of California, Mendocino and Humboldt, where many "back–to–the–landers" have built their own small homes, tilled gardens and generally recreated the America of the 1900s. If you don't need a formal structure to your commune, I suggest that you simply go to the area of your choice and start making friends.

Religious Communes

These are common, and they can be found throughout the United States. Many have created successful farming ventures on large, otherwise unused parcels of land. There is a religious commune in Nevada City where the emphasis is on natural food and spiritual growth; which is also the major objective of a Zen community at Tassajara in the east Carmel Valley, California.

Starting Your Own Commune

Nothing could be easier. Just gather those of a similar mindset about you, and then proceed to acquire the space you need. It doesn't even need to be land; I also envision floating communes. After all, many fishermen spend most of their time tied to each others' boats. Once you have the people and the place together, it's up to the members to create their own favorite world. There are so many variations on this theme that it would require an entire book to cite even the rudimentary details. But as an alternative lifestyle, it surely bears further investigation and study.

Ad Infinitums...For Good Measure

Escaping the rat race, finding an alternative lifestyle that is more conducive to good health and self–fulfillment, and learning how to make the most of your life is really no problem if you open your mind to the many possibilities and opportunities. Here, for example, are some capsule descriptions.

Caretaking

There are so many possibilities in this category that it boggles the mind. All over the world, there are unused boats, buildings, land and so on, that require someone to watch over them to prevent vandalism and fire damage. To obtain free shelter as a caretaker, just start searching in the area of your choice. My favorite method for this has been to ride a bicycle or small motorcycle. On these modes of transportation, you can easily go down back roads and alley ways or over rough terrain to find places to live that might otherwise go undiscovered. For example, once needing a temporary place to park a trailer, I canvassed a series of ranches along a lovely river. At the second try, I connected. Ask and the answer is possibly "yes". Don't ask, and the answer is always "no."

Consultant

Almost everyone has a special skill. You can sell this as a commodity by offering it to those who would benefit. Often this can also be incorporated with living space. For example, if you are an expert in boat repair, try for living quarters aboard a boat at someone's marina or boatyard. I've always thought it would be fun to work as a nutritional consultant for a large institution on a live–in basis. That way I could help the institution cut costs and improve the health of those concerned—and at the same time cover my own room and board.

Photojournalism

There are more than five thousand periodicals published in the United States. All require good articles in every issue—well–written and –illustrated. Thus there are many opportunities for a person to combine travel with an income. I visualize a well–equipped RV containing typewriter and photo gear. Then the operators thereof could enjoy both travel and an income. Often it is possible to work steadily for a trade journal. For example, if you specialized in articles on computers, you could research every town you visit for new and innovative uses of computer hard–and software. A great guide for this work would be *Writer's Market*, a standard reference book in any library, or you can buy a copy at your local bookstore.

Seminars

One of the most innovative techniques of teaching in the 80's has been the traveling seminar. In this, the expert hires a hall, sends out publicity and then proceeds to instruct his clients in his own expertise for a substantial sum. There is also the possibility of income by selling books and other reference material. It is similar in nature to becoming a consultant; only in this capacity you have a willing and temporary audience. Check your local newspapers for announcements of seminars, and study the methods used. From then on it's up to you and your assistants. One of the best features of this lifestyle is that you not only get to travel, you can estimate your income by the advance sale of tickets to a particular event. Thus you have the best of both worlds: a novel style of living and a predictable income.

Building Microhouses, the Backyard Bedrooms of the 80's and 90's

Housing, the affordable type, is sadly lacking in many parts of the United States. Thus, there is a great demand for shelter that people can really afford. In the shelter section, of this book, there are details and plans of a unit called a *minigranny*. Why not consider becoming a contractor in your area for this type of structure. The need is great, the process is very simple, and you can earn a living doing good works. What could be better?

The same applies to the Kaysite process. Anyone living in a seacoast area will have plenty of opportunities to restore old boats by this method.

Summary: Look around you at those who are successful at what they do. Also, check out the newer methods of providing an income. They are proliferating daily as new ideas are put into action. Then take necessary action. Don't procrastinate. Write down a plan of action, and follow it.

NETTLE

How to Totally Eliminate Fear from Your Life

Most books are too long. They are like cheap hamburger full of fat and water. Take *The Bridge of San Luis Rey*, by Thornton Wilder for example. It's a virtually endless, recital of the pedestrian lives of some South American natives. The author should have presented his closing words first: "There is a land of the living and a land of the dead and the bridge is love," and chucked the balance in the circular file.

Joan Didion's works often read like a computer programmed to endlessly recycle terminal depression.

Even the venerable Twain is largely unread today because most of his works read like the author was paid by the word. *Life on the Mississippi* starts brilliantly and then trails off disappointingly.

Conversely, some authors know how to condense their work. One of the reasons people lined up to buy Edgar Lee Master's *Spoon River Anthology* was that the writer knew how to pack a lot of information in a few words. The saving grace of *Johathan Livingston Seagull* is its merciful brevity.

For the ultimate in the most information with the fewest words, read the New Testament. Where else does one find gems like:

- "Heal the sick"

- "Let not thy heart be troubled"

If you accept the London Principle on faith, you will be free of fear instantly. If you don't, read on. But it's short, so take heart.

The London Principle

"I couldn't change anyone until I changed myself."—Jerry Rubin

In 1972, I received a contract to write a book entitled *The Robin Hood Handbook*. Casting about for a likely spot to plant my IBM, my wife and I decided on Sausalito, a lovely seaside community on San Francisco bay.

But there was a problem; even then rents were astronomical. But while looking for a place to land, I couldn't help notice how many people were living aboard boats at picturesque Gate 5.

So we began to search for a suitable boat. One morning I was actually *propelled* to obtain a fresh, early copy of the *San Francisco Chronicle*. There was a large ad for a large boat. It read in part:

> 76–foot ex–CG cutter. Needs lots of work to make livable but basically sound. Twin diesels…etc. $10,500

The price was fair for such a large vessel and the ad was correct: There *was* a lot of work to be done. But living on a boat is like being in a movie twenty–four hours a day—it's *fun*! The boat gently rocks when other boats pass, waterlights play on the ceilings, seagulls land on your roof, and many people come to visit—after all, boating is associated with play and vacations.

So we bought it and moved aboard. At the time, I did not know that Jack London once lived aboard *his* boat, *The Snark*, just a few hundred yards north of our Oakland marina location.

During the next two years, my career as a freelance writer progressed handsomely.

In 1974, I was back aboard the *Flying Goose*, the name we gave our monster, floating writing platform, doing two books; *Eat Well on a Dollar a Day*, and the controversial *We Never Went to the Moon*. Several friends warned me that I was treading on dangerous ground by leveling a charge of "hoax" at the Feds—NASA in particular.

Of late, I had been reading of the fascinating life of Jack London, particularly his autobiographical *Martin Eden* and his dynamic novel of the future, *The Iron Heel*. For fun, I visited several locations made famous by Jack during his lifetime, including Heinolds Bar. This historic and well–preserved saloon seemed to still possess the vibrations of the energetic writer. I also visited the Jack London room at the Oakland Public Library and here saw films taken just before his untimely death at age forty. My interest in Jack and his messages of social protest grew. I discovered, as many people have, that Jack was not really a writer of dog and Alaska stories; instead he was an *expert* at describing socio–political conditions. His predictions in the *Iron Heel* had, for the most part, come true.

Then one evening, while I was walking along the dock near my boat, I received a very clear message—not a voice, merely a thought that seemed to be written on the blackboard of my brain:

> "There is nothing to fear, now or later."
> Signed, Jack London; and then parenthetically,
>
> "I know because I have been on both sides."
> (For brevity we will refer to this as the London Principle.)

Prior to this moment in time, I had never had what might be termed an ESP or Psi experience. Thus, I was almost stunned by the clarity of the transmission. There was no qualification, no mincing of words—just the simple, crystal–clear words that I remember to this day.

As soon as I received this message, I knew that I had actually been contacted from or through another dimension. I discussed the incident with a psychologist in Nevada who said that Jack had accumulated a large amount of energy and used it in a single burst to break the barrier between his spiritual world and my temporal one.

For a few days, I did not concern myself too greatly with the message. However, early in the next week, I had occasion to fly a long distance by jet. While I had flown before, it was a form of transportation that did not fill me with joy; in fact, I almost always found myself with sweaty palms and feelings of vertigo as I looked down 35,000 feet through thin air.

But on this flight, I decided that I would put Jack's counsel to the test. If he assured me that there was nothing to fear now or later, crash or burn, land safely or not, then what would I have to lose by taking this statement as an act of faith?

A miracle occurred! I was not the least bit frightened. I found myself actually enjoying the view, chatting with stewardesses, even walking about when previously I had remained tightly belted to my seat, in the hope that by sitting quietly I would not perturb the aircraft.

I thought, Jack really had something.

There really is nothing to fear, now or later!

A real test of this principle came a few months later. I was flying into Las Vegas in a gale. The 727 bucked and pitched like a gigantic aluminum bronco. Passengers were beginning to emit little cries of anguish and fright. The pilot announced that he would attempt to land despite the counsel of the controller to return to San Francisco. We descended through even more turbulent air, and the gyrations were close to spins and stalls. The stewardess came by and sat next to me. As she buckled herself in she said, "I've never been in a storm as bad as this!"

"There, there," I said, patting her hand. "We'll make it down OK, I'm sure. And even if we don't, I'll be here with you."

She looked at me appreciatively, gratitude showing in her beautiful blue eyes.

The plane came to a jolting touchdown, and the passengers and crew sighed in collective relief. There were many smiles from the relieved safe–arrivals and animated expressions of elation at finding themselves alive on the ground in one solid piece. But no one was as elated as I.

Jack London's transmitted wisdom *had triumphed in an acid test*! From that moment on, I have felt free of fear in all situations and conditions. No longer do I fear rejection slips from publishers. No longer do rebuffs from individuals cause me any anguish. Gone are fears of illness and death—my own or of those others close to me.

After all, Jack's advice was *not qualified in any way*; I took it to mean that it was all—encompassing, valid in *any and all* situations. And in the ensuing years, I've found that this assumption was correct.

Now if you wish, you can stop reading this. I have nothing more to offer in the way of revelation—only further proofs. If you can and will accept Jack London's dictum on faith, there is nothing more for me to teach you. You are free and can go forth and live the rest of your life without fear (as I do now). But if you need more convincing, read on. Or, if you are just curious to learn what corroboration I've found, the following may be of interest.

A Logical Analysis of the London Principle

Aristotelian logic has its place. Often fallacious in its reasoning (apes have two eyes, I have two eyes, therefore I am an ape), it can be a tool.

Premise: Let's assume that London did, indeed break through the barrier between his world and mine to deliver his valuable message. On that basis, it is then true that the London Principle originated from a source of information far more sophisticated and advanced than our own terrestrial sources. The London Principle must then be based on knowledge available only to those who:

1. Have experienced life and death.

2. Are able to communicate to those living on earth.

This produces some heavy thoughts. If the London Principle is truly of a Psi nature, we should accept it as being of far greater value than principles drawn from our own limited secular or theological concepts. It can, because of its origin, be accepted as an ultimate truth. And once accepted as truth, we can have no doubts as to its validity. It *will* work for us in our daily lives.

Premise: Let's assume that the delivery of the London Principle was merely my own imagination at work—that Jack London had nothing to do with it.

Does it really matter *what* the source is if it *actually works in daily life*? No, of course not. Vonnegut speaks of "granfaloons," or harmless untruths that make life bearable. Well, if the London Principle is a granfaloon, it is no less valuable for me. I have been able to devote 100 percent of my time to productive effort wasting *none* of fearful thoughts.

The London Principle is like a *blanket insurance policy*, it covers every situation; all contingencies from the most trivial to the most important!

To summarize for review:

1. The London Principle is actually true.

2. The London Principle is not true.

It makes no difference which of the above is correct. As long as you *accept* the principle and practice it in your daily life, it will be effective, and you can toss your Valliums in the toilet where they belong.

Both 1 and 2 require an act of faith. But is an act of faith too big a price to pay for a life that is free of fear? That's a question that only you can answer.

The London Principle in Literary History

"Once we experience the transformation of a fear we have trouble recapturing it, as if we have stepped far enough back from the fire to see that the burning buildings are only a part of a stage set or that the wizard is creating smoke from behind the curtain. Fear, it becomes evident, is a special effect of our consciousness.**"**
—Marilyn Ferguson
The Aquarian Conspiracy

Great truths are simple:

God is love.
A thing of beauty is a joy forever.
He who cares naught for death, cares naught for threats.

Throughout literature we find cogent statements by profound philosophers that provide substantive support for belief in the London Principle. For example, Thomas Carlyle wrote an autobiographical book entitled *Sartor Resartus or the Tailor Patched*. His hero, Diogenes Teufelsdrockh, has lost his work, his love, his religion and even hope had departed. He is at the nadir of despair, and to him the universe appears to be "a huge immeasurable engine rolling on in dead indifference to grind him limb from limb."

But he realizes that all suffering must end, and in the meantime he can shoulder the crushing burdens. As Carlyle describes Diogenes renaissance:

"Despicable biped! What is the sum total of the worst that lies before thee? Death? Well, Death and say the pangs of Tophet too and all that the

261

devil and man may, will or can do against thee. Has thou not a heart; canst thou not suffer whatsoever it be; and as a child of freedom, though outcast trample Tophet itself under thy feed while it consumes thee? Let it come then; I will meet it and defy it!

And as I so thought, there rushed like a stream of fire over my whole soul; and *I shook base fear away from me forever*, I was strong, of unknown strength; a spirit, almost a god. Ever from that time, the temper of my misery was changed; not fear or whining sorrow was it but indignation and grim, fire–eyed defiance."

Carlyle's hero is now fearless but has one more step to achieve the ultimate in moral growth—renunciation of self.

As he passes through this phase, he says,

"And ye too, haggard spectres·of Fear, I care not for you; ye too are all shadows and a lie."

Shadows and a lie!

In his book *Equilibrium*, John Kiley espouses his theory that what we are experiencing in life is nothing more than a role in a cosmic motion picture. We are God's TV! In the haunting story, *The Planet of the Dreamers*, earthlings are taken over by minds from another galaxy and used for amusement.

In her definitive work, *The Aquarian Conspiracy*, Marilyn Ferguson cites Karl Pribham, a Stanford neuroscientist, as conceiving of the world as a hologram. And for centuries, religions of the East described the universe as being maya, an illusion.

Perhaps the best delineation of Carlyle's contention that fear is a shadow and a lie appears in Shakespeare. At the end of his life he wrote the mystical *Tempest*, in which we read:

"Our revels now are ended. These our actors,
As I foretold you, were all spirits and
Are melted into air, into thin air;
And, like the baseless fabric of this vision,
The cloud–clapped towers, the gorgeous palaces,
The solemn temples, the great globe itself,
Yea, all which it inherit, shall dissolve;
And, like this insubstantial pageant faded,
Leave not a rack behind. We are such stuff
As dreams are made on, and our little life
Is rounded with a sleep."

—Act IV Sc 1 Line 148

There is much evidence that we serve some unique purpose in the Universe. What this purpose is.is not known at present. We do know this: We have been programmed to react to "reality" with responses of fear. And this response, in light of what we now know, is totally unnecessary.

Defining Fear

In the early fifties, I began to race motorcycles at a track in Malibu Canyon called Crater Camp. Here would gather some of the great racers of the era. Bud Ekins, Dick Dorrestyn, Don Surplice. It was always a colorful and dramatic scene reminiscent of the jousting tournaments of King Arthur's Court. Vivid pennants snapped in the brisk breeze, helmets of rainbow hues decorated the vulnerable heads of the contenders while powerful metal steeds with flashing chrome growled and roared. Set against a background of deep green grass, of strips of rich brown earth that composed the track, with fleecy clouds in a clear blue sky, it was a vision of paradise for avid motorcyclists.

But there was an alien element to the beauty and dynamics: Fear. After all, nearly every race yielded a crash or two, and, often, unconscious and bloody riders were loaded into ambulances and driven away. So despite the joy of action, fear often made one's stomach writhe in anticipation.

As one's race time drew near, palms would sweat, foreheads became clammy. But inexorably, like an execution date, the time for one's own race would arrive. With trembling fingers, riders would buckle on helmets, draw on gloves and kick their snorting beasts to life.

In jerky surges, the racers would approach the starting gate. Then, with motors revving, they would await the starting flag. The tension became almost unbearable as though a frenzied beast was merely out of control within each rider's mind. Then, with all hearts pounding, the flag would drop and the pack would leap forward as though propelled by a giant slingshot.

In a single instant, all fear would dissolve as the rider's attention was directed to the task at hand—to get around the track as fast as possible without being killed.

This experience gave me one of the keys to the elimination of fear—an important element in laying one's fears to rest forever. I'm sure from my story you can guess. *Inaction breeds fear.*

Why Belief Works so Well

In the film *DOA* (Dead on Arrival), Edmund O'Brien plays the part of a San Francisco visitor who is inadvertently poisoned by members of a "hit"team. When he learns he is terminal, he sets about to find his killers. In the ensuing adventures, he is faced with many fearful situations but *he has no fear*! He is like a man in a play who can thus consider himself invulnerable to all dangers. This concept was also dramatized in Stoppard's *Rosenkrantz and Guildenstern Are Dead*.

Consider this. O'Brien knew he had only a day or so to live and acted accordingly. Are you, the reader, not also aware of your own mortality? You *may* have more than a day or so left, to be sure, but *what if you didn't*?

Seneca expressed this thought best with his aphorism, "Live each day as though it were your last, gain knowledge as though you were to live forever."

A young racer friend was very swift around the track. He would win or crash and seemed absolutely nerveless before and after any race. After he died of a heart ailment, we learned the truth. Doctors had given him a year or two at most to live since his congenital heart condition was inoperable. Thus, Tommy had nothing to lose. He could die on the track or in bed. He was actually *DOA*, either way!

In the embarkation ports during World War II, I found this "What the hell" attitude prevalent. No one shipping out knew for sure whether he would return. So it was "eat, drink, and be merry" continuously.

Not one of us knows when he steps into a car or plane if he or she will return safely. Then why should we be so all–fired concerned *all the time*? All fears can be eliminated by a simple change of attitude. And once this attitude becomes a habit, fears evaporate like mists on sunrise.

How to Make a Little Extra Money Even if It's Hard Times

❝Ninety–nine percent of accomplishment is getting started.❞
—Anonymous

Prologue

Back in the early thirties, when times were really tough, I discovered how to make a little extra money. There was a place called the Ultra Violet Ray Ice Company in South Pasadena. Few people had refrigerators, and most of us relied on ice. But ice was expensive—15 cents for a 24–pound block, and remember that in those days 15 cents would buy three loaves of bread. So some people couldn't afford ice, and that's where my little business got its start.

The big blocks of ice were slit by giant saws so they could be split into smaller pieces. In the process, a lot of ice chips were created. These fell under the screaming machine were little Willie was waiting with his cardboard boxes. I would fill them and then go on my route, pulling my "snow" in my little red wagon. I sold a big box of snow for a nickel, and it lasted the customer almost as long as a 15 cent block of ice.

So I was able to earn a little extra money and help out some poor people in the process. This was a real, hard–times–proof business because it was based on the fact that people didn't have much money and were willing to try alternatives. But the message for today is this: You don't need a lot of capital to start an extra money business. You can invoke ingenuity, simplicity, and common sense.

Creative Income Possibilities

> ❝Why limit yourself to something that will kill your mind when the whole world is a storehouse of possibilities.❞
>
> —Sylvan Hart, *Mountain Man*

Sylvan Hart is a remarkable man. He chose to leave a big city behind and carved out a comfortable home for himself along the banks of the Salmon River in Idaho. He taught himself to make his own tools, grew all of his food and became a legend in his own time. All of this is documented in a book about him entitled, *Last of the Mountain Men*, which you may find in your library. I strongly recommend you read it. It is an inspiration to anyone who has ever thought about escaping the rat race and living close to nature like a modern Thoreau.

Sylvan's story and philosophy is appropriate to cite in this chapter, since both prove that, if you really want to live a joyful, exciting and adventurous life, it can be done. The world will accommodate you most generously. Let's take a look at some possibilities.

Why a Business of Your Own?

If you work for someone, a large percentage of your pay is deducted for income taxes, social security, and other bureaucratic shenanigans. Often you would be better off taking the deductions rather than your net check.

If you work for yourself, you can deduct your expenses of doing business from your gross income and often pay little or nothing to the tax collector. In that way you don't have to earn as much money to have the same net income. Also, many self-employment enterprises are in the home, so the high cost of going to work is eliminated. And there's less stress since you are the boss. But most importantly, you can use your talents, creativity, and skills to the fullest extent rather than having to adapt them to a conventional, often deadend job.

While it often takes some time to build a business of your own to where it is returning an income suitable to your needs, in the long run it's worth the effort. Ask anyone who's done it!

Recycling Glass

One evening after dining at a local restaurant, I noticed one of the cooks carrying out cartons containing gallon bottles that had held house wine. I asked how many bottles they threw away every week, and it was an astounding number. About that time I had been buying wine from a small winery in Martinez, California, so I asked the owner of the winery if he would like the bottles.

"Sure," he said, "bring them up. I'll trade you wine for the bottles." Shortly thereafter, I got a book contract which took me to another city, so I never followed through on this "extra money" possibility.

But just think of the potentials in recycling such common items as glass bottles. Hundreds of millions are used every year in this country alone, and since glass is recyclable, many opportunities represent themselves. Bottles of different sizes could be collected and redistributed to fruit juice, vinegar, and water companies.

Spring Water

Speaking of water reminds me of a friend in Santa Barbara who collected gallon bottles and developed his own business with them.

My friend had access to a spring that gushes a never–ending stream of cold, crystal–clear water from one of the mountains back of Santa Barbara. Every day he drove to the spring with his well–scrubbed bottles and filled them. He pasted on a good–looking label and then delivered the water to a route of grateful customers. (For some reason, Santa Barbara city water has always tasted like it was run through a horse.) So my friend generated a profitable one–man enterprise with just some one–gallon bottles and an old pickup truck. Incidentally, he parlayed this business into one of the largest orchid farms in California.

The Wedding Florist

One of the most beautiful people I have ever met in my life is a spiritual lady named Nancy Lingemann. To help her husband pay for some property, she started growing vegetables and flowers. For many years she has sold the flowers in the Santa Cruz area and now concentrates on providing floral arrangements to enhance the joys of a wedding.

This "extra money business" required only seeds, water, and a patch of land, plus plenty of hard work. Her service is complete from design through delivery.

Delivery Service

Another friend of mine once rolled into a Southern California town in his old Buick with just a dollar in his pocket. He used the dollar to buy some 3 x 5 cards, and on them he lettered the following information:

> Any package delivered within 3 miles of city center for $1. Dave's Delivery 372–0569.

He talked a phone–answering service into giving him a week of service on credit, and his business was launched! The first day, he made about ten bucks, and, deducting a couple of dollars for gas, he had enough to enjoy a good meal before going to sleep in his car. Within a month, he was producing enough income to rent a small office, which doubled as his apartment. Within a year, Dave had two people running most of the errands on bicycles, while he sat back as dispatcher.

This is a prime example of making money on a totally bootstrap basis. When people tell me they need a lot of capital to go into business, I tell them about good old Dave and his entrepreneurial ingenuity and energy.

Typing Service

I know a beautiful lady in her 60s who, needing some extra money to supplement her social security, started a typing service for attorneys. In these increasingly difficult times, a number of attorneys have taken to minimizing their staffs and are ready customers for independent typing services. The major point here is that often extra money can be made *because* of hard times. As people's budgets grow tighter, they seek out alternative skilled services, such as the one my friend provides.

Freelance Writing

Whenever I find myself short of bucks, I wander over to the local newspaper to see if they need a feature article, a book review, or maybe a column. There are more than 8,500 weekly newspapers in the United States. All need fresh material from time to time, which gives lots of employment to gypsy writers.

Hip–Pocket Business Enterprises

We call them hip–pocket because, in many cases, you can start them with your shoestrings, bootstrap them with their own earnings, and keep all your records and cash in your hip–pocket or purse. Of course, some require some capital, tools, or significant space, but most have been selected because almost anyone can be their own boss *now*. You learn as you earn, and you prosper in accordance with your efforts. Best of all, you can keep most of what you earn, since any small business has many deductions that are completely legal. Here's one to start you off that can be profitable almost anywhere.

Washers and Dryers

After he lost his job during an aerospace layoff this man cast about for something useful as well as profitable. He noticed that many people discard washers and dryers, since the purveyors of new ones don't want trade–ins. Having a small pickup truck, he decided to pick up several and see if they couldn't be fixed. He discovered that in most cases a washer was junked because of problems with the pump unit, and, with dryers, the problems were belts and power transmission. It was easy to obtain new pumps and other parts from a major appliance wholesaler, and relatively easy to install them. Before long, he had several washers and dryers ready to sell.

Rather than rent a store, he decided to work out of his home. He placed ads in the paper for his modestly–priced units and was pleased to sell out his stock in one day. From then on, his enterprise had only one direction—up. He was able to obtain discarded units from many sources: dealers who took them in just to get them off the street, people who were moving, charity organizations that didn't want to bother with repairs, and so on. When one thinks of the many millions of washers and dryers in the United States, it's understandable how anyone could keep quite busy making sure at least some of them keep on running.

Anyone with a handyman bent could start this with no more investment than some screwdrivers, wrenches and the right parts. These items plus a few ads would be all that is required to be self–sufficient indefinitely. Incidentally, this technique works well with other appliances such as dishwashers, stoves and refrigerators.

Furniture Refinishing

If you're not mechanically inclined and prefer to work with woods and fabrics, here's a similar enterprise. Restoring furniture is quite simple It usually entails removing the old finish, making minor repairs, and then applying new coatings. There are many books on the subject in your local library so we won't go into detail on that part. Here's what you can do:

1. Acquire some space. Your own garage would be fine for starters, or you can rent a shed nearby.

2. You may already have all the tools you need, since they consist of scrapers, sandpaper, and brushes for finish work. An electric sander would be fine, but it's not necessary at startup.

3. Find old furniture by running ads offering to pick up discards free, respond to ads wherein people are leaving town and selling most everything, or just travel around looking for furniture that people toss out.

A friend of mine has made a good living restoring furniture and other artifacts from a wealthy neighborhood near his home. Try garage sales and flea markets, particularly at the end of the day when people are inclined to let things go for low prices. Another friend of mine lets furniture for sale ads "age" for a week or two and then calls the sellers to see if they will liquidate any leftovers for low prices. He often buys a roomful for the price of single pieces, and the people are delighted to be rid of it!

One good method is to offer to clean up someone's garage or shed in exchange for the unwanted items. Also, try the "as–is" yards of the Salvation Army. They often let items go cheaply that they don't wish to repair themselves.

4. From this point on, it's strictly up to your energy and ability. Hard work, yes, but so rewarding to see a scratched and neglected piece of fine furniture emerge shining and beautiful. You can retail or wholesale your restored pieces through ads and phone calls, or try your local flea market.

This same routine works for upholstered pieces, but you need a little more training to handle this work professionally. A good way to get experience would be to apprentice yourself to someone in the business. They get your free help in exchange for training you in the skills.

Vinyl Repairs

There are hundreds of square miles of vinyl coverings in the United States on furniture, in cars, boats, and just about every restaurant and motel and hotel. Naturally, this material gets scuffed, torn, damaged or otherwise rendered unsightly. Fortunately, there are methods to repair vinyl that are almost undetectable. The following trade magazines would be likely sources for information or try your library:

Modern Plastics

Plastics World

Progressive Plastics Magazine

To get started, prepare a portfolio of repairs so you can show potential customers what they can expect. Then, further armed with business cards that you can leave, show your expertise to restaurants and hotel owners, car dealers, airplane and boat facilities and the hundreds of other places where vinyl–covered items are in daily use. From then on it's just a matter of keeping up your reputation by performing expert work.

This certainly qualifies as a hip–pocket enterprise since the materials to repair vinyl shouldn't cost you more than twenty– five dollars plus another twenty dollars or so for the cards. The portfolio can be free since you can find vinyl scraps at any upholstery store.

Automotive Electrical Repair

One of my friends discovered that almost every car's horn stops working when the car is a few years old. So he advertised that he would "fix any car horn for $5, no ups." While he occasionally lost money on a tough job, most of the time he made a profit since he became an expert in the common causes of horn failure. From this beginning, he branched out into other areas of auto electrical repair, including voltage regulators, alternators and so forth. He ended up with a new van completely rigged for on–the–spot auto electrical–repair work. He travels to his customer's homes, eliminating the overhead of a shop and making it more convenient for his clients. Electrical–repair work is light, usually clean (as contrasted to doing motor overhaul or brakes), and well–paid, since few people are dedicated to fixing their own systems.

The key to this one is to start small on a single automotive item until you become so expert you have the time and energy to branch out into other areas. With cars becoming more complex yearly, the field is one that staggers the imagination. And at last report, there was a significant lack of trained people to do this kind of work.

No–Investment Tire Company of Your Own

Here's another hip–pocket enterprise that requires even less training. It has been tried and proven successful by a number of entrepreneurs, including one on the east coast who makes about twenty–five thousand dollars a year. His procedure was as follows: First he had some cards printed showing the four tires on a car sketched in diagram with a rating from good to poor for each tire. He then went to parking lots and places of high car concentration and inspected the tires of parked cars, placing his written inspection on the windshield of each car. On the back of each card was a note advising the car owner to contact the man for wholesale prices on replacement tires. When they phoned, he would drive out to their homes giving quotations for one or more new tires. He then had a tire–mounting expert install the tires on a regular basis. Thus, the man did no actual work himself; he was simply a dealer without a regular shop and got his tires from major distributors at very low prices. Incidentally, the markup on tires is fantastic, so there's plenty of profit margin and room for generous discounts. The man had 30–day credit with his distributor but dealt on a strictly cash basis with his clients. Customers liked the idea of having the tires installed without having to go to a shop, and they certainly enjoyed the lower prices.

This is a basic business, involves selling a quality product without the overhead of a store and has only one employee on a piece–work basis. Think of the potential! This can be extended to other car–related items, including seat covers, convertible tops, paint jobs, body–and–fender work, mufflers and other visible items. If one category doesn't make the money you need, add more until you have an adequate income. But check with the proper agencies as to licenses and permits so you won't have any hassles with the bureaucrats.

Pictures from Remnants

Recently, I visited a clothing factory and was amazed at the enormous quantity of scrap material that was discarded. Of course, the pieces are not large, but then, with ingenuity, they don't have to be.

For example, a retired woman has supplemented her income by making colorful pictures from fabric remnants. She leaves cartons at various upholstery and similar stores for the collection of scraps of all kinds. She sorts them into various color and texture combinations and then glues cut out pieces to various sizes of masonite. The effect is most appealing, since the fabric simulates oils in both texture and color. I recall one cloth "painting" of a New York skyline that was stunning: each building was slightly different; shade and shadow effects were created by darker versions of each basic color. Any kind of glue can be used to cement the fabric to the backing, including a simple paste of flour and water.

When the picture is done, it is framed and displayed at gift stores and tourist facilities. This creative craft idea is one that lends itself to any age, sex or talent. Furthermore it could be a joint effort for a couple, with one person doing the framing and selling and the other the artistic effort.

A follow—on idea: Cut out scraps the same size, provide a picture guide, and sell the boxed components as a creative kit in toy and craft stores.

Poster Printing

There's an inexpensive way of printing the common poster using a silk—screen and stencil. It's a simple process that can be learned in a few hours. Books on the technique are in any library, and you can get supplies from any graphic—arts supplier. Check around your town, or any place for that matter, and see how many posters there are. The market for this service is wide in scope and constant throughout the year.

Beyond doing the poster printing as a service, you can produce your own repro-ductions of old fashioned posters, which sell well in tourist areas, or create your own artistic renderings in multi—colors. Paper and ink are cheap, but the results often bring top prices. In this hip—pocket enterprise you can exercise your talent and get paid for it to the limit of your ability and energy.

Incidentally, don't forget that stores often need posters for advertising and win-dow display, and this could be a regular source of income.

A Hip—Pocket Ad Agency

How would you like to have an income from your local post office with virtually no investment? First obtain an assortment of magazines and search through them for ads that show a distinct lack of appeal. Cut out these "dogs" and send them with a cover letter to the advertiser offering to improve the ad and thus the advertiser's re-turn. You might send along a rough sketch of your improved version. Include an estimate of what your fee would be to do the final version ready—for—print. There's lots of competition in advertising, but, if you have a flair for this field, you might well end up as a top "ad doctor."

Once you have had a few ads of yours printed, you can use them as proof that you know what you're doing. Every advertiser wants the maximum return for his space dollar, so you are going to be working in an area where people will listen to you if you can produce. And think about the billions of dollars spent on advertising with much of it going to waste because of ineptitude. Even the better ads can stand improvement.

It's obvious that this is a field in which anyone with talent and ability can be successful. Remember, there's plenty of room at the top.

Writing

Few people are aware that there is a tremendous demand for top quality nonfiction. While many would–be writers are grinding out bad fiction for a saturated market, a select few are living well by pursuing the nonfiction field. *Writers Market* is a book that should be in your local library and lists more than 5,500 markets for nonfiction material.

Rather than go into detail here, let me recommend that you check out some of the many books on writing from your local library. Also, take a tip from me as to achieving success: It's persistence that pays off. Don't *ever* give up, and remember that the only person who can defeat you is you.

Melody and Her Cookies

Mendocino looks so much like a New England town it's been used as one by the movie people. Sharply angular Victorian clapboard houses painted stark white are silhouetted against a rocky coast where blue–green waves dash against stolid rocky outcroppings. Daisies wind in and out of arrow–tipped picket fences. The wind hardly ever stops blowing. Sometimes at night, you are certain that it's going to tip your house over.

There was something about this community and its rugged charm that enchanted Melody, a young woman searching for a few answers in a confusing world. One problem—how to support a modest lifestyle.

Away from the main street was a tiny, former real–estate office. It was really just a large phone booth, but Melody felt that it would be perfect for an idea she had. Among her other talents was an expertise in baking gigantic cookies—huge oatmeal, chocolate chip, and raisin cookies over a foot in diameter. If giants ate cookies, Melody's would satisfy them.

With the help of a friend, she built a counter, put up a sign and opened for business with her giant cookies, freshly baked, on display. It doesn't take long for the word to get around in a small town, and before noon she was completely sold out—even to the broken giants, which she discounted. It was an instant success and remained that way until Melody went on to bigger and better achievements.

I often think that the current cookie craze might have been launched by her creativity. I'm fond of telling this story because it has all the characteristics that make up a fulfilling alternative lifestyle:

- Someone doing what they do well

- Everyone enjoying their output

- An easy sell

- Simple to organize and execute

- A modest income but an assured one, since people's penchant for cookies is likely to continue for quite some time

- Relatively short hours...Melody baked early in the morning; was through with all her work by noon. The rest of the day was hers.

She lived in a small cabin within walking distance of her shop. With no car to support, her income from the cookie project was more than adequate.

Gold Country Souvenirs

Hanging on my studio wall is a treasured handicraft. It is a fragment of an old 1849'er pistol mounted on brown calfskin and framed with weathered wood from an antique window. It's what the maker calls an *assemblage*, an artistic composition of several related items.

Rick Harper gave this *assemblage* to me one Christmas many years ago, and I've enjoyed it since. It's one of hundreds, perhaps thousands, that Rick has made since he moved to the Mother Lode from southern California years ago to escape that choking smog.

"It's a fascinating hobby and business, Bill," he told me, and went on to describe how he roams the back country finding all kinds of items to use. Almost anything with some historical value and the patina of age is grist for his creative mill. Rick uses old harnesses, tools, mining equipment, photos, bottles and nails along with natural woods, rocks and plants to create an intriguing spectrum of handsome and durable conversation pieces. They sell well in the local tourist shops and antique houses.

Like many innovative craftsmen, Rick lives in his studio workshop and often gets his ideas from just observing the various items he's collected. As he puts it, "Things just naturally go together, and it's fun to experiment until the right combination is found."

Harper points out that this is the kind of enterprise that could be pursued in almost any location. For example, if one lived along the coast of Maine, there are any number of maritime relics that could be "assemblaged" and marketed to the hordes of tourists that roam that picturesque area. Another good place to find both antique artifacts as well as natural "settings" would be around abandoned houses in the back country of any region. Then there's the cornucopia of a beach near the mouth of a river. Here, naturally sculptured driftwood, shells, bits of sand–worn glass abound, along with the detritus of our throwaway civilization.

There are few things in life more satisfying than to fulfill one's creative urge and earn one's living simultaneously. Rick's done it, and so could you, if you have that bent.

Bad Brad

From the outside, the building looked all but abandoned. However, once through the door you might think you had wandered into Santa's workshop, a Santa who was into stained glass. Cutting and soldering the colorful bits were a half–dozen young men and women. The final products were striking: multi–hued lamps, planters and jewel boxes ready to be packed and shipped to customers nationwide.

The owner of this back–bay operation was a young man we called Bad Brad, bad in the sense that he pretended to be a grouch when in reality he enjoyed giving work to a group of drifters who couldn't or wouldn't be employed elsewhere. The job was on a piece–work basis so that a worker could earn just what he needed for the day and then amble off to fish, swim or just meditate on the mysteries of life in Oakland's estuary.

It's understandable why a segment of our population seeks alternative income solutions; many orthodox jobs are boring, repetitive and generally maddening. Think of how much illness must come from the frustration of stamping insurance claims "Closed Without Payment" for eight hours a day or watching boxes of Crispy Crunchees go by in an endless stream. Bad Brad was the type of man who would have thrown the claims out the tenth–story window or rerouted the Crunchees into the trash bin. Creative, and his own man in every sense of the word, he had to have an outlet that would give his restless spirit some room to grow yet produce enough wherewithal to fund his love for sailboats. Designing, making and selling stained–glass artifacts proved to be a perfect fix.

Brad found an unused warehouse, rented it for the proverbial song, brought in some power, built benches and hauled in supplies of glass and lead wire. In the loft, he constructed a mini–apartment complete with a hotplate, a stereo, a stained–glass portal and a king–size bed. Thus, he had no additional rent to pay or commute to make. He made up his own samples, photographed them and sent them to exclusive gift shops all over the United States. Orders came back, and he was off on his chosen career. Soon business became so good he hired back–bay denizens to manufacture his creations on a "work–when–you–feel–like–it" basis.

The last I saw of Bad Brad, he was designing some fantastic lamps that would have done credit to an Arabian–Nights setting.

The Sinclairs

Have you ever seen baby goats playing with one another? If you have then I don't have to describe them. If you haven't then bear with me, because there just aren't words to picture how absolutely delightful and charming they can be. And they are even more so when they have teeter–totters, ramps and other toys on which they can play their sprightly games. That's what the Sinclairs have built for their continuous crop of "kids." It's better entertainment than any TV. The setting is idyllic. The Sinclairs live on a 15–acre ranch not far from the coast in northern California. Their comfortable old ranchhouse has been there as long as anyone in the area remembers. It's surrounded by tall, second–growth redwoods, wild blackberries, and few neighbors.

The main enterprise is goat cheese, and to facilitate this business they have created the state's smallest approved dairy. Not long ago, I watched John Sinclair go through the process of making cheese from the milking of the nannies to wrapping the cheese for shipment. It's really not difficult, but, when you make several hundred pounds, it can be a lot of work. However, there's one basic consideration to review— John is his own boss and always will be.

It's a long way in distance and in time from the frantic aerospace industry of southern California where John once worked. Caught in that mad pace, he dreamed of having his own self–sufficient ranchette somewhere in the north woods. And like any dreams that are accompanied by hard work, it came true.

"Sure, it can be a drag, milking goats seven days a week," admitted John. "But consider the alternative: chasing yourself around some big building in search of fulfillment or bucking the traffic on a bumper–to–bumper freeway."

There was no question that the rural life was far more satisfying and conducive to a longer and more relaxed life.

Afterthought

Recently I saw the headline on an article: "Make $30,000 a Year With Milk Goats." Personally, I believe that one would be well–advised to search out a John Sinclair or his equivalent to find out if this is really true. It would make sense to offer to work alongside an operation of this nature to see if you are compatible on a long term basis. As John admitted, milking goats seven days a week can be a drag. And this type of tedious, repetitive work is common to many occupations. As Mark Twain said, "It's easier to stay out than to get out." So before you take on any ventures, investigate them thoroughly.

Retirement Hobby Has Many Rewards

When Bill Falk retired he expected that life would be continuously enjoyable without any effort on his part. It didn't take long to dispel this erroneous notion. Walking, playing cards with cronies, and reading the paper soon became boring, so Bill began looking around for something interesting to do.

He noticed that original paintings displayed in the hotel near his home moved rather rapidly; visitors to his tourist–oriented town liked having a souvenir if the price was right. The one factor that often moved a painting was low price—good or bad, simple or complex, if the picture and frame were under thirty or forty dollars, it would sell quickly.

So Bill sat down to figure out if he could produce worthwhile landscapes for that figure. Masonite was cheap and so were paints. He could make his own frames from old or scrap wood. And that was it, plus his time, which had been hanging rather heavy on his hands lately. He was willing to sell that "heavy time" for a mighty low price.

He began by painting desert scenes, since they are simple and uncomplicated— just lots of sand and sagebrush. His technique was to coat a smooth piece of masonite with a flat white paint and then add oils, pen and ink, and acrylics as necessary. With pen and ink he could present the minutiae of a scene with great accuracy: hawks on the wing, individual blades of rabbit grass, spokes of weathered wagon wheels.

His first work sold the first day it hung in the hotel, and that changed Bill's life completely. Never before had he felt he had any artistic talent, because he had never tried to express it. But now he realized that he had a lot, as the increasing number of sales proved. Despite his popularity, he never raised his prices. "Why should I," he told me. "I'm happy that someone likes my work and whatever I make is frosting on my financial cake anyway."

What he was saying was that he got his major reward from being creative. Money was a secondary or tertiary.

Corn and Pumpkins

As urban areas expand, much former farmland is being used to build homes. However, between the time it is rezoned and finally developed could be anywhere from a month to several years. A man I once met in the San Fernando Valley made good use of this time lapse. He would offer to sharecrop on the unused land, providing seeds, cultivation and harvest with a share of the crop proceeds in barter for the use of the land. Inasmuch as the land wouldn't bring in any revenue prior to development, the owners would usually agree; after all, to them it was like finding money in the street. Corn was the usual crop since it yields high returns in the sale of sweet corn. Pumpkins were another good choice since they are great sellers during Halloween and Thanksgiving.

The effort involved a lot of work for about three months, plowing, planting, irrigating, cultivating and weeding, plus setting up a stand to sell the produce. But then the greenbacks would roll in seven days a week as the corn was picked and sold fresh daily. Later, pumpkins produced the same income with somewhat less labor and less concern over freshness, since the orange globes keep well without refrigeration for months.

What is so interesting about this method of earning an income doing what is of benefit to people is that you get so much time off! Even if you did both corn and pumpkins, you would still enjoy about six months of leisure! One could travel in high style using the same trailer as an office for the farm venture.

Freedom of Choice

One of the most advantageous aspects of having your own enterprise is that you can expand or diversify anytime you wish. For example, in the case of the farmer, he could have easily increased the area of sharecropped land. Or he could have planted tomatoes between the corn or pumpkins. The cookie girl could have bagged her cookies and offered them through markets in nearby towns. With the same oven equipment, she could have made giant bran muffins with a variety of fillings. These opportunities extend to having sidelines, so if you don't make enough income with one enterprise, start another.

Wildflowers

If there is one thing in abundance in the rural regions of America, it's the wildflower. Every spring, billions of them leap out of the ground to display their colorful blossoms to one and all. A young lady, whose name I've long forgotten, felt the urge to preserve this beauty beyond springtime. She gathered many varieties and dried them between the pages of old books. Then she arranged them in artistic ways between sheets of thin glass. The edges were sealed with "came" or lead wire with a groove on one side, and the borders were decorated with scraps of colored glass that matched the colors of the wildflowers. A ring was soldered to the top so that they could be displayed in a window where the light streaming through would bring them back almost to their original outdoor beauty. In all, it was an inspired, if not entirely new, way to preserve and present some of the bounties of nature. I found the lady and her work at a flea market and, in the process of buying some, learned about how she made them.

There are lots of books on this subject in almost every library. The work is simple, easy and fun, plus you get to wander around picking wildflowers. Now what could be better than that?

The Connection

A young married man with two children and a large mortgage worked for an advanced electronics firm as a software programmer and consultant. Every day he fought the bumper–to–bumper traffic to his office until he reached the limit of his endurance. "Why," he said to his boss, "why can't I just stay home and send in my work over a phone line to a computer?" "No reason why it won't work," the boss replied and sure enough, it *did* work. The next step was to eliminate that big mortgage by moving to a small town some four hundred miles away. The phone line worked just as well and output of work improved.

This is just one example of what is now happening worldwide. Many people are finding that they don't have to physically appear at their jobs. It's sufficient to send their work in by phone, mail or other communication links. I know it works; I've done it for years. I work at home (or wherever I happen to be) and send my proposals and manuscripts to potential buyers.

So, no matter what means of information transfer you use, whether it's mail or modem (the electronic link), you can consider living where it's better and cheaper and still maintain a high–income level. To find out more about the high–tech approach, visit your local library and be amazed and delighted by the number of books and magazines on the subject. Although it might at first appear complicated, it's really as simple as I've described above.

This technique opens up a cornucopia of opportunities for those who can use their talents in this way. Imagine living in a remote and scenic area (Alaska, British Columbia, Baja), enjoying all that this implies while still earning a substantial income via mail or electronic links. One could also travel, do the work en route, and then phone in the output from any small town. The possibilities are unlimited.

Amaranth

If you haven't heard of this grain, then you have a surprise. It was a staple of the Aztecs, grows in poor soil with little water, and produces a seed that has more protein than most grains. It looks like sesame, has a nutty flavor, pops like popcorn, and can be steamed and flaked or ground into flour.

What a great staple item for your lower forty or upper 10 x 20. Seeds are available at most agriculture experiment stations and large seed companies.

Kiwi and Beyond

By now, most of us have enjoyed this delicious green fruit which has proliferated widely in many states. You can get in on the ground floor of a new fruit called the pepino. Hundreds of acres are being planted in California, and soon people will enjoy the pepino, which tastes like a cross between a strawberry and a melon. If your local nursery can't supply you with seeds or seedlings, write to Native Plants Inc., 417 Wakara Way, Salt Lake City, UT.

Arcosanti

Can an experimental city become a reality? The answer is definitely yes, as you'll find when you visit the legend in its own time, Arcosanti. The brainchild of Paolo Soleri, an Italian architect–visionary, it is located about sixty–five miles north of Phoenix, Arizona. Much too elaborate to describe in words, pay a visit and see what persistent effort plus imagination can accomplish with apprentice labor.

Could you do the same in your area? Why not? For more information, write: Arcosanti, Mayer, AZ 86333 and ask for a brochure.

Out of Thin Air

That's what Jane Parker did. She created a marvelous business in Saratoga, California that allows her to travel with her husband on deluxe cruises in all parts of the world. It's called Retirement Exploration, offering preretirement seminars that are held on board luxury liners for those who are looking forward to an active life after they quit the 8–to–5.

Anyone could do this. All it would take is some inquiries, a bit of research and up–front money for advertising, probably via mail, to pre–retirees.

250 New Ways to Earn Money Independently

Many of the successes of this decade did not even exist in the last. Can you recall a baked potato restaurant, a hot tub distributor, electronic security services, one–

hour photo processing or an aerobic dance studio being around ten years ago? Obviously, there are many, many new ways to earn a full– or part–time living on your own, often with a small investment.

A company that specializes in describing how to go into new enterprises is the American Entrepreneurs Association, 2311 Pontius Avenue, Los Angeles, CA 90064. Send for their free catalog and see what's available in the new business field. Costs are mostly under fifty dollars for a manual of instructions—a modest price to pay if the new enterprise works out for you. I look at information of this nature as insurance against possible failure. I have attempted many ventures without knowing what pitfalls lay ahead; a good guide would have been invaluable in most cases.

MUSTARD

Sources

The GPO: You pay for it; you should use it. That's the Government Printing Office in Washington, D.C. 20402. Write them for a catalog of publications on any subject that interests you. I've found the ones on food to be biased in favor of large food manufacturers, but those on gardening and shelter are quite good. Just beware of the use of chemicals with respect to the former subject.

The Whole Earth Catalog: You'll find old issues of this fat catalog in many used book stores. The new edition is rather expensive but does contain a lot of well–documented data. For more information along these lines, write Whole Earth Access, 2990 Seventh Street, Berkeley, CA 93710

Chambers of Commerce: Most cities have them, and you only need that title and the zip to get all the data you need for possible relocation. Ask for a copy of the daily newspaper (or weekly) since, as we've mentioned before, it will tell you more than any other source what's really happening. If there are no jobs offered, then you can assume that the economy is either static or down.

Growing Your Own: You can get all the information you need from your local county agricultural agent. Or, if not available, write to United States Department of Agriculture, Washington, D.C. 20520. There are many free booklets available from the USDA, especially on small garden plots.

City, County, State and Federal Agencies: Ask the reference clerk at your local library to give you the directories for the various agencies. Take advantage of the mountains of data that these agencies have accumulated and the services they provide. For example:

U S Customs: Takes charge of all boats and vehicles seized in drug busts and sell them at auction or by closed bid. If you want a 150–foot freighter for trading in the South Pacific, get in touch with them at 1301 Constitution Avenue, N.W., Washington, D.C. 20229.

Peace Corps: Probably one of the most useful agencies. You can work in a foreign country, learn a language, and do some good in the world all at one time. Get your application from Peace Corps, 806 Connecticut Avenue,N.W., Washington, D.C. 20526.

Association Directory: Most industries form associations. For example, the plywood industry has one supported by manufacturers. You can find this directory in almost any library. It is a goldmine of valuable information, since any association will deluge you with free publications.

Publishers: Many will be glad to send you a catalog of their books, usually requiring a 9 x 12 manila envelope with two first class stamps attached. For a list of many publishers see, the latest editions of *Writer's Market* or of *LMP* (*Literary Market Place*) in your local library.

Speaking of Your Local Library: I make it a practice to go to my local library at least once a week just to browse. They have a section of new books, and the periodicals have even more timely information. I can't think of a better way to keep up with the times than to visit and use all the libraries you can. Even while I'm traveling, I check into libraries just to see what they are offering that is new and interesting.

Great Hot Springs of the West: This is a typical reference work that describes seventeen hundred hot springs in the eleven Western states. There are many opportunities connected with hot water, and this book describes some. If not in your local library, send $10 to *Great Hot Springs of the West*, Suite 29, 999 Old San Jose Road, Soquel, CA 95073.

Income Tax: How can a single book save you thousands of dollars? Quite simply, if it's one that proves you don't have to file an income tax return or pay any taxes. It's typical of how a book can change your life overnight. Available from Laissez Faire Books, 532 Broadway, 7th Floor, New York, NY 10012. Ask for their complete catalog...it's illuminating!

United Nations: They have booklets on various subjects. Write them at New York, NY 10017

VITA: Lots of booklets on the general subject of rural development. VITA, College Campus, Schenectady, NY 12308

Learning By Mail: Want to improve your mind? You can, with lessons from various correspondence courses. Write to UC Extension Service, 2223 Fulton Street, Berkeley, CA 94720, for their free directory of schools that offer this service

Free Teaching Materials: There are books in your library that list companies and agencies that provide free teaching materials. One of the books is entitled *Where to Get and How to Use Free And Inexpensive Teaching Aids.*

Source of Back to the Land Books: Rodale Books, 33 East Minor Street, Emmaus, PA 18049. Ask for their latest catalog. Their periodicals seem to have capitulated to corporate demands and are advertising junk foods, but their books are top flight.

Ranch and Farm Equipment: Nasco has a great catalog of just about everything you would need to be self–reliant. In the east it's Nasco, Fort Atkinson, WI 53538; in the west, Nasco, PO Box 3837, Modesto, CA 95352

Scientific Data: Want to know how to make diamonds? Drill for hot water? Make a windmill from an old auto differential? Then contact U S Department of Commerce, Clearinghouse of Federal Scientific and Technical Information, Springfield, VA 22151

Local Schools, Colleges and Universities: All have libraries and all are in the business of providing information. In my own community, I contact nearby universities by computer for free! Take advantage of this free storehouse of information. Usually the librarians are happy to help you with a special search.

The Thomas Register: Want a product? Want to know about who is making what? Then check your local library for this astounding, multi–volume reference file on American manufacturers. For example, if you are going into the boat business, it will provide you with all firms manufacturing marine hardware and accessories.

Note: We are now in an information explosion. If you don't keep up, you'll be left behind in every way.

Summary, Conclusions, and Plan of Action

Summary

This book has presented a diversified spectrum of alternatives in the important areas of food, shelter, health and other subjects of general interest. The material was drawn from real life—recent and earlier experiences of the author. Everything presented was factual and will bear the most rigorous investigation as to authenticity.

Conclusions

No one need go hungry or without a roof in America. There are too many alternatives, too many creative possibilities, and in most cases they are there for the taking.

If a person is homeless, there are an abundance of live–in jobs taking care of the older generation. I've done it myself just recently and learned how much one should appreciate good health and the ability to walk and talk without difficulty. It's rare that I take a step that I don't thank God for the privilege.

Food is everywhere in the U.S. The oceans are full of fish, and most fields and orchards are left with thirty percent or more of their crops unharvested.

Opportunities abound. No one need be jobless since the chance of self–employment is so great. We have millions of people with billions of real needs and trillions of desires. Just fill a few of these needs and desires, and you will have all the income you need. We all have been programmed to spend a lot more than we need. And this causes us to work too hard. As the bumper sticker says,

"I owe, I owe, so off to work I go"

But it does not have to be that way. We can limit ourselves to real needs rather than insidiously engendered wants. Who really needs a hair dryer, a microwave, a Porsche? You'll recall that when you went camping, the best feature was that you were having so much fun with so little!

Plan of Action

Make a list of what you *really* want out of life, not what someone else has programmed you to *believe* you want. It might be difficult to discriminate, since corporate programming is so clever, but make an effort. What would really make you truly happy.

Now, make a list of what you need to obtain your wants.

Acorn

QUERCUS *spp.*

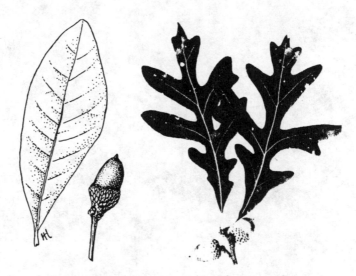

live oak, *Quercus virginiana*   white oak, *Quercus alba*

Index